FOUL
Best of Football's Alternative Paper 1972–1976

The Alternative Football Paper

October 1972
Number 1, 5p

WOULER IF MR CLOUGH WOULD HAVE ME, AFTER ALL...

WHO SAYS WE'RE JUST PRETTY BOYS THEN ?

RS'
NE
L

MAN. UTD GET THE ELBOW

inside: DANNY BLANCHFLOWER INTERVIEW / DESMOND HACK / BRIBES:PICKING UP A STINK / CLOUGHY SPEAKS / THE 'NEW' ARSENAL / AMATEUR WAGES - LATEST PRICES / 'RON GREENWOOD' / PRESS WE DESERVE ? / FOUL OF THE MONTH / THE RANGERS MEMORANDUM /

FOUL
The Alternative Football Paper

November 1972
Number 2, 5p

TOLD YOU IT WAS LEFT FOR THE MARKET, FLO...

SPURS IN THE RAW, AND A WHITE HART LANE

Pic: Colorsport

inside: WITCH-HUNT, pp 2&3
DES HACK ON THE UP AND UP, p4
'SUNDAY PEOPLE' PUNCH-UP, p5 / COACHING THE SWEET FA WAY, p7
LOW-DOWN ON BLACKBURN AND COVENTRY, pp 8&9 / KROSSWORD, p10
plus MRS WILSON / BIG MAL AND FRANK O'FOUL / BREMNEATCH ???

FOUL

Best of Football's Alternative Paper 1972–1976

Edited by Mike Ticher

SIMON & SCHUSTER

Acknowledgements

We would like to thank Steve Tongue and Andrew Nickolds for all the help they have given us in compiling this book and for giving us access to many documents and press cuttings relating to FOUL, as well as copies of the original magazines. Thanks also to Douglas Allen, Steve Gilbert and Chris Tiratsoo for the loan of their precious copies of the FOUL Book of Football and back issues of the magazine.

A SPORTSPAGES BOOK

First published in Great Britain by
Simon & Schuster Ltd in 1987

© Foul Publications Ltd, 1972, 1973, 1974, 1975, 1976
Introduction © Simon and Schuster Ltd, 1987

SPORTSPAGES
The Specialist Sports Bookshop
Cambridge Circus Shopping Centre
Charing Cross Road
London WC2H OJG

Simon & Schuster Ltd
West Garden Place
Kendal Street
London W2 2AQ

Simon & Schuster of Australia Pty Ltd
Sydney

British Library Cataloguing-in-Publication Data available

ISBN 0-671-65521-3

Printed and bound in Great Britain by
Martin's of Berwick

Introduction

It has been said that *FOUL*, like Martin Peters, was ten years ahead of its time. If so, then it's about time that it was available to be read once again, as the very last *FOUL* appeared in October 1976. Since *FOUL*'s demise, it has achieved near-legendary status, a position which has more than a little to do with the fact that those people lucky enough to own the original copies have hoarded them so carefully that the rest of us have found it almost impossible to get hold of them. For anyone who was too young to appreciate *FOUL*, or who was simply unaware of it at the time, it has remained little more than a rumour, whose very existence, never mind content, has been open to doubt.

The aim of this book is to bring *FOUL* to a whole new audience, to revive some distant memories for its original readers (and contributors) and to look back on the magazine from a viewpoint more than a decade on, trying to put it in context in a rapidly-changing football world. We have tried to indicate how some of the main issues have changed since the days of *FOUL* (though many more have stayed the same), but to be sparing in comments on the actual text, since most of it speaks plainly and eloquently for itself.

The book is divided into three main sections, loosely grouping together similar issues, though much of the material is equally at home in any of them. The articles were chosen from every issue of *FOUL* (1–34) and the *FOUL BOOK OF FOOTBALL* no.1 (see below). At the risk of sounding like a beauty contest judge, it was a thoroughly enjoyable task, and a very difficult choice, much that was worthy of inclusion having to be omitted because of lack of space. The main characters in the book need, as they say, no introduction, although some have faded into obscurity (Sir Alf Wit where are you now?), left football altogether, or swapped the riches of the United Arab Emirates for the glory (sic) of managing England. Brian Clough, it seems, goes on forever . . .

THE STORY OF *FOUL*

FOUL's history begins in the summer of 1972, with two Cambridge undergraduates, Steven Tongue and Alan Stewart. Fed up with the bland pap of the glossy football magazines and the shallow cynicism of the national papers, and realising for the first time how

cheaply a magazine could be produced, they created *The Alternative Football Paper* (later to be boldly re-named *Football's Alternative Paper*). The name *FOUL* was chosen as a direct parody of magazines such as *GOAL* and *SHOOT!*, which had flourished since England's World Cup triumph, and the first issue saw the light of day in October 1972. In true 'underground' style, it was knocked up on a borrowed typewriter in the Student Union, printed for just £54.00 (1,000 copies) and distributed to outlets in Cambridge from the back of a car.

It was an appropriate time for football's first alternative magazine to appear (if indeed it was the first). The brief resurgence of English football following the 1966 World Cup was well and truly over. The national team had been not merely eliminated, but humiliated by West Germany in the European Nations Cup in 1972, playing sterile and dirty football, and Arsenal had just won the double, placing more emphasis on effort, commitment and organisation than skill or entertainment. Don Revie's Leeds were exerting a dominant influence on the domestic game with their equally joyless football and attendances had resumed their steady decline.

Perhaps the most eloquent testimony to this loss of flamboyance and excitement was Manchester United, whose stylish 1968 European Cup-winning team was in the last stages of disintegration. In *FOUL* no.5 (February 1973), Matt Busby is pictured with that European Cup, sitting next to a laughing Denis Law. The caption reads: "*In five years, Denis, you'll be playing no.4 and United will get relegated*". Law's goal for Manchester City, which duly did send United down in 1974 was a deeply ironic symbol of what they, and the rest of football, had lost in those five years. Chelsea were another relatively attractive side in rapid decline (the Trident Fair Play League printed regularly in *FOUL* shows graphically how they kicked their way into the 2nd Division in 1974–75) while the no-nonsense, no frills sides typified by Leeds, Arsenal and Liverpool won the trophies. It was about time someone started pointing the finger.

So *FOUL*, spurred on by what they later called "a mountain of disgust", set out to raise a small banner of idealism in a football world obsessed with win-at-all-costs and determined to maintain its antiquated power-structure. The first nine issues ran to only 1,000 copies each and were laid out, printed and distributed in Cambridge and London, mainly by the editors (Tongue and Stewart) and Andrew Nickolds who was then (to put it politely) 'freelancing' in the capital, following a spell in Players cigarette factory, having left Cambridge the previous year. Also contributing regularly almost from the beginning were Peter Ball (then working for *Time Out*), Geoff McDonald and Steve Gleadall, who drew the *FOUL* masthead which graced its front page from issue no.2 until the very end.

Tongue and Stewart finished their degrees in 1973 and so, by the start of the 1973–74 season, all of the people most closely involved in *FOUL* had arrived in London. Steve Tongue got a job with the new independent radio station, LBC, while Alan Stewart went to Thames TV. The previous season had been one in which

"predictability was more sought after than spontaneity" (*FOUL* no.9), in which perhaps the greatest satisfaction could be taken from Leeds losing in two Cup Finals (F.A. and Cup-Winners). *FOUL*'s own response was to take two major steps forward. The magazine was typeset for the first time (no.10, September '73) and began to be 'professionally' (but somewhat erratically) distributed by Moore-Harness Ltd, who were also handling *Private Eye* at the time. The print run went straight up to 9,000 and from then until issue no.30, circulation grew steadily from about 6,000 to almost 12,000.

Much of this expansion was made possible by the involvement of Tim Rice, then recently made famous by *Jesus Christ Superstar*, and his brother Jonathan through their company, Heartaches Ltd. Their initial contribution was to "guarantee *FOUL*'s debts", a process which eventually could be more accurately described as "subsidising their losses". The Rices also let *FOUL* have free use of part of their offices at 40 Craven Road, near Paddington Station, which became *FOUL*'s permanent home from issue no.20 (summer 1974) until their investment ended with issue no.30 (June 1975).

These two seasons (1973–74–75) perhaps represented *FOUL*'s golden years. The quality of the content fully justified the more ambitious production and several famous or near-famous names contributed, including Eamon Dunphy, Derek Dougan, Bill Grundy, Bill Tidy and Barry Fantoni, as well as the old lags and others just starting to make their mark in the media, like Tony Wilson, Chris Lightbown, Terry Bushell and cartoonist Kevin Macey. *FOUL* continued to irritate those who deserved to be irritated (Malcolm Allison threatened to throw them in the bath) and give a good laugh to those who desperately needed one, for they remained pretty grim football years. The Ramsey era ended, but only to usher in 'The Godfather', Revie, whose unloved Leeds team had won the title in 1973–74.

Revie was an obvious target for *FOUL*. A serious and austere man, he built the England team in his own image, and it played duly frightened football. *FOUL* awarded him the 'Pope John XXIII Francis of Assisi Nobel Peace Prize Pulitzer' in their 1974 New Year's Honours and invited comparisons with Al Capone and Hitler. Revie's overcoached, negative and physical teams and his materialistic approach which brought in cash incentives for the England players and a lucrative (for him) sponsorship deal with Admiral, represented everything which *FOUL* was against. The fact that Norman Hunter won the very first PFA Footballer of the Year award in 1974 showed how accepted his ideas had become.

There were many others too, of course. Apart from a whole succession of dodgy chairmen, there was Alan Hardaker, always ready with a torrent of reactionary nonsense; the ever reliable Clough and Allison; and of course the players, whose foul exploits provided an unlimited supply of material for the 'Foul Award' and 'Foul of the Month'. But *FOUL* wasn't just about taking the game's characters down a peg or two. It railed against the whole structure of football and often did fine investigative jobs on individual clubs and their masters. Most importantly of all, it was very funny.

As *FOUL* developed, Stan Hey, who had also been at Cambridge, became more involved in the lay-out and production, as others found they had to devote more time to their 'proper' jobs. He and Andrew Nickolds were then working together on scripts for the BBC, but also found time to put *FOUL* together in between playing darts at 40 Craven Road. However, *FOUL* now had serious financial problems, largely brought on by a failure to attract sufficient advertising, and the indulgence of Heartaches could not last forever. Tim and Jo Rice finally decided to pull the plug at the end of the 1974–75 season, by which time it had become apparent that they were not going to recoup their investment in the magazine. It is *FOUL*'s proud boast that they are the only project on which Tim Rice has ever lost money. Although the Rices did not finance any further issues of *FOUL*, they remained involved, with Jo as a director of *FOUL* Publications Ltd, and they continued to pay the outstanding bills. Issue no.30 (June 1975) carried emotional farewells and the question on the cover: "Is this the end of *FOUL*?" The answer was, "not quite".

In order to raise some capital to finance further issues, and to put on record some of the best material from the first 30 issues, Hey and Nickolds hurriedly compiled *THE FOUL BOOK OF FOOTBALL no.1*. Dedicated to Billy Bremner and sub-titled *The Chelsea Book of Unnatural Acts* (the cover photo explains why), it also contained a substantial amount of new material written especially for the occasion. It took until April 1976 for the book to be published (by New English Library), by which time two more issues of the magazine had also come out. Until then, *FOUL* had appeared regularly every month, with a break in the summer, but the last four issues spanned a whole year. *FOUL* was limping along, desperately needing to be re-financed from the proceeds of the book.

At first things went well, and 5,500 of the 20,000 copies had been sold by July. It was then that they were finally undone by the nightmare of all satirical magazines – a libel case. Mike Langley of the *Sunday People*, threatened to sue over *FOUL'S PRESS GUIDE*, an article in the book which made some scathing comments about Fleet Street journalists, implying that some of them were lazy, poor writers and even (shock horror!) that they liked a drink occasionally. Langley's failure to see the funny side cost *FOUL* dear. Rather than face the potentially massive costs of a court case and withdraw the book indefinitely, the editors decided to fall back on the goodwill of their readers and made the best of a bad job. When the book was recalled they transported all the copies from the warehouse of the New English Library in West London to an empty house in Blackheath, where over 20 volunteers had answered the call and set about snipping the offending paragraph from the book and replacing it with an apology. For a week in the middle of that legendary hot summer, nearly 15,000 copies of the book were amended and returned to the distributors, who by now seemed less than fully committed to the project.

Eventually, a further 5,000 copies were sold, but the damage had been done. During the two months that the book was off the shelves, *FOUL*'s promised payments to their printers had dried up and they were now unable to print any more issues of the magazine until part of their debt of £2,500 had been repaid. In addition they also owed Heartaches Ltd about £8,000 and the bank was refusing to honour their cheques.

The end was in sight, but it was decided to try to produce another three issues up to Christmas 1976, which would have 'paid-off' the 1,000 subscribers who would otherwise have been owed another £750 (the price of *FOUL* having risen from 12p to 25p since the end of Heartaches' subsidy). In the end, only one issue came out (no.34), in October 1976 – the last *FOUL* of all.

The final meeting of *FOUL*'s shareholders was held on April 21st 1977 (the Queen's birthday, so it is recorded in the minutes). It was decided to terminate the contract for distributing the book with NEL and attempt to get rid of the remaining 10,000 by whatever means possible. Tim Rice offered to store the books in his barn, and eventually most of them wound up on the bonfire. *FOUL*'s only remaining assets were an addressing machine and fifty *FOUL* t-shirts. Very few of the subscribers (still owed 50p each) asked for any money back, but their support for *FOUL* through subscription drives and straightforward appeals for money was not enough, loyal and generous though it was, once it was clear that the book could not be the hoped-for salvation. In the immortal phrase of Danny Williams, then manager of Swindon Town, *FOUL*'s pig was dead.

SUCCESSES AND FAILURES

' "Previous philosophers have interpreted the game: our task is to change it" – B. Clough (attrib)' – *FOUL* no.1

In concrete terms, *FOUL* achieved very little during its four year existence. It didn't carry any dramatic exposés which would have led to public resignations, sackings, scandal etc. It didn't even begin to bring about any changes in the way football is run in this country. However, that is hardly surprising. It wasn't, as many lazy journalists tagged it, 'the *Private Eye* of Football', because not enough people in football ever read it, and so its power to offend on a large scale was limited, although some individuals certainly resented their inclusion.

The influential people who read it the most were certainly journalists, but even they dismissed it as an irrelevance on the whole, although they occasionally supplied interesting pieces of information for publication. Apathy towards *FOUL* was rampant among footballers themselves (with the notable exception of Eamon Dunphy) and Chairmen, Directors and officals of the League and F.A. were obviously completely beyond the pale.

Perhaps *FOUL* needed another couple of years to establish itself on a firmer financial base before it could start to even make its presence known to these people. If it had got to a stage where it could have employed two or three people full-time, they would then have had the time and resources to dig a bit deeper into the murkier parts of the football world and come up with more revealing stories, as well as planning ahead more effectively for the magazine itself. Alan Stewart's brilliant article on the aftermath of the Ibrox disaster (Issue 24) is an example of what could have been achieved more often.

The key to this advance was advertising, but *FOUL* was never able to find someone who was willing and able to find an advertising market for them. The Leyton Whippet Club, and Sajid Khan's Sheepskin Coat Warehouse in Whitechapel, who advertised in early issues, would hardly sustain the magazine for long. This failure was probably due to the fact that *FOUL* appealed to intelligent football fans – a group which the world of marketing does not acknowledge. *FOUL*'s readership survey, sent out with issue no.22 concluded that their typical reader was "a twenty-five year-old, footballing, hard-drinking rock music fan who likes 4.28% of what is happening in the theatre".

In retrospect, one of *FOUL*'s greatest achievements was to bring together that very group – the people who for years had been grumbling to themselves about the state of football, not realising how many other fans felt the same. *FOUL* provided a focus for their discontent and gave them space to express it, which many of them did. *FOUL*'s influence also extended to other publications. Whereas they were the only 'alternative' magazine covering sport when they began, others outside the national press included it later, particularly the listings magazines such as *Time Out*, and even predominantly music publications. They can perhaps also claim credit for the introduction of *Private Eye*'s Colemanballs column, which only began to appear during *FOUL*'s lifetime. Now there are several new magazines, particularly *When Saturday Comes*, *Off the Ball*, and *The Absolute Game*, which appeal to many of *FOUL*'s readers and have their origins firmly in that same "mountain of disgust".

Perhaps the greatest tribute to the quality of *FOUL* is how little the material has dated in 10 years. The width of the trousers (see 1974–75 season review) gives them away and certainly no magazine daring to call itself 'alternative' would run something as crassly sexist as 'Norma Huntress' in the late 1980s, but otherwise it remains remarkably fresh.

In the end, *FOUL*'s succcess or failure can be summed up by its ability to survive. Thirty-four issues over four years was a much greater achievement than could have been expected at the very start. *FOUL* found a niche in the hearts of many hundreds of fans and the fact that people are still asking about it ten years on proves that the impression was a lasting one. *FOUL*'s 'failure' was only that it could not sustain itself further.

In some ways it was apt that it should finish when it did. *FOUL* is an honest record of a particular period in British football which few (except perhaps Derby County fans) will look back on with any affection. By the time it folded, the new generation of Ted Croker and Graham Kelly were taking over from Denis Follows and Hardaker at the F.A. and League respectively. Revie was about to do his moonlight flit, and Ron Greenwood, whom *FOUL* had often held up as an example to others, hardly aroused the same revulsion as his predecessor, despite his mediocre record as England manager. The Leeds era ended with the European Cup Final fiasco against Bayern Munich in Paris in 1975 and the Liverpool team that was to dominate the next decade was not quite so grim in its efficiency as its counterpart in the early 70s. Nottingham Forest, Ipswich, W.B.A., Aston Villa, West Ham, Tottenham and, eventually, Watford, among others, started to challenge for trophies playing slightly more imaginative football than we had come to expect. Of course, much remained that was mediocre, uninspiring, shady and downright crooked, but until the twin horrors of Bradford and Heysel in 1985, some of the more appalling excesses, on the field at least, seemed to have withered slightly. It was *FOUL*'s historic task to record faithfully those excesses.

WHERE ARE THEY NOW?

ALAN STEWART continued to work for Thames Television on the *TV Eye* programme, until he was tragically killed in a landmine explosion in the Sudan while researching a programme in October 1986

STEVE TONGUE stayed with LBC Radio as a sports reporter until 1986 when he joined Robert Maxwell's ill-fated *London Daily News*.

ANDREW NICKOLDS and STAN HEY have been writing plays and scripts for the BBC, including the series *Hold the Back Page!*

PETER BALL was sports editor of *Time Out* until 1982, when he went freelance, and then also worked on the *London Daily News* until its closure in July 1987. He has co-edited *The Book of Football Quotations* (with Phil Shaw), worked with Eamon Dunphy on *Only a Game?* and also collaborated on the autobiographies of Steve Perryman, Tony Woodcock and Peter Reid.

GEOFF MCDONALD remained a teacher after *FOUL*'s demise, mainly at Holland Park comprehensive in West London.

STEVE GLEADALL, who drew the *FOUL* logo and many other cartoons for the magazine, was a commercial artist at the time of *FOUL*, working for the *Star* newspaper in Sheffield. He is now publicity manager at the same paper, and has also contributed extensively to Sheffield Wednesday's programme, both writing and drawing.

CONTENTS

"Didn't say anything original"
JEFF POWELL, DAILY MAIL

1 Let's look at it another way . . .

FOUL and the media were natural enemies from the start. The very reason for FOUL's existence was that no-one else on TV or in the press was doing the job of supplying informed and articulate criticism of the more unsavoury aspects of football. So it's hardly surprising that the media were so frequently on the receiving end of FOUL's barbed comment. Brian Glanville sniffed that this was because FOUL's writers were themselves anxious to hop on the media bandwagon. In fact two of them (Peter Ball and Steve Tongue) were already working at Time Out and LBC respectively, and this was to FOUL's benefit, since they thus had access to the press-boxes and were able to observe the newspapermen at close quarters, and strip away their veneer of omniscience. (A brief paragraph in FOUL no.31 quoted the Sunday People man on the phone to his office from Stamford Bridge: "No-one seems to know who this Garry Stanley is, so we'll give him 5 and not mention him.")

The excesses and omissions of the tabloids inevitably provided an endless source of material for FOUL's satirists, editorial-writers and cuttings columns, but Ball and Tongue's presence in their midst meant that the press were an even softer target than they would otherwise have been. Mike Langley's libel action and the fact that Glanville and Frank Keating, to name but two, were genuinely offended by FOUL's parodies of them, prove that FOUL was doing a good job. Glanville's amazing personal attacks on FOUL's writers only serve to hold him up to further ridicule. Keating's rather patronising 'obituary' after issue 30 ("if the result was often trying, at least the lads were always trying") earned him a good dose of Andrew Nickolds when FOUL reappeared. He was not amused.

With The Sun and others hitting new depths daily in their search for the ultimate in trivia, sensationalism and bigotry, it can hardly be argued that things have improved since then. Perhaps it is an accurate indication of how things have gone that one of FOUL's favourite bogey-men, Frank McGhee, has now transferred his talents from the Mirror to the 'quality' of The Observer.

FOUL was on slightly less firm ground in their assaults on TV, although the personalities were equally alluring targets. FOUL correctly predicted that "the big switch-off is getting closer all the time", but could not have foreseen that this would actually only serve to strengthen TV's hand. The complete victory won by the TV companies over the League in their negotiations in 1986 has now, ironically, led to the introduction of regular live matches and the virtual elimination of the goal highlights berated by FOUL. It can hardly be said that this has been an improvement, though the current set-up is far from their ideal.

FOUL may have failed to unravel completely football's complicated relationship with television, but at least they gave the subject a proper airing, long before football's administrators had woken up to the fact that TV might be detracting from, rather than adding to, the well-being of the game. And there's no doubt that FOUL was accurate in pinpointing the problem from the League's point of view, then and now: "All they can think about is the money".

Foul

THE ALTERNATIVE FOOTBALL PAPER   10p   December 1973

Big "Chiv" — the end of the roab?

CHIVERS RIDDLE ROW FLARES ANGER FEAR SHOCK SHOT INQUIRY BIG BIAS DRAMA

TOTTENHAM HOTSPUR striker Martin Chivers is thought to be unhappy with his recent performances for First Divison Spurs.

I understand that he is not too hapy either with his recent England team performances at International level.

No comment has been recieved from England boss Sir Alf Ramsey — but Chivers was dropped for the recent England/Italy international; though he had an injury.

But Chivers' goal against Manchester United the other week should boost his self-confidence, and should keep the fans happy, who are understandbly puzzled by the shock decision.

WHAT'S PETER BATT UP TO? WHO CARES?

ATOM WAR MEANS ENGLAND COULD PLAY IN WORLD CUP FINALS!

See Back Page

No. 13   December 1973

THE PRESS WE DESERVE ??

The state of football journalism is so appalling that there is a very real danger it will damage the professional game it publicises and feeds on.Match reports apart-for they are toolimited to convey specific information,the standard of criticism and comment is so low that journalists whose thoughts on the game are worth reading make a very short list: Brian Glanville and Brian James, Geoffrey Green and Ken Jones perhaps. Now even Hugh McIlvaney has embraced the Beaverbrook ethos.

The situation with periodicals is even worse. SHOOT and STRIKER are boys comics, except that Peter Osgood replaces Roy of the Rovers: SOCCER STAR and JIMMY HILL'S FOOTBALL WEEKLY have sunk without trace in the face of the challenge from GOAL, a weekly whose banality of expression fits neatly into the adulation/platitude tone of article and pin-ups of facial muscles. FOOTBALL MONTHLY carries this even further with My Story articles of how the current rave was spotted playing for Ashington schools.WORLD SOCCER attempts a more intelligent assessment of the world game, but is frequently a month out of date by the time it appears, and tends to get blocked with league tables of the Zambian second division. There are also Football Association and Football League propaganda magazines, neither likely to bite the hand which owns them.

The reasons for this state are complex. Most football material is written for males with an undemanding intellect, or for those whose interest lies mainly in the pools (hence the high incidence of team news). Far more fundamental is the net of self-interest which surrounds the game. If a journalist writes an offensive piece about Sunderland FC as a club, he will be refused a place in the press box, and any facilities he may have for gleaning news about the team will be withdrawn:for a local journalist,this is suicide. The same attitude applies to those who voice their ipinions in public; Jackie Charlton was suspended last year for'bringing the game into disrepute': Peter Eustace's statements about Sheffield Wednesday and West Ham made him publicly unpopular with both of them and, although his ability remained constant, his value to West Ham dropped by about £90,000.

True assessments of players are desireable. But a GOAL preview of a match will cite a number of players with their particular skill -"good in the air" - without balancing the picture - "a regular own goal scorer". If a journalist were to write "Peter Cormack is yellow", "Chopper Harris is dirty" or even "Peter Storey is a bad player", he is wide open to an undefendable libel charge, since it is impossible to prove any of these statements. Therefore the press must harp on a player's good points, and simply not write about those who are doing badly.No player can criticise his manager or his team-mates because they can always get back at him,and anyway their own articles are probably ghosted by the same man. The illiteracy of most soccer players is well-known,but the SUN insists on £1,000,000 worth of soccer talent writing weekly -it is what they do on the field that matters,not their filleted opinions.

Somehow love of the game is rarely apparent in what most journalists write. That is why the contributions of Michael Parkinson and Hunter Davies are so refreshing, as they are not strictly sports journalists at all. Hunter Davies' sketch of Alan Gilzean as the outsider at Tottenham, the old man at 33, who had done National Service and wore grey flannel suits compared to the hairy flash gladiators in the rest of the team, stands out in the trailers from his book The Glory Game (Weidenfeld & Nicolson, published Oct 26 at £2.95), the first-ever attempt to explain to SUNDAY TIMES -type readers the reality of a football club's year. But of course none of the players actually read the newspaper.

The outlook for a football journalist is therefore bleak. Conditions of self - interest in the game prevent him from writing what he feels. Intellectualisation of soccer is met with apathy or derision. And as for revealing the true facts behind soccer's public facade, it is very difficult to define where objective journalism ends ,and sheer mischief-making begins.In these circumstances is it reasonable to expect football writers to discover an idiom?

***

No. 1   October 1972

No. 6   March 1973

DESMOND HACK

THE MAN THEY COULDN'T BE BOTHERED TO GAG.

Allison pays his gambling debts

SOCCER manager Malcolm Allison and comedian Des O'Connor yesterday settled betting debts totalling over £3,000.

Mr Allison, £13,000-a-year boss of Crystal Palace, sent a cheque for £1,360 to bookmakers William Hill.

Hills claimed that Mr Allison had been 'warned off'—barred from all racecourses—in January, 1972, after a report to the Jockey Club by Tattersalls' Committee, which rules on betting.

Daily Mail, Thursday, April 5, 1973

SO BIG MAL is back in town. And it's going to be like an alcoholic in a brewery. It is not news that has been greeted with shouts of delight by bookmaker friends of mine; Mal is about the closest thing there is in sport to an underworld figure. Many have been the times when bookies have considered refusing to pay out, after spectacular coups by Mal which have looked too true to be good - no welcome for Mal at the dogtracks. Nor from bookies who concern themselves with big-time soccer. They still remember a time when Brentford experienced a rather unexpected result that redounded rather to Mal's favour. And they remember, more specifically, an Upton Park result in the late fifties that read: West Ham 3 Newcastle 5, which cost them all a packet. And they remember that West Ham's goalkeeper that day, one Noel Dwyer, was absolutely inseparable from Mal, going with him to Bath, and then following him back into the League with Plymouth. Bookies have long memories.

Joe Mercer once described himself to me as a Mahoot riding an elephant; the question is whether this one is a rogue elephant - but that is Oh! Bloye's problem. He must just be hoping that Mal does not sign Dwyer to replace the sea-green Jackson.

No. 7 April 1973

A Nod From Rod

BY the time this appears we should know whether or not Rodney Marsh, grateful for a ready-made excuse at last to go home, has followed his greatest fan and apologist to Selhurst.

Although I haven't got a transfer tip right since forecasting that Alex James would sign for Arsenal, I'm betting that Hot Rod will face the same choice that Ron Greenwood put to Macdougall and Possee: "D'you want money, or d'you want to play football?" And that being a nice guy, but one that likes his £sd, Rodney won't make the same choice as Macdougall.

But then Ted had had some strange offers anyway. One of which was from Sheffield United, who promised him their standard £10-a-point bonus, which...er... could be increased if...um...he didn't - nudge nudge - tell the other players.

Our Ref: Your Ref:

MY GROANING desk has been deluged with floods of mail lately about the recent activities of Arsenal FC, and "the refs who referee with a jaundiced eye".

One letter points out that the men in black have long been received even more hospitably at Highbury than everywhere else, in a boardroom where "everything is on the house, SCOTCH, CHAMPERS, FOOD, the lot, with all the trimmings".

What's more, an old Arsenal captain reveals that "the club have always sent half a bottle of scotch round to the ref's changing room before a match".

A mischievous connection is drawn between Jeff Blockley being allowed to punch away a certain goal, when referee Hill was as close to it as anyone, and the way Leicester were twice disallowed good scores in the Cup. And the Arsenal/Chelsea tie only added weight to the argument: "Our old friend HILL done another Franny Lee act, and disallowed two penalties at least", I'm told. "Then he handed over to his red friend NORM BURTENSHAW to do his act, and he duly gave them the goal I told you they'd get, come what may".

Being a straightforward sort of fellow, I can't of course afford to lend an ounce of credibility to any of this. After all, a ban from the Arsenal press box may have its attractions, but as the man says, where else do you get champers and ALL THE TRIMMINGS on a Saturday afternoon?

£££££££££££

Gracious,what a month it's been! Crowned by Bob's triumphant return,even though Dr Mahmoud at the clinic still isn't entirely convinced about his bad knee.

"They don't know anything about it,they only play cricket," Bob snorts whenever I exhort him to have a care. "Anyway Barnett's beginning to forget he was only bought for the reserves."

Of course, Mrs Smyth next door had to try and spoil it all when I called for high tea again last Tuesday. All these absurd idées reçues about how we'll soon be off to Leicester then, once Mr Mee signs Peter Stilton or someone: and won't it be nice for Bob to be near Loughborough again, the thought of which turned me quite pale in spite of myself.

And he'shad proper time at last for his newspapaer articles and TV work. That Mr Leech does rather keep on,though, about him doing an action analyst thing of this new way Arsenal are supposed to be playing and the poor love must have told him a hundred times that he doesn't understand it either.

Except that he's supposed to throw the ball out instead of kick it,he says, but it always comes back just as quickly anyway.

Not that his devotion to the game has waned in any way. "I owe it to the club and my agent to get fit as soon as possible," he says in his Match of the Day voice whenever I remark how nice it is to have him helping round the house. He's taken to doing the drying-up every meal-time,the idea being that the maid throws the crocks to him from the draining-board, and Henry, our gardener, has to stand by the 'fridge pretending he's Frank McLintock and shouting "Offside,offside,ref!"

You can imagine the chaos! Ever since I've known him, Bob has had this remarkable talent for dropping things,and what with being a trifle out of practice as well... We're nearly reduced to the Charlie George teacups now,and when he tried to turn Mother's best butter-dish round the post, I almost wept.

So within a very short while we'll be back to the old routine: action replays all through Sunday lunch, Supporters Club dances at the Town Hall, and stern admonitions about 'Never on a Friday' - doubtless the man with the AFC blazer who hides in the front garden pretending he's from Social Security will be back as well.

But,as Bob never tires of saying, that's all part of being a Wife at the Top !

SOMETHING is frustrating Arsenal manager Bertie Mee. It is a problem so elusive that it haunts this meticulous man and taunts him with its mystery.

Mee defines the problem in a simple question. He asks "Can you tell me why Arsenal have such a bad image? Why do we get such bad reports? "

Colchester Evening Gazette 17/1/75

soccer as I see it ALAN BALL

First one is from Terry Montem of Guildford, who says: "You don't seem to show as much dissent these days as you have done in the past. Why is this?"

I think, Terry, it's because I'm now captain of Arsenal and more concerned with stopping my teammates from arguing with the ref than doing it myself.

It's not always easy to remember it at the time, but it is pointless trying to persuade the ref to change a decision by telling him he's wrong. The laws state that his decision is final and that's that.

Shoot/Goal 15/2/75

Ball ignored a warning to keep the comments about his 14th-minute booking to himself and was sent off for continued dissent. McNab committed a similar sin in the 66th minute and it invited the same punishment.

Daily Mail 24/2/75

Six million dollar woman

What the stars predict for Sheffield Wednesday

Sheffield Star 3/3/75

FOULM @!*!✱!! UTH

THIS summer has seen the biggest upheaval in televised soccer since *Match of the Day* moved off BBC2. There have been dramatic incidents: Coleman left an embarrassed BBC in a pall of mystery; Jimmy Hill moved to the BBC after long hesitation and talk of a £25,000 p.a. salary; and London Weekend Television sports supremo John Bromley drummed up a ridiculous pseudo-drama over his replacement, involving Brian Clough — who finally refused to join the Sunday show — and Malcolm Allison. This successfully drove the BBC off the sports pages, and nothing Jimmy Hill could do, even with cover-stories in *Radio Times* and *Time Out* magazine, disguised London Weekend's publicity victory.

This was the big opportunity for TV to recognise some of its responsibilities towards football and the football-watching public. The BBC clearly had no new ideas so they bought Hill, who was ITV's best idea in years. It is hard to be disappointed then, as *Match of the Day* admitted its lack of inspiration before the shake-up began; and the appearance of Norman Burtenshaw as someone whose views are respected in the game shows just how much Sam Leitch is out of touch. The verdict on *Match of the Day* is relief that David Coleman has gone, and sad acceptance that no one really expected them to do any better.

But London Weekend's *The Big Match* was expected to improve. They had the real opportunity, for they had initiated Hill's post-match analysis. They had also recognised the potential during Mexico 70 of a 'panel', which gained cohesion from personal obsession and prejudice, when the BBC just had a gaggle of experts. The mistake the controllers of *The Big Match* made was to assume that if they extracted the personalities from the panel and promoted them individually, their views would stand up, without the sniping from the others. This is what landed Allison and Clough back on our screens this autumn, Mal performing much the same role as Hill, Brian indulging in self-parody.

However, this error was rooted deep in long-established misconceptions about televised football held by both channels. Because of their subjection to the ratings, they feel that football should appear on the screen not as Football, but as Entertainment, a sort of Saturday Night at White Hart Lane. Everything is subordinated to this.

The content of the game founders under the weight of loud-mouthed egotism; the dull bits are edited out, destroying any rhythm a match might have had; goals are lauded to the skies by near-hysterical commentators. Football is packaged into an hour of family amusement, with no violence that might upset anybody. The analysis sessions are really a sop; ITV is determined to show action from three games, instead of covering one game properly, and the BBC continues its Goal-of-the-Month competition — an excuse for showing less football and more goals.

Football is often mean, boring, frustrating and punctuated by bouts of petty viciousness and violence. But television, by excising the tiresome aspects, allows no hint of the real thing to seep through.

In this way it is doing serious damage to the game it misrepresents. Goal-worship as it is plugged on the box means that anyone going to a game for the first time might expect to see half a dozen of the best goals Barry Davies has ever seen, in their 90 minutes on the terraces. They would expect incident and action and excitement following each other end to end. The wouldn't enjoy what they actually see, because television has never taught them what to look for. The pattern of the game, the shifts of emphasis in midfield, the way dominance moves from one side to the other without being reflected in goals — all this would escape notice. We are now in an era when teenage fans have been brought up on a pre-digested diet of televised football. They are abandoning the terraces in increasing numbers. Telly, and the fictionalised version of version of football it portrays, is one of the most potent reasons why.

What then should it do to prevent itself from emasculating the game it professes to love?

1) It must liberate itself from exclusive use of the camera on the halfway line. Just as theatre needed to be freed from the restrictions of the proscenium, and cinema developed once it cottoned on to moving the camera around, so TV must accept that there are other places from which to view a match than the eyrie halfway down the grandstand. LWT has taken steps toward this with their cameras on the touchline and behind the goal (the credit must again go to producer Bob Gardam) — but they haven't gone far enough.

If a game is a goal-less draw, what better place to view it from than from behind the defences, watching how every attack is sealed off? If the game hinges on the confrontation between big striker and centre-back, then put one camera on them for the entire match. Examine the idea that violence on the field provokes violence off it, by delegating cameras to cover both. Another time, instruct the cameras to watch for fouls and nothing else, purely to examine what effect fouling has in determining the pattern of the match. Above all, the camera must learn as the supporter learned long ago, to stop ball-watching.

2) It is time for honest commentary. If it was a bad goal, as a lot of them are, say so. If it was a disgraceful foul, say so, instead of saying "Oooh, a Mighty tackle there"

If the ref looks as if he's bent, as in the Leeds/Milan Final in April, say so. If the cameras are following what is happening on the ball, then the commentator should tell us what is happening off it. And if one commentator isn't enough (and one man can rarely see all that is happening on the field, the same as one camera or one official can't), then there ought to be two. Radio has long ago recognised the value of using more than one commentator, just as in the BBC TV and radio coverage of Test matches. Like football, TV is a subjective medium — so no commentator should pretend he has no prejudice, a fact of football that TV is loath to accept.

3) It is up to football's administrators to control the

Continued

Continued

way that football is televised, As usual, the men of Lytham have misunderstood the problem: it isn't the amount of televised football that is damaging the game, but the way it is televised, and the attitude that TV inculates. What the League should do is to attempt to protect the game from the editor's scissors. (Ideally, it would mean that no game should be televised — a more realistic target is that not more than one match should be covered in one hour of television). If the League do not take drastic steps, football in this country could end up like American football — a small number of games with blanket TV coverage. The money earned from the television companies means that these games could easily be played behind closed doors.

4) Television must come to terms with its 'experts'. The reason that LWT had such trouble in replacing Jimmy Hill is that they had fallen into the trap of believing that only former players or managers are qualified to comment on the game. This myth that they are the only ones that understand it is propogated by people in the game itself, but football has never really had a reputation for encouraging intelligent and articulate characters — the Hills, Blanchflowers and Dunphys are exceptional.

Yet television insists on ignoring the opinions of the Hopcrafts, McIlvaneys and Hans Kellers, because they have never played the game. What is more, television has misjudged the atmosphere of the time: now more than ever there is a mistrust of the figures in authority and a willingness to listen to grassroot spokesmen. Until television people learn that they are not the only ones who know about and care about football, it will never drag itself out of the banal mire clogging it now.

This summer, TV lost its best opportunity to re-establish itself on more honest, productive and ultimately entertaining lines. Although both channels were forced into sweeping personnel changes, none of their basic misconceptions have even been recognised. It defends itself with the argument that a more intelligent and adventurous approach would not be appreciated by the viewing public. If that is true, then it only has itself to blame. Instead of describing in pictures what football is really like, TV has conditioned the viewer to accept a version that is neither stimulating nor comprehensible. If, as Jeff Powell wrote in the *Mail* (27/8/73) the average viewer could not understand Allison's elementary tactical dissection of the Manchester United defence, then television must again take the blame.

Futhermore, the longer it continues with its present attitude, the less will be the demand for it to be overthrown; banality of output breeds thoughtless acceptance by those who have not already switched off. Unless television adopts a more enlightened viewpoint soon, it will remain forever in the Dark Ages.

Dear FOUL,

The editorial last month on televised soccer was not, I feel, the stuff of which alternative football papers are made.

You mentioned that ratings-conscious producers are keen to present football in the form of variety shows and "everything is subordinated to this", Had you really believed this, then you would not have wasted space on four pie-in-the-sky notions for improving the package. Exciting camera angles and unsycophantic commentary would merely serve further to disguise the deep-rooted malaise afflicting TV soccer. Before we set about preventing television "emasculating the game it professes to love" we have to be sure that producers do even protess to love football as she is played. On the evidence of their programme, they never give the game a thought.

There was another glaring inconsistency in what you wrote about Jimmy Hill. In para 2, you say that Hill's post-match analysis had been "ITV's best idea for years" — yet in para 5, the analysis sessions are "just a sop". If we are to accept that the BBC and the commercial companies are bitter rivals over weekend football coverage, and it's a conclusion impossible to deny, then we must also admit that Hill's nauseous and adolescent rituals of worship are just an unusually successful gimmick. And BBC's motives in buying him over were precisely those which governed the transfer of Morecambe and Wise. Until the basic philosophy behind televised soccer undergoes a radical change for the better, FOUL ought not to confine itself to suggesting obvious improvements which will never be implemented. We must come out and say that televised soccer is an insult to the game and the fans.

Geoff McDonald,
London SE 27.

Wit and Wisdom

> E.H.   What of the First Division? Who do you rate as the top teams now?
> I.St.J.   The top teams in the First Division are the teams who eventually will end up in the top bracket. Because that's what the First Division is about. The good teams don't go down. The good teams get to the top and stay there, and the bad teams go down or the unlucky teams go down. The teams who have had a bad season go down, but the teams who are the best teams that season get to the top of the table and stay at the top of the table. I think that you cannot argue that a team three-quarters of the way down the table is a better team than Liverpool, for instance, who are at the top or whoever else happens to be there.
>
> *Football News Vol. 1 No. 2*

> I PREFER the Beeb because of ITV'S infuriating habit of interrupting those thrilling musical adverts with shots of racehorses and wrestlers. And they waste at least 10 minutes of The Big Match by showing football.
>
> F. A. LAMB, Beaminster, Dorset.
>
> *The Sun*

> "The crowd think that Todd handled the ball there . . . they must have seen something that nobody else did."
> Barry Davies, *Match of the Day.*

FALLING

THERE IS a row of numbers along the top of the terraces at the East end of the Rangers' Ibrox Park stadium in Glasgow. They run from 12 to 16 and they omit number 13. It is not just superstition; on January 2 1971, 66 men died in trying to leave the ground after the New Year 'Old Firm' game against Celtic. They died on the Cairnlea Drive stairway, Stairway Thirteen.

They died in the most horrible circumstances. Some died underneath a pile of bodies ten feet high, all laid the same way, a wall of heads and faces, most with their tongues lolling out. Some died on their feet, squeezed out of their shoes by the crush of bodies, shoes which were later found on the stairway slimy with urine and vomit.

For three of them the cause of death was simple asphyxiation, for five of them suffocation, for one of them asphyxia due to inhalation of stomach contents. Charles Dougan, 31, a boilermaker from Clydebank died, as did 56 others, from traumatic asphyxia.

But his death has greater implications for the Rangers Football Club than any of the others, for on October 23 1973 his wife and two sons were awarded £26,261 damages against the club by a Glasgow Court. Sheriff James Irvine Smith found that *the said accident was due to the fault and negligence of the defenders'*, on no less than four counts. And there are 60 other cases against Rangers in the pipeline.

The effect of this ruling on Glasgow is unimaginable in any English city. Founded 101 years ago, the Rangers are as venerable an institution as the Church of Scotland, and they have a lot more prestige and a greater public following. They embody all those old-fashioned virtues that seem to be evaporating all around them, and wallow in the power of tradition. Their players are not allowed to play with their shirts outside shorts or socks rolled down; moustaches are banned. They know they are playing for a club that insists on a concept of total authority, a patrician member of the Scottish establishment, a vital member of the Protestant mafia that rules Glasgow.

Over the years the club has received much assistance from a compliant City Corporation and Lord Provost. Much of the slum clearance in Glasgow has been done by construction companies controlled by two Rangers directors, the late Ian McLaren and former chairman John Lawrence, and the City has been duly grateful.

The directors of the Rangers (not Glasgow Rangers, or just Rangers) are powerful men in a city that has a very small elite. Planning permission has never been much of a problem, nor has the provision of alcoholic licences at a time when it is the declared intention of the judiciary to reduce the number of licensed premises in the city.

The Press in Scotland rarely bothers the Club. Sir Hugh Fraser, the most powerful of the Glasgow proprietors, is inevitably a Rangers shareholder. And, as Jock Stein says, 'how many Catholic journalists are there in Glasgow?' Aside from that, there are only two football clubs in Scotland that anyone wants to read about, and to lose the cooperation of Rangers, or to get the reputation of being anti-Rangers would be suicide in terms of circulation; half the readership would defect. And so the habit has developed of ignoring the bad things about Rangers; there has been no investigation into their affairs in the Press, and the ruling of Sheriff Irvine Smith and its staggering implications were relegated to page 5 of the *Daily Record*, and page 8 of *The Scotsman*. This sycophancy has even spread to the BBC, who had to send a man up from London on the day of the disaster, because they could not trust

MASONRY

their man on the spot to ask the right questions. In the business and legal circles inhabited by the Glasgow elite, protecting and furthering the interests of the Rangers is traditional.

'In that word tradition lies the secret and power of Rangers', wrote general manager Willie Waddell. *'Rangers were built on discipline and character. Their discipline, code of conduct and demeanour must be exemplary.'* The team is the visible sign of an ideal, and it is a Protestant, Unionist and conservative one. At the Supporters Club, the Queen is saluted at closing time every night, and a notice on the wall warns that anyone who does not intend to comply will not be allowed entry. Opposite the portrait of the Queen is a painting of Robbie Burns, founder of Kilwinning Masonic Lodge. Freemasonry is a strand that is woven so deeply into the history of the Rangers that the two are inseparable. The true Rangers player and the true Rangers supporter rise from the slough of poverty through exercising the disciplines of obedience and self-restraint reinforced by religion. So the club celebrates the Masonic ideal and a brotherhood whose secrets are too precious for public knowledge. Each week the faithful are summoned to the game, the Eucharist, when the values are put to the test; it is not the private hopes of eleven men, but a way

of thinking, the pursuit of an ideal that is on trial.

And now it is the judgement of a Glasgow Sheriff that the hands of the directors of the Rangers are stained by the blood of 66 men.

These deaths were not the first to occur on Stairway Thirteen. In September 1961 70 persons were injured, and two died. Certain alterations and repairs were carried out on the Stairway, and a consulting civil engineer was instructed to supervise the work, but around 1967 the Rangers ceased to instruct him and they did not use the services of any civil engineer or other expert in relation to their ground until after January 1971. This was in spite of another accident in September 1967 when 11 people were taken to hospital, although it was scarcely surprising in view of the fact that there is no record in the minute book that the Board of Directors ever discussed this accident.

It was only two years before there was another accident, when 29 people were injured on January 2 1969, and still Rangers took no steps to consult a civil engineer on the question of potential danger from crowds on Stairway Thirteen. This time at least there was a meeting at the ground between two members of the Glasgow Master of Works Dept., two senior policemen and **David Hope**, a Rangers director, in the presence of whom no less than eight suggestions were made to reduce the risk of crowd pressure causing injury. Hope told the others that he would bring the matters discussed before the Rangers board, but *there is no evidence that this meeting or the suggestions made at it were ever brought to the notice of Rangers' board, and at no time did the board discuss the particular question of safety on that Stairway following this, or any other accident.*

John Lawrence

The attitude of the Rangers to this meeting is significant, and is a pointer to their attitude to the whole affair. David Hope denies ever having attended the meeting at all, although he did not stick to that story under cross-examination. In the words of Sheriff Irvine Smith, *Mr Hope vacillated between his being unable to recall such a meeting, his denying any such meeting, his possibly having got the dates wrong,*

being mistaken, admitting he could
have forgotten, stating that if he had
attended such a meeting he would
certainly have recalled it, and so on.
There was hardly any variation on the
theme of equivocation to which he did
not resort. The evidence here is such
that it has to be read to be believed.

But even more important than the
evidence of Rangers directors and em-
ployees is the evidence of **David
White**, who was manager at the time,
and was mercilessly sacked later that
year after the team had been knocked
out of Europe. He if anyone had an
interest in getting back at the club that
had so ruthlessly ejected him. But the
secret society had reached out and put
the finger of loyalty on his lips. When
called to give evidence, White said that
he had been present at the meeting, in
order to be able not to recall that David
Hope was there, and also to assert that
he left the meeting feeling that no one
thought there was anything amiss with
the staircase.

There is no doubt in the mind of
Sheriff Irvine Smith that Davie White
(now manager of Dundee) invented
the story from start to finish. *The impression created in evidence by Mr
White became increasingly unimpressive
as his cross-examination progressed. . . I
am satisfied that he took no part in the
discussion, nor was he even present at
the relevant time. Mr Cowie (counsel
for Mrs Dougan, who could afford to
be generous at this stage) said he was
prepared to accept that Mr Hope had a
genuine blockage of memory. I fear,
however, the matter cannot be left in
so innocent a light.*

And he had this to say about the
credibility of Rangers FC:
*Making due allowance for the passage
of time and its effects on the witnesses'
recollection, and having regard to the
demeanour of Mr Hope and Mr White
in the witness box there is, I fear, no
escape from the conclusion that on this
matter their evidence must be rejected
as wholly unreliable and untrust-
worthy. . .*

But it was rather difficult for the
Court to be certain about exactly what
the Rangers Board did or did not discuss owing to the confusion, accidental
or intentional, of the records kept by
the club:
*If the verbal testimony of the defen-
ders' witnesses, however, revealed little,
their written records revealed even less*

*. . . Rarely can an organisation of the
size and significance of Rangers FC
have succeeded in conducting their
business with records so sparse, so
carelessly kept, so inaccurately
written up, and so indifferently stored.*

Rangers, then, have been desperately
attempting to cover up for what seems
to have been a boardroom game of pass
the parcel. The decision was that the
buck should stop with Ian McLaren,
and that was one story that they were
all agreed on:
*All the Rangers witnesses were in
the fortunate position of being able to
lay responsibility upon the shoulders
of Mr McLaren who, being now dead,
was in no position to dispute their
evidence.* McLaren, as David Hope
pointed out, must have been some
kind of expert on safety, because of his
experience in repairing tenement
chimneys. ·

The verdict, when it came, was a
damning one:
*So far as the evidence is concerned,
the Board never so much as considered
that it ought to apply its mind to the
question of safety on that particular
stairway. . . and would appear – I put
it no higher – to have proceeded on the
view that if the problem was ignored
long enough it would eventually go
away. . . Indeed it goes further than
this because certain of their actions can
only be interpreted as a deliberate and
apparently successful attempt to decei-
ve others that they were doing something, when in fact they were doing
nothing.*

David Hope

The impact of this judgement upon
the Rangers has been less than devastat-
ing, even though they are facing a bill
for damages that could top £2 million.
This sum would bankrupt every other
club in the Scottish League and would
certainly put even the mighty Rangers
into extreme financial distress. Between
clenched teeth, and through a barrage
of no comments, the word 'insurance'
is to be heard. However, Rangers have

always considered meanness a virtue,
and it is very unlikely they would be
insured for such a sum. But the amount
for which they are insured may not be
very relevant. For although their insur-
ers, the Norwich Union, are giving
nothing away, few accident policies of
this nature remain in operation once
negligence has been proved in a court
of law.

Rangers now have the right to appeal,
and this they will surely do. The case
will go to the Court of Session, and if
this does not produce the right result,
it will end up being fought in the House
of Lords. If the verdict is not over-
turned by them, the money will have to
be found, and if the club cannot find it,
then the shareholders will have to.
Rangers have a registered share capital
of £345,600 and this might mean that
every Rangers shareholder would have
to find £6 for every share he holds,
which can hardly be good news for
Chairman **Matt Taylor** who holds about
40,000 of them.

This is all speculation, but not plea-
sing to the Rangers shareholders,
traditionally the most dormant of
bodies. Already a mood of resentment
is spreading among them, about the
secrecy and incompetence of the way
the club has been run, and the will to
purify the club is growing. The General
Meeting this year is on December 30,
and will prove a rough one for the
Board. They are likely to offer up a
sacrificial victim, and the choice is
David Hope. Hope was badly instructed before he gave his evidence, and that
can hardly be accidental. He had had,
after all, 3½ years to think of a con-
vincing story. He is in bad health, and
his position on the Board has hung on
a thread ever since his bid for the Chairmanship in 1973 failed. Although he
was the choice of retiring Chairman
John Lawrence, he became immediately unacceptable when it was revealed
that some thirty years ago he had
married a Catholic girl in a Catholic
church; that she died more than fifteen
years ago availed him nothing. It is
possible that he will turn on the Board
that left him out on a limb in the
Court, and if he does he will find many
shareholders to support him. But it is
not a likely development – secrecy is a
habit that becomes instinctive, and
Masonic oaths bind the initiate beyond
the grave.

The end to this story is not yet in
sight, and silence will be preserved for
many months yet, as immediately Rangers appeal the case it will be *sub judice*
again until the process of appeal has
been worked through. But nobody in
Glasgow expects the club to fall apart,
even after what has happened. For the
club has many friends, and in the words
of the first official club publication
(1923), *'all who look upon the old
club with a freindly eye stand prepared,
by precept and example, to protect its
interests and its good name.'*

Alan Stewart

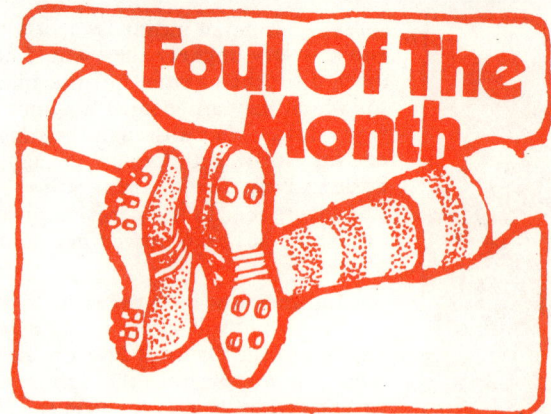

Foul Of The Month

Sunday Express 25/11/73

WELL, don't say you weren't warned. In FOUL 12, two Brummie lads drew attention to their club's "creditable attempt to transform themselves from a good footballing team to a team of hard-men"; one of them commending Tony **Want**, "whose tackling was too fearsome for even Spurs to keep him." Last month, a Newcastle fan pointed out that **Jim Smith's** skills are "balanced by a temperament which is able to absorb assaults and return them with interest."

The run-up to the Texaco game at St James's was about par for such a ludicrous number of meetings between the teams — 5 bookings in 4 matches, Moncur and Macdonald out of action. But even hardened FOUL Award judges paled at the 5th and 6th kickabouts, fortunately dealt with at length by Fleet Street ghouls who'd always led us to believe that such things Just Didn't Happen Here.

Suffice it to quote Mr Joe Harvey "I didn't see the incident, but the players told me Want appeared to stumble just before he was tackled": and note a name for the future, wee winger **Paul Hendrie** of City, who in the final match got a booking and two Newcastle defenders. Other than that — blame Texaco.

Hendrie should have known better than to attack **Pat Howard** from behind: he got the same treatment as poor McLaughlin of Everton, graphically captured (right) by the S. EXPRESS. Reader Nigel French suggests "official recognition for adding a new dimension to the art of fouling."

The rest of the first division boot boys weren't letting Newcastle and Birmingham monopolise the violence though.

Perhaps the most efficient foul of this month came from the normally pacific **John Hollins** against Leicester. Chelsea were two down just before half-time, and most of the damage had been done by Steve Earle. The doughty Hollins turned the game in a five-minute spell when he immobilised Earle, who had to limp off a few minutes later, and then knocked a penalty past Shilton. Chelsea never looked back, and won 3–2. The real pro only needs one tackle to achieve his ends; it took **Dave Clements** just 3 minutes of the Everpool derby before he had lined up Kevin Keegan, and prevented Keegan from having any further effect upon the course of the game.

Which brings us to Leeds. Some of the best fouls, the really artistic ones, are the combination fouls. As in boxing, much more damage can be done by a flurry of assaults than by a one-off job. A good example of this was displayed in the Derby v Leeds game when, in one smooth movement, **Gordon McQueen** hammered O'Hare to the deck and kicked him when he got there.

Several nominations for the way in which Emlyn 'Babyface' Hughes has taken over from Tommy the Smith in Liverpool's back four — as exemplified in the drawn game away to QPR. Reader John Smithard of London SW15 suggests that "At last Emlyn has found a use for the left foot which he used to carry around so ineffectually. Attempted amputation of feet, legs and other parts of the lower anatomy do not look too pleasant on the field, and we can only be thankful that the lights weren't on to highlight the spectacle."

Rangers also copped it from Man City, who are promising great things under Ron "it's-a-man's-game" Saunders. Reader G.R. Murray of Stockport wants an honourable mention for **Mike Summerbee** "who celebrated City's goal by racing 50 yards across the pitch and burying his studs in Clements' thigh." But **Rodney Marsh** gets the Supreme Irony Award for winning a penalty by falling over the leg of an old team-mate. We didn't think he'd dare. . . . Helen Morgan, from Pinner, rebukes us for not mentioning **Big Bopper Holton's** part in the Spurs-United punch-up, and suggests that we award him an electrified jockstrap. And Julie Galloway of Rugby (sic) nominates **Terry Paine** ("a right-hook and over-the-top all at once") for almost turning the Chelsea-Southampton game into a niggler's nirvana.

Keep 'em coming, guys and gals.

ALL TIME GREATS

Previous Foul Of The Month winners:
FOUL 1: **Mike England** FOUL 2: not awarded FOUL 3: **Hunter** FOUL 4: **Jefferson** FOUL 5: **K.J. Croft** of Birkenhead (knocking referee out) FOUL 6: Sheff Weds defender (anon: still hasn't owned up) FOUL 7: **Holton** FOUL 8: **Pitt** FOUL 9: **Ball** FOUL 10: Foul Award starts FOUL 11: **Craven** FOUL 12: **McGrath** tribute FOUL 13: **Mike Elwiss** (Chester)

YOUR VOTE COUNTS! Nominations for REF/Foul of Month received with delight by C.I.D. Dept, FOUL House.

BBC1

8.30am
Breakfast with Bremner

We join the chirpy Leeds skipper as he tucks into a light meal of crunchy Stokopops, and a low-fat Cherry-flavoured Yorath.

9.0 It's A Knock-Out!

Including Wrestling from Highbury Stadium, Princess Anne riding the Grand National course, and stock-car racing from Wembley Turf.

11.0 You can take a White Horse Anywhere

Historic Film of the 1923 Cup Final

11.50 Giles

Cartoon

12.0 Final Score

TV's panel of soccer experts predict the result of this afternoon's big match.

12.30pm
When Comedy was King

Highlights from last year's Cup Final.

2.0 Lunch with Lorimer

3.0 The F.A. Cuppa

Sponsored by the Milk Marketing Board

5.0 Final Score

TV's panel of soccer experts predict the result of this afternoon's big match.

5.5 We Want to Spit

DON REVIE leeds 20,000 supporters in a rousing sing-song as they travel homewards

5.45
This is Your Life

EAMONN ANDREWS

springs another surprise

on an unsuspecting celebrity

6.30 All Our Yesterdays

This afternoon's Cup Final

8.0 I'm All Right Jack

Film starring TERRY COOPER

9.30 Supper with Stokoe

(This replaces the advertised 'DINNER WITH DON')

10.15 Match of the Day

Tonight's match is an exciting tussle between a team from the North-East, and a leading First Division club from the North with ten internationals, fought on neutral ground. The commentator is a balding former athlete from Staffordshire who has given his name to a brand of well-known English and French mustard.

No. 8   May 1973

I FINISHED the 1973-4 Season disgusted with the Club I have followed for 10 years. If you report football instead of watching it for entertainment, you start looking for different things from before; who holds the ball while space is tight? Who runs into space to receive it and takes the load off someone else for a moment? Who will tackle back while his team-mate who should be doing the job is out of position for a moment? By those standards West Ham are a disgrace to the game.

What finally did it for me was the final game of the season, a 2-2 home draw with Liverpool. By Hammers supporters' standards, it was yet another classic: the ball was lashed around the field something rotten, plenty of mind-boggling flicks, passing movements that ran geometry into the ground, and all the other old favourites. It was the sort of match that makes you feel great if you are a West Ham supporter — the Old Loveleys might not be going to win anything, but as long as they turn on Honky Stuff like that, it does not matter.

I cannot look at it that way any more, and the match left me disgusted. Some incidents from the afternoon, will show why. The first was an utterly needless handball by Tommy Taylor that led to a penalty. Then not long after that, Taylor gave a free kick away in a dangerous position by levering up on an opponents back while knocking out a cross. Something which all centre-halfs do, but few as blatantly as Taylor. He did the same thing 2 years ago with Wyn Davies, until it turned into a running battle from the centre circle back to Taylor's penalty area, and another penalty. Alf Ramsey was there, and it probably cost Taylor the international career he was on the verge of. He does not seem to have lost any sleepless

nights over it — he just does not seem to care. And as if those sort of antics needed any showing up, there was the time of Liverpool's second equaliser to do it — 89 minutes, 58 seconds, scored by a team that was playing in the Cup Final a week later.

Players that care: when Billy Bonds walked up to receive his inevitable Player of the Year award, I could not help thinking of my nomination of Player of the Year; one who has had his worst-ever season, and has not played in the First Team since October — Bobby Ferguson. Ferguson was dropped after he exploded to the press about players here "who can make a thousand passes and not one tackle". It was showing unparalleld guts for a professional footballer to talk like that, and within a short time he was out on loan to Sheffield Wednesday and open to anyone who would take him away. Tommy Taylor's horsing around, the fullbacks' inability to tackle or mark   and Brooking's ball tricks, have cost Bobby Ferguson his career. I wonder if they lose any sleep over that? Its doubtful; Ferguson and Taylor had a fight on the pitch at Newcastle last year when Ferguson got tired of Taylor's sloppy marking of Malcolm Macdonald. Ron Greenwood apparently thinks Taylor will grow out of his casualness; I wish Greenwood would grow out of putting faith in players that obviously have no intention of returning it.

This year, nature did Greenwood's job, and it's just as well. Injury removed a lot of the stars from the side, and then things started to move. Eight superstars were missing from the victory over Manchester United that was probably the very start of the revival.

Then there is the old Professionals standard test; what are they like away

from home? Well, what can you say? When it comes to hiding on alien pitches, some of them beat the Wombles in going to earth. This season, until the Billy Bonds revival, they had etched one away victory — at Coventry, who were rapidly going off the boil anyway. Does 20 minutes of whirlwind aggression at Upton Park one week compensate for a disgusting 1-0 fold-up at Sheffield United the next? The mind boggles at next season's away performances at Carlisle and Middlesborough.

While all the time, the ultimate sickener is that when the mood takes them, they can turn anyone over, home or away. Players are great at storming into space when the other team gives it to them — McDowell spent Easter running down the middle of the pitch at Wolves and Southampton: teams that were hardly coming out of their own areas. But no one will go out and fight for space when it is not being given away on a plate. The exception of course, is Billy Bonds, who looks outstanding at least partly because all around him are holding back in resigned apathy.

It's been chic this year in the limited radical football circles, to talk about the remoteness of footballers from their community. Al 1 footballers are a million miles away from their supporters, but those with passion in their game can at least claim some blood relation to the fans. West Ham's uncommitted indifference — in an area that is being socially battered to its knees — makes them more remote from their public than any other team in the country. I wonder if any of them lose any sleep over *that?*

Chris Lightbown

No. 19   June 1974

DOYLE, LEE, BOOTH UNMARKED AS ANOTHER SOFT GOAL GOES IN.

Dear *FOUL*,

These two cuttings from the Northern edition of the *Daily Mirror* illustrate just how widespread the philosophy of 'if it moves, kick it' has become, and how niggly certain writers can get when for once, a season draws to its close without a northern team carrying off a major domestic trophy. With all this season's accolades falling on the likes of Ipswich, Derby, Stoke, and West Ham, these two hacks are reduced to carping about the cleanest Final for years, and bemoaning the lack of 'commitment' and 'passion' — i.e. over-the-top tackles, the subtle art of ankle-tapping, arguing the toss over every decision.

As a Fulham-ite of 20 years, now exiled in the north, and someone who cares a bit about the way the game is going generally, it gave this jaundiced old soul a good feeling to see two of soccer's more eccentric and amiable sides make it to the Final, and then proceed to play the game in the manner in which (in my foolish ignorance) I understood it was meant to be played. With a League season chock-full of clogging, fighting, and violence just behind us (all of which has been lovingly action-replayed on our *Match of the Day* screens), some of us actually felt that a Cup Final with only 17 free-kicks might leave a more agreeable taste in the mouth.

Messrs McGhee and Wallis must have short memories, anyway — I can recall some pretty colourless Finals recently, involving some of their beloved northern sides. Besides, we Londoners know how to behave ourselves on a nice sunny day when there's Royalty about. Incidentally, who had more right to be on the pitch, anyway, Frank — His Royal Highness, or the Hammers' fans in their totally good-humoured post-match invasion? At least they'd paid to get in.

Still, never mind: we Londoners have had our bit of fun, and I've seen my heroes tread the sacred turf at last, and next year I've no doubt we shall once again be treated to those fine old sights so traditional at Wembley — the trainers pelting to-and-fro tending to the victims of those manly skills we have come to savour throughout the season from Elland Road to Ayresome Park; not forgetting, of course, the witty exchanges with the men in black; the subtle art of time-wasting; the amusing shirt-pull.

Sorry we spoilt your party this time — we'll both arrange to bow out tamely in the 3rd Round next year; mind you, didn't we provide you with lots of easy copy? You know the kind of thing — 'The Cockney Sparrer Final', 'Bobby's last golden chance', 'Grandads' Final' etc. etc.

'Homely little Goodison' won't have quite the same ring somehow, but the resourceful men from the *Mirror* (Northern) will come up with something, rest assured.

Yours, only a bit cynically,
Pete Taylor,
Salford

FRANK McGHEE, brought up on roast beef, says:

I wouldn't care to watch games

like this every week

YOU would have to be deaf, blind, daft or living on a desert island not to be familiar by now with the single statistic that dominated soccer's final flourish—West Ham two goals, Fulham none.

But it is another fact-in-figures which nags at me constantly—the number of free-kicks whistled at Wembley. There were just 17 in 90 minutes. And, incidentally, neither trainer had to treat an injury.

For the purists that might sound like the gateway to a soccer Utopia—the signal for a return to standards the rest of the game should seek to achieve. And maybe the purists are right. Maybe.

For the cynics amongst us, however, it does tend to suggest that the game which has been called the 'Friendly Cup Final' was too much like a friendly, too little like a Cup Final. It lacked competition, commitment. It lacked passion.

Even the crowd didn't help. The West Ham yobbos who, by invading the pitch at the end, soured and spoiled a presentation ceremony that belongs exclusively to the participants, had done so little to support their team before it was won they were not entitled to join in the celebrations.

I've heard more noise in a public library than those fans raised until it was settled. Their actions at the end were indefensible—as out of place as garbage in a cathedral.

And it didn't help that all the significant scoring action was crammed into five second-half minutes which one player—Alan "Two Goals" Taylor—will always remember and another — Peter "Two Mistakes" Mellor — will never forget.

WEMBLEY MAGIC HAS GONE

SAYS DEREK WALLIS

WELL, Wembley definitely isn't the same without a Northern team playing in the Cup Final.

That is not the cynical view of someone who has now seen 20 Cup Finals. I still get a kick out of Wembley on Cup Final day — or I did until Saturday.

I used to enjoy the pageantry of it all before the kick-off, the community singing which was guaranteed to get everybody in a good humour, the emotional moments of "Abide With Me."

Bewildered

There was none of it on Saturday. The match didn't improve my mood. It was all too matey, with more pats on the head from one opponent to another than shots at goal — until two Northerners intervened.

I thought Fulham goalkeeper Peter Mellor, who used to play for Burnley, should have held the shots from Billy Jennings and Graham Paddon which led to Alan Taylor scoring the goals and becoming the slightly reluctant and certainly bewildered hero.

For those who like their football laced with romance and fairy tales it couldn't have been better, because Taylor — "Sparrer" as they call him at West Ham — had completed a dream season which began modestly at Rochdale and ended gloriously at Wembley.

The normally efficient Wembley information service slipped up here because the match had been on half an hour before those in the crowd who didn't know were told that Taylor was wearing No. 9 and Jennings No. 7.

The game was sprinkled not too liberally with notable individual performances like Trevor Brooking's for West Ham and Bobby Moore's for Fulham.

But I was left with the feeling that if this is the best these London chaps can do, the sooner Northern teams take over Wembley again the better.

Right first time with THE SUN 3.5.75

FULHAM CAN ROAR ON TO GLORY

By FRANK CLOUGH

DAVE CLEMENT'S TV SPOT

HOW the hell can West Ham win? Just about every armchair fan outside the East End is rooting for Fulham . . . and even the television companies are biased.

I mean, how can the BBC claim to be impartial with Jimmy Hill as their soccer sage? They don't come any crazier about the Cottagers than Jim, so there's no need to ask which way he will be sticking his chin out today.

They've even signed up Fulham's greatest ever player for the day. Johnny Haynes joins England boss Don Revie and Bobby Charlton for the big talk-in on the game.

Attractive

As for ITV. Well, they're virtually the Fulham mascots. Or to be more precise, Margaret Booker is.

Margaret is the attractive personal assistant to soccer director Bob Gardam. And, as London Weekend have covered all Fulham's Cup games, the players look on her as their lucky charm.

WHY I BACK FULHAM

By BRIAN WOOLNOUGH

THERE are two big reasons why Fulham will beat West Ham in the FA Cup at Wembley and Bob . . . . They . . .

BOB WILSON'S CUP COLUMN

I go for Second Division Fulham. Normally I would have taken the First Division side but West Ham have won only three of their past 21 League games.

Colin's Column

Cor! It looks like this is going to be the worst winter for football since the Munich disaster of 1958. What with the oil crisis preventing Dad getting to the match, and the electricity crisis causing games to be played on Tuesday afternoons, we're in a right old mess!

Not to worry, though, Christmas is coming and the old man (that's the editor) says we can have our office party indoors this year, so there'll be lots of pop and jelly and trifle and Christmas Crackers to keep our minds off things. Ian, the Office Junior, says he's going to come in his Portsmouth scarf, so I shall wear the West Ham scarf my Mum knitted for me. Talking of West Ham (and my mum says I never stop!) I hope they don't go down this year. I also hope Norwich, Birmingham, Manchester United and Stoke don't go down either, because relegation's not much fun, is it? Still, someone has to go down, don't they?

Well, that's enough from me, or else there won't be any room left for your letters.

Colin

Dear Colin,

I am a West Ham fan, and my hobby is collecting copies of the Football League Review. I would like to swap my entire collection (14,278) for a new centre-half. Would this be a record?

Louis Criminale, Plaistow

No. Bertie Mee, of Arsenal, got 120,000 pieces of green paper for George Graham.

Dear Colin,

My brother says George Young has won the record number of caps for Scotland, but my mum says it's Billy Bremner. I think they're both wrong; I think it's Denis Law. Please could you solve this for us before we go to press (January 11th).

Norris McWhirter

Well, Norris, the answer is that George and Denis both have 53 caps. What fine players they both have been.

Dear Colin,

I am a Gillingham fan, and I wonder if you could print a picture of my favourite player, Damien Richardson. I am eleven years old. I have never had a letter printed.

Oliver Croom-Johnson,

Oswaldtwistle

Well, you have now. Here's Damien. Quite a good-looking chap, eh? Aren't the Gills doing well this year? Good for them.

No. 14 January 1974

FOULNEWS

Ball kicked out

LAST month, a banned supporter; this month a banned reporter. When Peter Ball, Time Out sports man and FOUL contributor, rang Fulham to request a press pass for a recent game, unloveable secretary Graham Hortop told him with evident glee that they didn't want to see him at the ground again.

The reason given was that Ball's Time Out preview of the season, published two months ago, was "a disservice to the club and to football."

Bearing in mind that the truth didn't ought to be a 'disservice to football', even if it's an unusual embarrassment to Fulham, we reproduce the offending piece:

"FULHAM: The new stand is reported to have leg room for dwarfs only, but why pay for a seat when there's lots of room on the terraces? Get there 15 minutes before kick-off and pick your spot.

"And of course there's no atmosphere. There never was much, but the middle-class take-over in SW6 has ensured that it has only a small working-class community to draw on — which means no passion and no committment.

"The team aren't bad. For a time last season they were in third place in the second division — which was too high. The acquisition of Slough and Busby from Luton will strengthen them, and Mullery is still a first division wing-half. But the surrounding detachment undermines a team, and they certainly aren't good enough to win through without a crowd behind them.

"It's quite a pleasant place to go academically, but there's no involvement and no passion, which is what football is all about."

IS IT too much to hope that the closing down of *League Football* magazine will lead the League to consider blocking some of the other drains down which they're currently flushing much-needed cash?

When the original propaganda paper *Football League Review* went into liquidation in 1969-70 it had lost an astonishing £190,059 in just over three years. The League had sunk £234,000 into it initially, but waived the huge debt and produced *League Football* instead. The only difference was a profit of £5,000 in its first year, followed by a loss of £177,000 in the next two. "Justification" for this mismanagement is that the League nevertheless stays in the black, despite also losing £20,000 in 12 months on the 'Leagueliner' train, spending £11,000 on meetings of the Management (sic) Committee, and paying the secretary, Mr Alan Hardaker, a five-figure salary.

PS. Lest anyone should, however, begrudge the League their fee from the Pools Promoters Association — the main source of income — two companies, Corals and Ladbrokes, have recently announced their first returns of 1974. In six months, Ladbroke made £4,283,-000. Corals profits over nine months were £4,475,000: both substantially up on last year.

No. 12 November 1973

No. 23 November 1974

League
FOOTBALL

5p
Free

DEREK DOUGAN, popularly known as 'The Dog', has been a loyal servant to Wolverhampton Wanderers for longer than he cares to remember! But that's not all — Derek is also chairman of the influential Professional Footballers' Organisation (PFO), and a gifted novelist and broadcasting personality. The game can be proud of you, Dog — you're a credit to the game and an example to youngsters everywhere!

Here's the answer to how to make use of a football ground in the close season! Manchester City manager Tony Book says: "We give visitors to Maine Road such a bundle of laughs during the season that it seemed a pity we couldn't do the same in the summer!" It sounds like a good idea other League clubs might be well advised to follow — Book reports that by putting postcards in the shop window he was able to dispose of Ron Saunders and Francis Lee!

Figures? They don't mean a thing

THE FOLLOWING is the seventh part of my findings concerning the sale and readership of *League Football* at League grounds in all four divisions of the Football League. As usual they are divided into these categories: Average home attendance, copies of *League Football* sold, copies given away in programme, copies read, time screwed up and thrown away (GMT):

Rotherham United: 7961 — 0 — 6432 —
0 — 3.05.

Scunthorpe United: 5723 — 0 — 4358 —
0 — 2.59.

Sheffield United: 15,452 — 0 — 11,243 —
0 — 3.02.

Sheffield Wednesday: 15,452 — 0 —
11,243 — 0 — 3.02.

Shrewsbury Town: 4,300 — 0 — 3,756 —
0 — 2.54.

Southampton: 2,561 — 0 — 1,895 — 0 —
3.06.

Southend United: 5,397 — 0 — 5,003 —
0 — 3.00.

Southport: 2,864 — 1 — 2,611 — 1 — *

* Insufficient data received, as copies are taken away to Lytham and recycled.

The obvious conclusion to draw from the survey so far is that either a) No football spectators in the country can read, or b) *League Football* serves no useful or economic purpose, and should be wound up forthwith. But we all know, don't we, that statistics can be manipulated to prove anything.

Note: As this is the last issue of *League Football*, this survey is necessarily incomplete. Readers interested in the final, Swansea Town — York section can obtain it by sending me a stamped addressed envelope. For an extra 20p I will send a bound and signed copy of all data I have had published in *League Football*, plus a wallchart of my greatest triumph: *Alphabetical List of Tattooed Players Who Have Never Played In the Back Four of a Promoted Side South of the Humber in Midweek.* Keep in touch!

PORKY WANKERTON

Halftime Poser

WHAT was the match, WHO was the ref, and WHAT was the final score?

We must not be complacent

the self-appointed knockers would be simply this.

THIS IS the last edition of *League Football*. So the moaning minnies and dismal jimmies have had their way. I suppose they are satisfied to see the downfall of a magazine that, however albeit so humble, always tried to add that little bit of extra glamour to what remains for many the high point of the week – Saturday afternoon (*or Friday night if you live in Stockport*).

But let me say this. A few weeks ago at Blackpool – a club less than five miles from League Headquarters, mark you – only four thousand-odd people could be bothered to turn out to see Blackpool, a team with a chequered history and a fine ground, play Notts County, the oldest club in the League.

Turning to the fixture list, it is just not true to say that the League computer has been rigged to produce matches which tie in with my holiday arrangements. I am getting tired of this criticism, so let this be an end to it. *If a team loses fifteen away matches in consecutive weeks it only has itself to blame.* A good manager should keep his own house in order.

Let me make one final point. *League Football* has always catered proudly for the ordinary fan – the little chap who loves his team, is a bit of a collector, and still thinks football is a family game. Not the intellectual or the scruff *whose only use for a toilet roll is to throw it on the pitch.*

I do not deny that we have lost money. But I could number on the fingers of one hand some First Division managers – half a dozen at least – who have lost twice as much in half the time. . . *and have not received not one half of a per cent of the satisfaction we at League Football have had in doing it.*

By ALAN HARDAKER

I would have thought the dangers were clear enough for even a schoolboy to see. It comes as no surprise to me that this has happened in the same month that this publication is forced to cease publication.

Of course I have no doubt that some Mr Clever-Clever somewhere will point out that *League Football* has lost a figure in the region of a quarter of a million pounds in three years. All I would say by way of replying to

LEAGUE FOOTBALL

The official non-profitmaking journal of The Football League.
Published by The Football League Ltd (address liable to change without notice), Lancs. Telegraphic address FOOTLE.
Managing Editor, Public Relations Officer, Chief Accountant, Solicitor, Maintenance Engineer, Cleaning the Kit: Alan Hardaker.
Further Enquiries to Lytham and Fylde Waste Paper Merchants Ltd, Lancs.
Debts total £248,524 (telegram claims only).

---

the 'spurs are my team...

THE 'Spurs are my team
They play like a dream,
The manager's Neill, name of Terry;
So I say to the lads –
Keep the goals coming fast
And may Christmas and New Year be merry!
Paxton Rod, London N17.

I AM a firm believer in sticking to the rules, but I think the time has now come to make the game more interesting for spectators and players alike. *My suggestion is to use five balls – each one a different colour and constantly in play.* Everyone in the ground would then be watching some action the whole time, and there would be no need for attackers to stand around idly while the ball is in their half.

Each of the linesmen could be given a whistle, to spot anything missed by the referee. You could even have a 'goal-points' system – 5 for a goal scored with the red ball, 4 for the blue and so on. I feel that this or some similar system must be adopted if the crowds are to be brought back to football. . . *so come on, officialdom – wake up!*
Name and address supplied, Stranraer.

I HAVE over twenty twenty thousand Sporting Bratislau programmes, which I will exchange for a work permit so I can come to your country and watch my beloved Wrexham. In the meantime I would be happy to write to any male fan of Chesterfield goalie Phil Tingay living in the Havant area.
K. Lorenz, 17 Tubatewthpezst, Prague.

I AM a senior citizen of above average height. I can't post my letter to *League Football* because your pillar box is too low. How about giving us old folk a chance?
A. Lawson, 26 Heathcote Rd, Bignall End, Stoke-on-Trent.

I HAVE supported Gateshead for 57 years, and have seen every match, home and away, since they failed to be re-elected in 1961. Put that in your pipe and knock it, you smokers!
Tony Wilson (14), The Butts, Chaddesdon, Exeter St Marys.

Write to:
POSTBOX,
League Football,
Lytham St. Annes
FY8 1JG, Lancs.

CLASSIFIED ADVERTS

WANTED: Work of any sort, anything clean undertaken. I have a wizard brain for figures, which would ideally suit me for work in a shipping line office, on a traffic census etc. Apply W. Pilkington, Box 0602.

I HAVE a big centre-forward, which I will let go for a set of League club badges, plus cash adjustment of £25 o.n.o. Terry, Box 0603.

A MILLION copies of League Football can be yours, for less than 1p each. Or would exchange for piano. For details ring the League and ask for Mr H.

Service with a smile

EVER WONDERED how you get your football results? It may seem an easy business — which may be ranged along the terraces to you the spectator, listening to the results or up on a scoreboard tucked under a on your wireless or reading them in the floodlight.
'Pink One' on a Saturday night.

But in reality the providing of Football League half-time and full-time scores and results is a complicated task which a lot of people have to put a good deal of time, effort and even dedication into.

Crewe ... 0 Rochdale . 1
Half-time: 0—0
Doncaster 3 Hartlepool 0
Half-time: 1—0
Exeter ... 2 Northmptn 2
Half-time: 1—0
MANSFIELD 3 Shrewsbury
Half-time: 1—1
Newport ... * Scunthorpe
Half-time: 1—1
Rotherham 1 Chester
...... 0—1

udford C 1 Workngtn.
Half-time: —
'rentford 3 Darlington 0
Half-time: 2—0

Let us say you are enjoying watching your favourite club playing, home or away, in a League match. The half-time whistle is blown by the referee, who then leads both teams off the pitch. The chances are that if there is no brass band playing, nor no schoolboy penalty competition taking place in either of the two goalmouths, that you will look to the

'alphabetical guide' to the half-time scores

Under this system a number of matches are designated under letters of the alphabet – for example letter 'N' might stand for 'Hereford v Swindon', in your programme (although there is no hard and fast rule for programme codes up and down the country). One detail that is observed, though, is that out of the alphabet the letters 'I' and 'O' are not used, as a halftime scoreline of 0-1 or 1-0 under either letter (or vice-versa) might prove confusing to the spectator.

In simple terms, the operation goes like this: members of the Press Association, stationed at every ground, telephone scores and results in to their important main office in London's Fleet Street. And then League club secretaries ring up this office to find out the details they require. They can even get their own half-time score if they wish!

The League has always been grateful to these servants of the game who operate such systems – and also to the news and communications media, who are largely responsible for the accurate relaying of up-to-the-minute information to each and every Football League ground.

So what may seem like an easy business is in fact quite a complicated task. As ever, the League is concerned that YOU get the news YOU want, as quickly as possible. But spare a thought for the man behind the scenes... and beware of unofficial results.

gifts for all ages

Xmas is now not so very far away — so here's an idea! Why not shop for presents at your local League club kiosk? The following are a selection of moderately-priced gifts which every fan can afford... and will enjoy giving.

If you've a large back garden, then the Cup Final Pitch Jigsaw is for you! Sturdily made in stout green card, our stocks offer perfect reproductions of the pitches on which every FA and League Cup Final has been played since 1927! Actual Size! Exactly the way the pitch looked after the match! Over 50,000 pieces!

West Ham or East Fife, we have a colour and flavour to suit you! And if you'd rather concentrate on the match in hand, a handy League Gum Wallet will keep a lump of chewy moist and fresh from kick-off to the final whistle!

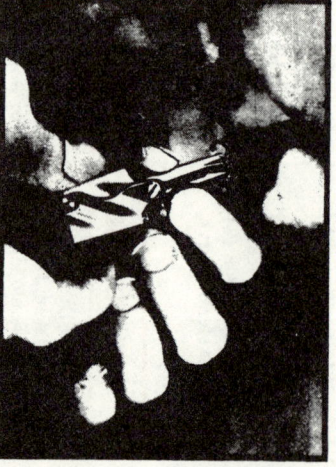

Give the ref in your life this combined Whistle-and-Radio! The man-in-charge will just love tuning in to find out how his favourite team are getting on — while his own match is actually in progress. Can pick up foreign commentaries too! Available at all souvenir shops.

Official Football League Chewing Gum is just the job for giving the game you are watching that extra zing! Whether you support Northampton or Southampton,

With this Meat-Pie Holder you can now eat, and read your programme without getting the pages greasy! Comes in four different club colours — with a built-in bonus: a clock which tells you how many minutes of half-time there are left... so you don't miss any of the action either!

Stocking-filler time! 100 Copies of LEAGUE FOOTBALL make a most attractive present, and what's more — they're all different! Collectors' Corner, Postbox, Manager's View, Walter Pilkington's Giant List of Facts — all your favourites are here. And buying in bulk this way means you pay just a fraction of the cost per copy than if you buy them at the match!

THE TELEPHONE rang and Al Malleson cradled its mouthpiece to his voice box in less time than it takes to say Another Manager Sacked. It was Arthur Glanville, an old chum of Al's from SPQR, approaching 35 and thinking of deserting the substitute's bench for a post in management.

"What can I do for you, Arth?" quipped Al.

"It's about the Doomcaster job, Al, what's it worth, you reckon? I mean, would I be wasting my time sticking an application in?"

There was a brief silence as Al calculated the odds.

"Is this off the record, Arth?"

"Aye."

"I'd rather be dead in Hell than alive in Doomcaster. It's a shit-hole. Honestly, Arth, don't go near the job; I'm telling you that as a friend. If you want to live in the sticks, okay, but do yourself a favour. . . avoid Doomcaster."

There was another brief silence as Arthur calculated some odds of his own.

"I've heard they pay well, Al."

"How well?"

"Twenty thousand plus car, help finding a house, all kinds of fringe benefits."

A third silence — this time profound.

"Money isn't everything, Arth. Not for money would I work in Doomcaster. Besides, the directors are dead mean. They charge for a parking spot at the ground."

"Well, if you say so, I'll maybe have a look at the Wrectham job. United might be on the lookout for a coach an' all."

"You qualified, Arth?"

"How do you mean?"

"Well, have you been to Lilleshall?"

"Twice."

"Twice!?!"

"Yeh, I left my jock strap first time, I had to go back. Picked up another badge, though, while I was there."

"Smart lad. Let us know how you get on."

"See you, Al."

* * * * * * * * *

Forty eight hours later Al was reclining in a leather armchair in the plush Directors' Lounge at Doomcaster Town, a neat Scotch in hand and up to his eyes in sycophancy. Chairman Jim Biddulph beamed triumphantly at the club cameraman, and slipped an arm around Al's brawny shoulders. The amenities

were inspected, the players smiled weakly and offered timid handshakes, and within half an hour nineteen journalists were speeding officewards with exclusive stories. Mr Biddulph drove Al in his Rolls Royce Corniche to a particularly grubby Service Station on the M6, where the deal was finalised.

MALLESON MOVES NORTH SHOCK! and **VILLA LOSE PLAYBOY AL!** are fairly typical of what appeared on the back pages the next morning, although the *Guardian* chipped in with a rare species of pun-crazed idiocy, and *The Times* allowed itself a sort of verbal yawn. Vince read all about it in the *Financial Times*, Matt Black in *The Scotsman*, Sambo Mbugwe in the *Sun*, and Reg Dwight picked it up in a news bulletin wedged claustrophobically between Minuetto Allegretto and an ad for singing breakfast cereals. Try as he might, Vince could not bring himself to feel disappointed or even surprised. Al Malleson was not the sort of man the sensitive, decent, honest and loyal Vincent Dearlove could be expected to work with, and they'd never begun to build a relationship. Good Riddance is an adequate summary of Vince's feelings.

Mere expletives were inadequate to express the surges of joy and triumph that ebbed and flowed in Matt Black's bosom when he read the news. He sprang out of bed like the man in the razor-blade ads, and placed a couple of phone calls to confirm the news; that done he donned his best black suit and hied him to Carr Park, double quick. Chairman Arthur Barr was already on the spot, resolutely

denying all knowledge of Al's impending move, while on the second floor the man himself was emptying his desk and the managerial drinks cupboard. Half an hour of unrelenting suppression of the truth was beginning to wear at Arthur's nerve-ends, and he was delighted to drag the normally dour Mr Black into the arena and see how he made out.

Matt was one of the century's masters of the polite No Comment. Five minutes of fierce questioning slid off him like water off a duck's back, until the doorman, ex-international left-half Giant Johnson, let the cat out of the bag. With the smug look of one who's just pocketed a £25 tip, Johnson waddled across the forecourt and deposited two cases and a bottle of hooch into the back of Al's Maserati. The game was up, and Matt knew it. There followed three minutes of frankness such as no journalist had ever heard from the wily Scot, and when Des Hack asked him about likely replacements he admitted that one name was certain to figure near the top of the list.

Blondie Brown — captain of Villa's European Cup-winning side.

The sportswriters had to admit that, of all the interviews they'd done at all the managerless London clubs that day, Matt Black was the best value.

A triumphant return for the still popular, though receding, Blondie Brown. . . or more upheaval for the Villa? See next month's satire-soaked FOUL! — The Force for Sanity in a Wacky World of Insecurity and Panic.

LAST month's article (by Terry Bushell) on Leeds as the biggest con since Hitler was a very thought-provoking one. In fact, although in sympathy with much of what he said, I felt that he really failed in the end to give an adequate analysis of Leeds, seeing them in the context of English football as a whole; and he also went over the top in his dismissal of their footballing abilities.

It's certainly true (and worth constantly repeating) that Leeds can still clog with the best. Of course, although Hunter is the main culprit, Bremner and Giles both contribute mightily to the cause on occasions. And there's always Jack Charlton, Cherry, Ellam or whoever to lend a hand. But one should do more than just state that, or ally it to a charge that the only reason people think they are entertaining is because they do pre-match circus routines on the pitch. The truth about Leeds, as the side of the last five years or so, can reveal a lot about English football generally.

Leeds at their best can reach a level of sophistication that no other current English side can match. Certainly to compare them to the old Real Madrid as some more chauvinistic commentators have done is fatuous. They also cannot stand

and all the other ills that beset English football as a whole. And as Leeds have a greater collective class than any other side in England, they play this football with a high level of ability. But when one sees them playing this way against sides of far less ability, one can only despair for them and for football generally. If a side of their class descend to time-wasting, from choice, against a limited side like Norwich, what hope is there? It is this perversion of great talent that seems even more distasteful than their clogging.

Even more than Arsenal, Leeds represent the alienation inherent in modern English football. For whereas Arsenal as a team have little capacity for flair, and apparently even less desire for it - why else would they leave their two creative footballers George and Marinello in the reserves? - Leeds have it in abundance. But through fear, or cold but ultimately mistaken calculation, they refuse to give it expression away from home. The abuse of great talent which one sees in Leeds is a tragedy.

leeds: the ultimate defence

comparison with the Ajax or Bayern Munchen sides, or the old Spurs or Manchester United sides. But watching Bremner and Giles controlling midfield, probing for openings and flighting carefully weighted balls for their front line is the nearest football gets to a game of high level chess. Even if one's preference is for the more flamboyantly passionate artistry of the sides mentioned above, one still has to admire the intellectual sophistication of Leeds at their best. And besides Giles and Bremner, the skills of Lorimer, Gray and Clarke should also dismiss canards about them being just a team of heavies.

But of course Leeds reserve these talents almost exclusively for home games. Away from home, even when the clogging isn't paramount, Leeds display as much sense of adventure as the average Women's Institute committee. Safety First becomes the be-all and end-all. If they fail behind then some of their undoubted talent is harnessed to the search for an equaliser. But as soon as that is achieved back comes their defence in depth, possession football

They aren't - as Terry Bushell said - a great team. Great teams have always been true to themselves and their abilities. There is something small and mean about Leeds which has always prevented them from being that. For example, the following comparison makes the point. In the 1948 Cup Final, Matt Busby told United, who were 2-0 down at half-time, to keep playing football. United won 4-2. At Palace recently Leeds, also 2-0 down, clogged Palace into submission for 15 minutes, played beautiful football for the next 20, scoring two goals, and spent the last ten minutes playing out time when they might easily have carried on to get the winner. A great team would not have needed the clogging, and would, if equalising, have gone on for the winner. Leeds' calculation tells them that a point away from home is championship material. But football is not only about calculation. I don't think Leeds will be a great side; but instead of dismissing them as just a bunch of cloggers, it is a cause for regret. And we might ask where that leaves football, when probably the best side over the last five years or more puts timidity before flair and expression.

11. 52AM   WORCESTER 1
SOBERS THE STUMBLING BLACK
GARY SOBERS, SEEMINGLY THE ONE MAN BETWEEN

Exchange Telegraph tape 1/8/74

Next Saturday here League Staines v Harwich and Pakistan K.O. 3 pm.

Staines Town v Enfield programme (could be)

FOUL Sport

The mystery men

★ WHO are the faceless figures behind the by-lines on the World's livliest Sports Pages? WHAT is the truth about "Steve Allan"?? WHO is the mysterious "Peter" who ghosts every cricket column in Fleet Street — under different surnames??? WHICH is the otherwise reputable Sports Agency whose long-suffering reporters jack their SHOOT articles to bring you the latest greatest SUN-SPORT Series????

Meet THE MYSTERY MEN! In the SUN!! and only the SUN!!!

SPORTIEST LETTERS

We asked SUN readers to write in for £1. The response was overwhelming.

SURELY a home draw at Wembley is good enough to qualify for the World Cup Finals, especially when no extra time was played. Come on you Poles, play the game!

SAM FRANCISCO,
Gosport.

I THINK England is the greatest team in the world — therefore they should go to Munich I say.

ALICE MARTIN,
Overton.

COME off it! Mr. C.L. Cowley.

DOES anyone else agree with me that there is too much football on television? Every night before going to sleep, my husband turns over and falls out of bed!
HARRY GLITTER,
Knebworth.

YOU CAN keep your Big Mals and your Brian Cloughs! As far as I'm concerned my dreamboat is the SUN's own Peter Batt! When I see him swaying in the press box my legs turn to blancmange as I watch the sweat trickling down his lean face! Please send me big poster.
Ps. I vote Daventry the sexiest town in Britain.
JAN TONCAR,
Daventry.

Well, what do YOU think? Should Alf go? Write to Sex, Sun, London.

LAST NIGHT'S SOCCER

LEAGUE CUP (3rd rd replays)
Hull 4 Stockport 1 Carlisle 0
(extra time being played)

WE'RE GONNA WIN THE LEAGUE!

■ WHO's going to win the league? The Sun put that question to its unique team of top sportswriting talent. Here are their in-depth replies — candid, forthright, controversial — but never dull!

LET'S BE CLEAR about one thing — England has the best football league in the world

Having said that doesn't solve my problem though. Because let's face it I'm a man who has loyalties to two sides — one in the First and one in the second Division.

Don't forget Nobby Stiles and David Sadler both came from United — so you could say I'm marking my cards in that direction!

But right now for R. Charlton, Esq., Preston's the name of the game!

says BOBBY CHARLTON

BILLY BREMNER

WILL EVERYONE please get off our backs?

Let me hasten to qualify this aggressive statement. Look, at the start of the season there was a lot of comment—fair enough — about the 'new' Leeds. And one or two people were laughing up their sleeves I'll bet. But now look what's happenned. We now have points from matches, and if that doesn't speak for itself what does for heaven's sake? Ask the boss. He'll tell you the same.

The Brains of Soccer are always in THE SUN

Malcolm Macdonald...

PUT YOUR money on us to win the League.

Because the spectator sees more of the game, as the bloke said to the undertaker, and I can tell you from where I'm sitting with my leg up that we look a very very good prospect

But there's a hell of a lot of difference between teams you look forward to playing against and teams you respect.

But like I say, tip us for honours

 Bob Wilson

LET'S BE rational about this — not every team can win the league.

And while I have the deepest respect for teams with the reputations of Leeds, Everton, Burnley, Newcastle, Derby etc — don't forget one thing. Arsenal begins with an 'A'. The first letter in the alphabet. And I reckon sincerely that that counts for something.

EXCLUSIVE

I'M NOT a man who takes sides.

In the European Cup we made the mistake of taking on a side like Red Star Belgrade. But, like the man says, there are mistakes — and mistakes. Some you can learn from.

If my lads have learnt a little respect from that encounter it'll make it that much easier for them when we eventually sail past Leeds and take the League title.

By BILL SHANKLY

LOU MACARI

Don't write us off just yet

Interview by TONY CARTER

IT'S ALL IN YOUR SUPER, SIZZLING SUNSPORT!

PROS AND CONS

THE PFA Awards beanfeast, eccentric though it was, threw up some important points about the attitudes of The Pro: firstly to fellow-pros, secondly to all those outside the game, which has come to include journalists, spectators, even administrators. It's handy to consider Eric Batty's book in this light too, not least because he is a disciple, if not worshipper, of Ron Greenwood, and implicitly accepts Greenwood's distinction between Football People and the rest: his book, and Jago's, illustrate the gap, but may also help bridge it, if we let them.

First though, the Players' Player, a choice so uncontentious this year that even Wislon got it right. What was apparently bizarre was that 12 months after picking Norman Hunter as their fave man, the players could come up with a list of nominees including the likes of McKenzie and Hudson. Even given that most players in the lower divisions only see these people in TV highlights, does this mark a change in standards and priorities to match that which has arguably occurred in the Press? Probably so, but don't over-estimate it. Intimidation may have dropped two places, but the number one quality required of a fellow-pro is still reliability: the key test is still who you want in your side when you're two-down away from home on a muddy afternoon. Players may join the campaign for more skill, but in a horribly competitive team game you pick Todd and Bonds before Bowles and Marsh.

Though this slight shift — from Hunter to Todd — is reflected by Press opinion, the concern allegedly felt by all factions for the future of the game hasn't brought any reconciliation between those outside the game, in particular the journalists, and the chosen few hundred. An essential goal of the PFA 'do' is to upstage the Football Writers Association award: it's a rare opportunity to have a go at the Press, to remind us of the venom felt towards your friendly local (and national) newspaperman.

"I've no confidence in any soccer reporter," said Steve Heighway in his famous *Sunday Times* interview. Greenwood, championed by many journalists, still lumps them and their readers together as "the blind leading the blind."

At worst, of course, the argument gets reduced to the age-old one of performer versus critic. "They haven't played (therefore) they know nothing about it," (Heighway). "It was Dr Johnson who said he did not know how to make a table, but he could tell a good table when he saw one," (Max Marquis). Equally superficial, really. Many journalists have and still do play, with varying ability. And what Marquis and the rest tend to do is not admire the table, but criticise the dove-tail joints.

Suspicion of journalists obviously isn't confined to footballers: a recent poll purported to show that only politicians were trusted less. Non-stories, misquotes, sensationalism and the search for an 'angle', are objectionable features of the gutter press in general. Where footballers come off particularly badly is that the people reporting their activities can survive quite happily with virtually no technical knowledge at all. This is the biggest beef. Our budding Jeff Powell is assumed to have a rudimentary knowledge of the laws and get the scorers' names right; beyond that, ordinary journalistic criteria apply — 'ability to dig out off-beat stories and write crisp, punchy copy under pressure.'

The result is that most journalists are simply not qualified to help people understand what's happening on the pitch. Hence the concentration on other things altogether. There are even Fleet Street reporters who make a virtue out of their ignorance and who, without much serious opposition, have made Coaching into a dirty word. That there are good coaches and bad, the public would never imagine: which are which, and why, they're never told.

The professionals, in turn, don't accord Fleet Street very much respect. So attacks on the Method Men, and Technical Jargon (from the very people who coin terms like Wingless Wonders and Total Football) don't cut too much ice either. When, like the boy who cried Wolves, a Voice Of Sport gets it right, derides dirty football, or runs down the low level of skill, managers and coaches feel obliged to defend their calling, insist that they should only write about the good things. Coaches grow more resentful, more introverted, when we desperately need them to talk . . .

Jack Charlton came into the press-room after another disgusting Middlesbrough performance (at QPR recently) smiling his goal-less draw smile, mentally waving two fingers at them all. "We got a good point, didn't we?" Dave Sexton refused to contradict him, to take the side of the newspaper tigers. And the gap yawned wider.

No. 28   April 1975

FRANK KEATING

"Y'KNOW. . . ", began that lovely player Gordon Hill (not Gordon Hill the referee, and lovely man to boot. To boot indeed — alas, no more: his licorice suit hung up, referee Gordon's gang aglae). Where was I. "Y'know. . . " began the chirpy dockland flipperti-gibbet, the former Lion (yellow in emblem only), the young man gone first West, to Euston, thence to Old Trafford. "Y'know. . . " And suddenly, there was the season summed up, rounded off, smooth as a ball, the ball that makes the game, bless it.

It's been a "Y'know. . . " sort of a season. 75-76! 75 — three-quarters of a century, last lap, lads, almost there, but steady, thrice three years merely from 1984, think on, 75! Thrusting on to 76, synonymous with trombones (and, there's no gainsaying, looking ahead there follows that Sunset Strip year, all the sevens, Bingo!).

Anyroad, point is, what's been achieved this year, has the game attacked or defended, stepped forward or back, y'know? Let's look at facts. Scouse on top once more. And Geordies too, hooray. But looky here, what's this? Saints preserve us! (And they do, McMenemy hasn't an enemy in the world). Bejasus — Hereford and Lincoln promoted. . . cathedral towns, both, can't be bad.

And yet, y'know. . . what of England and St George? 75-76 has been kind to The Doc, but what of The Don? With Hampden Roar died down, Sat'day fortnight last, what was left? Bedraggled Revie, out on the field, the tears of a million Englishmen watering grass and him like rain. A man at sea? Well, God bless all who sail in him, on t'quest against the alien Finn. And God bless all of you, too. Y'know it makes sense, even if the piece doesn't.

No. 33   May/June 1976

No. 27   March 1975

Press

Give them their due. It's not easy writing about an event which 400 million people have seen as it happens; and then, in the most civilised parts of the world, seen again in slow motion; then seen from a different angle; then had analysed ad tedium; then the best bits one more time; 'til eventually, light years later, Jeff Powell At The Big Match plops through the letterbox.

By about the third week, most papers had got with this, and were giving the whole thing a fairly low profile. Many of the troops – at least the foot-sloggers – were called home with Scotland, and in, say the *Mirror* or the *Mail* you had to wade backwards through a lot of Test matches and Wimbledon to get to

WM 74. Yet overall there seemed little recognition that we might need something different this time. McLuhan may have smirked at the *Mail* having one man to report on Brazil v Yugoslavia and two to cover what BBC and ITV said about it: but for our men at the match, Global Village Sports Day might have been Sheffield United v Norwich.

Coolest of all were the *Times* who proved that the whole thing could be covered by sending out one respected, if eccentric gentleman who watched the most important games and filed his worthwhile opinions on them. The *Guardian* managed perfectly with two reporters and one newsman (Peter Cole) who got into areas that TV completely ignored – commercialism, security, black market. And the never-ending copy which the press agencies sent winging into all newspaper offices did the rest – quotes, gossip, statistics, interviews, features: everything you needed, and plenty you didn't.

Force of circumstance stopped the *Express* going overboard, when Scottish camp-follower John Mackenzie was banned from

official contact after screaming that miscreant Bremner should be sent home and locked in the Tower. The *Express* raved about the Man They Couldn't Gag, then dropped him like a Rivelino free-kick: and soon realised that David Miller couldn't go on for ever writing the whole back page himself.

But at the Sensational Sizzling *Sun,* 'low profile' is the way the model girls wear their panties. If a story doesn't stand up and shout, it's spiked for life; likewise a *Sun* reporter. So from Wednesday June 12, it was one big footballing gang-bang.

Tip and Tap, the special 1974 World Cup mascots feel on top of the world about the whole exciting event.

"ROUS GOES: IS IT THE END?" Of Sir Stanley? Of the Coppa del Monda?? Of the World??? We never found out.   And Peter Batt (Sportswriter of the Year, need I remind you?) had hit Hunland, witnessing things that no-one else had: (**"I saw the indefatigable Oblak traverse each blade of grass 100 times over"**) and doing his bit for Anglo-German relations:

"Triumphant at having broken through enemy lines, I cockily asked the friendly neighbourhood copper 'Var ist de Toiletten bitte?' He replied 'Down in the cellar, where your English football is' ".

Nice one, Sohn. But not enough to dissuade big Pete from persevering with his role as the new Des Hackett; the one man among 2,500 journalists really where the action was, plague of the authorities and confidant to the stars. You'll just never guess who it was that told Peter Cormack he was playing against Brazil. . . Willie Ormond? Don't be wet:

"Bewildered Cormack spent yesterday trying to believe in fairies as I tried to convince him he was in at last. . . "

Writing about the football though presented problems. On June 17, the day of his marvellous pot-and-the-kettle complaints about the German press splattering football **'splendour and trivia across the front, middle and back pages'**, Peter Batt's view was, reasonably enough, that Haiti with their performance against Italy had brightened up the tournament considerably. They were **'breathtaking. . . thrilling. . . exhilarating. . . brave. . . primitive'.** But the party line back in Bouverie Street, you'll remember, didn't include support for Third World teams which dirty dago Havelange wanted out there instead of our European lads. So within three days, Sunsport Opinion

was declaring, in the biggest white-on-black headline you've ever seen that **IT'S ALL A BLOODY FARCE!** That (strapline) **The Great World Cup Show Is Just One Big Rabbit Shoot**. (Geddit?). And (opening sentence), **The World Cup is turning into a bloody great farce!**

Nice language for nine o'clock in the morning. There was more mileage in it, though, when the very next day UEFA president Franchi said that zonal qualification should be abolished. Not quite the first time he'd ever mentioned it, but justification (?) for the *Sun* to tell us

that **"The men who control soccer in Europe last night joined the SUN's fight for quality rather than quantity in future World Cup competitions."**

The *Mirror,* faced with the unenviable task of trying to outdo all this, began with a 1-4-1 formation (Voice of Sport, four reporters and a photographer) but soon brought in Pele In An Exclusive Interview With Steve Richards. A bold move, but one which had little lasting value: it was the same Pele, the same Steve Richards and the same exclusivity as *London Evening News* readers got for the rest of the tournament.

No points for originality either to the rival *Evening Standard,* which sent playwright Willis Hall to sit-in with the ITV panel – eight months after sporting voyeur Terry O'Neill had done the same thing for the *Observer.* Hall did at least cut through some of the crap – the absurd tartan jackets removed as soon as the lads were off-camera; the ecstatic producer ("You would not *believe* the shot we got of Paddy's face when Yugoslavia scored").

But a pic caption attached to his article really summed it all up. **"Derek Dougan – phrases charged with majestic eloquence".** It turned out that the Doog kept on saying "Oh shit!".

Steve Tongue

PANEL BEATING

Geoff McDonald looks at television

IF THERE AREN'T already two competing World Cup channels by 1978, it would be no surprise to find the Post Office issuing separate licences for ordinary sets and specially designed models for the reception of Summer Sport programmes. Trying to maintain an enthusiastic interest in this year's competition has been a daunting task, although the disappointments in the standard of the football served up might not have been so grave had it not been for the self-parodying antics of Brian Moore and Jimmy Hill, and their respective troupes.

Over the four years that the two concerns have been buying up the big voices in football, two definite house-styles have been established. The BBC continue to go for the Establishment figures — with the result that they end up with the completely inarticulate Joe Mercer — while ITV concentrate on men with personality, drive, go etc., and consequently get obscene squabbles between Crerand and Dougan. Both

have their own substitutes for informed argument, ITV's being to encourage personality clashes and statements like 'Tomaszewski is the worst goalkeeper in the World', BBC's to have five genial types sitting around earnestly agreeing with each other. C'est magnifique, mais ce n'est pas what we buy licences for.

There is light at the end of the tunnel, though, since virtually every paper and magazine going to press in the past month has carried a piece damning the panels to hell. The concept of an impartial and informed panel of experts sitting in judgement of the match we, the peons, have also been watching was created for the Mexico World Cup, and it looks as though it might well have been cremated at Munich. The gradual reductio ad absurdum has gained speed over the last year, and it's hard now to imagine where they go from here. They must surely now look away from the experts, and think about ways of improving presentation.

If anything, ITV were more fortunate in the games they showed than were the BBC, especially during the second round. They made nothing of it, because with the hysterical build-up Brian Moore gives even to schoolboys taking penalties at a one-eyed ex-international in a deserted stadium, there is no way left for him to convey the idea that what they have here, for a change, is really the genuine article. No matter how many times that man tells me West Germany v Australia is going to be a fascinating tussle, I'm going to judge for myself.

It wasn't until very late in the tournament that ITV's figures began to bear comparison with the BBC's, and, as ever, when given the choice between Hugh Johns and David Coleman the nation has looked to that master of hysterical tautology, and the stark contrast with whimsical Frank Bough taking it all in his immaculate stride back at base. The BBC audience for the vital, pulsating game between Scotland

Did you see that?

Continued

and Yugoslavia completely swamped ITV's, but you only had to look at the jackets Moore & Co. were wearing to know why.

It must be said that television coverage of the World Cup was comprehensive. With such huge audiences at stake, both sides planned their operations pretty thoroughly, it seems, and whatever we say about the lack of imagination and style, we have to admit that the lunatic football fan was well served. Every ball kicked was covered, every goal committed to memory, the prejudices of every panel member broadly publicised. Perhaps it's a little sad that I shall remember not Mueller's marvellous swivel to score the winning goal, nor Karasi's kick at Szarmach, nor Rivelino's goal against East Germany, not even Jordan's epic against Zaire. I shall remember David Coleman's "the pace of this match has been accelerating and it's getting faster all the time"... Barry Davies' "Holland look as if they could score any time

they liked – like now", as Rep stole in, right on cue, to pop in No. 3 against Argentina... and good old Bobby Charlton, his face a mask of torture and indignation, accusing Uruguay of cheating.

Action replays are made of this.

No. 20   July 1974

—Quotes—

Sir Alf, at the Scotland-Zaire game when the lights went out. On being asked by Huw Johns when he thought the game would be resumed, he replied: 'A em not an electrician'.

Brian Moore (in desperation when the phone-in turned into a fiasco): 'Is there nobody on the line?'
Big Mal: 'Yes. Jimmy Hill.'

Harold Wilson, after the Scotland-Brazil game: 'I know more about football than politics'.

Sam Leitch, when asked whether the BBC panel would be weakened by the withdrawal of Don Revie: 'Not at all'. (*Evening Standard*, 6.6.74)

Jimmy Bloomfield, much touted as the new England team manager, on being asked why he was not going to Munich at all: 'England's not qualifying is what persuaded me to stay behind'. (*Sun*, 22.6.74)

No. 20   July 1974

VICTORY FOR ENGLAND: Hugh Johns' Last Tape (an edited transcript)

"Referee Jack Taylor reaching into his pocket again, a scoreline of 1-1 but is this going to be the third booking? YES IT IS! Neeskens gets the yellow card, that's a goal and a booking for him and there's the incident that brought him to referee Jack Taylor's attention... Cruyff might get a booking there if he says anything more to Jack Taylor, still angrily Jack Taylor waves the players away from him... It looks very much as if Jack Taylor, yes, Jack Taylor has booked Cruyff, well that was sheer foolishness by Cruyff, great star that he is, he shouldn't show his temperament like that, Jack Taylor has been pretty firm in this half and obviously a very great deal for Brian Moore and the panel to discuss in London so without any more ado... " (Panel deleted).

"Maier makes a meal of it, they're squaring up to Cruyff, Mueller is there, Overath is there, Maier down on the ground, and referee Jack Taylor is right in on it... Manager Schoen back on his bench, his eyes had brightened for a moment there but now they're dull again as indeed the weather has been all afternoon... And Cruyff had a little dig at Vogts there, some advice being offered to referee Jack Taylor by the West Germans — Alf?" (Ramsey deleted). "Goalkick, but referee Jack Taylor saw a deflection... Maier showing referee Jack Taylor that it

didn't go completely over the line but I really can't see how he can get away with a con like that... And we look now as... Looking back at the game in fact whether referee Jack Taylor... making sure that the ten yards is back... " (unintelligible)

"Haan, that's Cruyff going to get a run against Vogts but he's there, Beckenbauer nods, NEESKENS!, but a foul is given anyway, a foul is given, referee Taylor looking at his watch and takes... a note of the time... Maier trying to instruct referee Jack Taylor that somebody else's name should be booked Franz Beckenbauer, the man who always looks cool but I get the feeling you could probably fry eggs on his forehead at the moment, his brain working overtime... about two minutes to play, Holland looking for the equaliser but Germany down to ten men and Benhof's had his treatment, wants to get back on the field, referee Jack Taylor signals him on... this game about 180 seconds away from the finish... Rep against Breitner, and Breitner falls, the free kick given, and Jack Taylor shakes his fist at Johnny Rep, it's getting very scrappy out there now, Mueller bundled out of it and referee Jack Taylor has... ENDED THE GAME... and West Germany... the whole stadium... the banners roaring... " (inaudible)

35

Press on Regardless

"For me the most refreshing feature of the current season so far, has been the behaviour of the Press. Gone are the adulatory tone, the overpraising of mediocre achievements and players. . . Spades are now most definitely called spades and a much more positive voice has been introduced into match reporting and feature writing."

Leslie Vernon, World Soccer (November).

LESLIE VERNON, late of Hungary and now of Hampstead, has always had an ambiguous relationship with Fleet Street and those who drink there. Joint-editor of *Rothmans,* and *World Soccer* columnist, he also writes and has written for the two publications most obviously guilty of the sins he mentions — namely *Goal* (R.I.P.) and the *Sun,* to which he contributes a regular column of foreign gossip and an occasional Cruyff For Arsenal story.

THERE is suddenly a host of Archie Gemmills dribbling through the playgrounds of England.

Six pictures of Gunther Netzer might just be worth one of Colin Todd.

Anyone can be Paul Breitner but there's a queue to be Charlie George.

Derby County, not Real Madrid, are playing in miniature towards the bicycle sheds.

Derby's memorable midweek performance against Real was not lost on future generations of footballers.

Skill

"I like it, I like it," says England manager Don Revie. It pleases him to think that Britons, not Brazilians, Dutchmen or Germans are currently top of the form.

For him to suggest that the British press has undergone a miracle cure in the close-season is asking us to believe a lot. Yet those who still read the back pages of, say, the *Express,* the *Mail* or the London *Evening Standard,* may have noticed a marked change in direction and emphasis. A change of the Sports Editorship at all these papers is not unconnected with apparent recognition that football is in trouble; that more entertainment is imperative (if only for commercial reasons); and that dirty players do not, short-term or long-term, improve anything.

So the *Mail,* for instance, has run an Entertainment League and now taken up the Fair Play League (which has become the *Daily Mail*-Trident League, for the same commercial reasons). The

Express, having risked a gamble with expensive signing David Miller, have taken his philosophy as their own and given him his head in return, with encouraging results: within a month this season he left an eloquent blank space as a report of all that was good in the Spurs/Arsenal game; and laid into Willie Young "who doesn't necessarily mean to kick lumps off the opposition, he's just built that way", criticising not only players like Young and clubs who employ them, but also "the system

MIKE LANGLEY
TALK OF SPORT

our 58,000 fans will lift us."

Granted that Czech crowds are near the top of the Decibels Division but noise won't intimidate the Todds, Bells, Keegans and Madeleys who live every Saturday with the volume turned up.

Nor do fans score goals, or Czech footballers overcome English.

which tolerates and even encourages such players to abuse the laws and the genuine skills of opponents — promotes negative craftsmen as ersatz heroes in the way London Weekend TV did yesterday afternoon". For a paper in which Hackett ruled only three years ago, I submit, m'Lads, that that is progress.

Now some doubts, criticisms, gripes, problems. . . and Victor Railton. Firstly, football journalists' conditions of work haven't changed. Popular papers still demand a big headline story each edition, even if there's no news to merit one; and for Monday mornings a new 'angle' has to be found on Saturday's match, which is now 18 hours old. If a story breaks early enough for the evening papers to cover it, the mornings must find a 'follow-up' or vice versa. When a manager is sacked, they must dream up some potential successors (note how many papers had the name Clough in their headlines the morning after Birmingham sacked Freddie Goodwin). Friday evening's paper carries the team news: Saturday morning's has the obligatory interview with a player who's been left out.

Most match reports still have to be started while the game is in progress, making considered judgement extremely difficult and observation of the second half rather haphazard. Even the Czechoslovakia/England reports were written in this way — a match beginning at one o'clock in the afternoon — and one Man at the Match spent literally half the game on the press box floor, trying to make himself heard down his phone.

Instant reporting begets instant judgement, and instant analysis of instant crises. So Derby beat Real by three goals and everything in the country is rosy: two weeks later Derby and England lose and English football is awaiting the last rites. After the first Derby match Ken Jones could write in the *Sunday Mirror* about the "host of Archie Gemmills dribbling through the playgrounds of England." (There must be a lot of bruised shins in the under-13 team.) And "it pleases Revie to think that Britons, not Brazilians, Dutchmen or Germans are currently top of the form." After the second leg, the new serious *Mail* asked: "Why Has It Suddenly All Gone Wrong For English Football?" The answer, of course, was that it hadn't *suddenly* gone wrong. It had been going wrong before and since Sam Leitch wrote the original line about kids in the playground: that they all wanted to be Nobby Stiles instead of Pele.

And hooliganism. . .? Try Frank Taylor of the *Mirror*: "I refuse to believe that morons who go on the terraces to chant their foolish ditties are true soccer fans. How can you sing when you are involved and excited by the thrills of soccer?" Treatment of the West Ham/Manchester United incidents was the stuff that Press Council complaints are made of: RIOT DAY! (*Sunday People*); THE MADHOUSE! (*News of the World*); THE MATCH THAT ALMOST DIED OF SHAME (*Sunday Mirror*). Victor Railton of the London *Evening News* ("If it's not shit, I'm not interested") actually wrote that "More than 1,000 rioters brought chaos. . . as fighting broke out all over the pitch"; and the week after these lies appeared, the *News* started to tag him "Fleet Street's Number 1 Soccer Reporter"

Steve Tongue

"*Life* is great for me with plenty of balls down the left from Graham and Frank Lampard.

"Billy Jennings and I have knitted together and we think alike. He's a good jumper"

Young Carl Jayes, the City's No. 3 goalkeeper was next tried and he acquitted himself admirably at Stoke

Nottingham Football Post

Something Completely the Same

Jonathan Croall

on The Box

'I really want to be just a performer on football,' says Jimmy Hill. He's certainly that. Saturday Night With Noddy (mysteriously billed as *Match of the Day*) gives our bearded ringmaster a regular chance to crack his own whip, manipulate a few other performers, and dazzle all the family with his virtuosity on the Action Replay, the Match Statistics and the Chat with the Stars. His show has been packing them in for a couple of years now; but the production's looking stale and flat, and the resident clowns aren't raising the laughs any more. Isn't it time for a change?

Of course it is — but it won't happen, will it? Though his breathless bonhomie and flip judgements make him an easier target than most, Jimmy Hill is no more than a symptom of the diseased state of televised soccer. The depressing fact is that, despite some heavy demolition work, some of it in highly respectable places (the BBC's own journal *The Listener* printed *three* critical articles on the coverage of the Munich World Cup), the unceasing banality and triviality of television football is here to stay. The battle of the ratings continues. David Coleman and his 'sheer professionalism' are a permanent fixture again. This show could run for ever.

May has been the cruellest month for those loyal viewers who remain in spite of everything. There we were on May Day, gaily thinking Dickie Davies had summed up the completed season by confessing, as a newly-revealed resident of Southampton, to being 'over the moon' at the Cup Final victory. But less than a week later Brian Moore was sitting us down to a 'glittering nine days of football' (he meant, would you believe, the Home Internationals). And before that we'd had a whole evening of West Ham's defence being taken apart by Anderlecht. And after that Liverpool's second leg against Bruges. Not to mention England's tour of America. . . Is this what they mean by total football?

Despite this barrage of coverage, there was one saving grace: a few of these matches were televised live, and in full. Much of the criticism of football on television, in *FOUL* and elsewhere, has focussed on the way edited highlights distort both the shape and the feel of the game. A comparison of the full and shortened versions of the Cup Final only serve to ram the point home. This year's game was scarcely distinguished by its flowing moves, explosive shooting or athletic goalmouth saves. Yet the way the Southampton players kept in the game and gradually took it over, the fact that the only goal came just a few minutes from time, gave the match its own fascination.

Little of this fascination was left by the time Jim came to fix it in the evening. We were showm McCalliog's incisive through passes, but not the similar number that went astray. Peter Osgood appeared to be playing an uncharacteristically prominent part in the action. Even Ian Turner seemed to be having a full afternoon. For once

1974 — the Expert embraces the Player.

you didn't have to be on the terraces to say, 'That wasn't the match I saw this afternoon'.

But can we even begin to imagine a world without the snippets we've been conditioned to? Obviously the TV companies are very unlikely to consider making drastic changes until there's more evidence of a big switch off. And they react as feebly to constructive ideas as they do to all the criticism that's been thrown at them since football coverage moved in to show business. Some of the most pungent criticism is buried away in a neglected pamphlet, *Football on Television*, published last year by the British Film Institute. A collection of essays from film and sociology academics dealing with the 1974 World Cup coverage, the pamphlet is streaked with hideous jargon and technical mystification. We're told, for instance, that Big Jack Charlton's attempts to compare Poland's style to that of England in their heyday 'serve only to locate us in an ethnocentric perceptual set'. Yet the essays also include some imaginative thoughts about camera positions, styles of match coverage, the stereotyping of players according to nationality, and the function and assumptions of the *Radio Times* and *TV Times*.

In one of the more readable essays, Andrew Tudor attacks Jimmy Hill for his domination of the BBC panel, noting that the only person to break the national front was the newest recruit, Lawrie McMenemy. 'In the half time discussion of the Holland/Brazil match, McMenemy. . . clearly annoyed, told the nation that he had spent the whole of the first half of the game listening to Hill shout each time a foul was committed'.

It was good to see the outspoken Geordie breaking a few tele rules again two years later, after his team's victory at Wembley. At the end of the match, when we'd been through the ritual 'Fantastic, David', and 'I won't believe it until I read the papers tomorrow' with some of the players, their manager took over Barry Davies' script: 'As the only religious man here, Barry, ask me what day it is today,' he suggested. The little man obliged (it's fairly easy to slip your own questions in when the man with the mike is preoccupied with signalling to 'the boys' to bring their milk bottles and sweaty faces nearer to the camera).

And the ex-Guardsman got away with something else on ITV the following day: he hazarded what might well have been the longest solo flight on a football programme since records began. For what must have been almost a minute, he gave us a year-by-year description of his managerial relationship with his predecessor, Ted Bates, who had remained at the club after McMenemy took over. OK, the speech was a touch sentimental, and was only indirectly to do with Southampton's Wembley win. But he was allowed to continue well past his usual interruption time — even though you could hear Brian Moore breathing heavily as time went by. A useful reminder of how rare it is for a programme to be allowed to meander off in directions uncontrolled by the production team.

The same post-match analysis offered quite incidentally an unintentional glimpse of the position of the players in the soccer hierarchy. Having lured Mike Channon and goalscorer Bobby Stokes into the London Weekend studio, Brian Moore spent the first three or four minutes ignoring them. And when Channon eventually popped in an observation, Moore said cryptically, 'I wondered when we'd get a word from the players!'

These small surprises shouldn't lead us to think that either channel is aiming to redesign their tired formats, let alone hire some intelligent commentators. David Coleman's bludgeoning style and paltry descriptive powers (the atmosphere was still 'electric' when West Ham came out to face Anderlecht) have survived all the critical shafts that might have felled a more self-critical performer. Will he never learn to keep quiet in those many moments when his voice is quite superfluous? And if he's paid to be something more than merely a commentator on the action, shouldn't he come up with analyses more penetrating than 'Anderlecht are certainly looking as if they are going about their business'? How many of us expend more passion reviling his barking

commentaries than reacting to the games he describes?

Brian Moore is certainly more restrained and less obtrusive — but that's not a great achievement. Indeed the *sameness* of the rival programme makes the duplication of coverage doubly crazy. Any thoughts of experiment are inevitably sacrificed to the bitch-goddess success. So both channels run the obligatory Meet the Cup Final Teams film. Both channels run highlights of the Wales v England game

1976 — Show Business embraces the Expert.

(though the BBC get 'the professionals at the game' to tell us that the Sunday papers had got it all wrong when they described the England display as rubbish). And both send their minions on to the pitch at Wembley, to get identical comments and predictions from the two Cup Final teams as they show off their new suits in front of the crowd.

We get all this, but never the passion of the regular supporter unaccustomed to press box or executive viewing suite. There is only the ritual two-minute encounter with an ordinary family or two in the Cup Final crowd — and TV has done its democratic bit for the year (apart from letting a few players run the programme at Christmas; but then that's the season of goodwill, innit?).

Ultimately, what the TV companies need — apart from new faces and voices — is a willingness to let the football sell itself as an event worth watching and a willingness to let the people in.

It's amazing that the recent access programmes and phone-ins have made no impression on the football programmes. If we have to be 'entertained' by discussion and argument after the game, let's not have the cast restricted to players and managers whose personalities and faces are 'good for television'. Hairy astrologers (especially when they get their predictions quite wrong) and adolescent commentators just aren't good enough any more. The big switch-off is getting closer all the time.

No. 33   May/June 1976

SOCCER FOR — SOPHISTICATES

HOW MANY TIMES HAVE YOU MARVELLED AT MARTIN PETERS' ABILITY TO LOSE HIMSELF IN A MATCH?

MARTIN? MARTIN? MARTIN? MARTIN? MARTIN?

HOW MANY TIMES HAVE YOU ASKED...

.."WHAT'S THE IDLE SOD UP TO?"

THE ANSWER IS...
HURRAY! BOOM HURRAH! BOOM!
CREATING SPACE
BUT WHAT'S IT MEAN?

'CREATING SPACE' IS WHAT THE BEST PLAYERS DO WHEN . . . .

THEY DON'T JUST STAND AROUND!

— THEY RUN OFF THE BALL.

...THEY HAVEN'T GOT THE BALL.

— MAKE THEMSELVES AVAILABLE.

SO THINK TWICE BEFORE SHOUTING, "WE WANT GEORGE GRAHAM!"

...HE'S AWAY CREATING SPACE!!

No. 13   December 1973

INTRODUCING...THE ONLY FIRST DIVISION SIDE WITHOUT A CHOPPER!

FOUL of the month

AS another thoroughly bloody season hobbled towards its close, it became more difficult than ever to select a single foul from a month of infinite variety, which had even spectators joining in the fun.

The home internationals began with Trevor Hockey of Wales, who two months earlier had kicked Poland into submission, trying the same tricks on Scotland. Yorath weighed in too, but David Hay apart, the visitors were clearly saving themselves for Wembley.

England-Scotland was once again a brutal disgrace, though David Miller in the Sunday Telegraph was the only reporter to say so. Ball and Bremner, those loveable little mid-field tigers, were soon kicking loveable little lumps out of each other, and for ten minutes just after half-time the Arsenal man seemed to go berserk: this provoked the ultimate in spectator participation, when a Scottish fan came flailing on to get himself a piece of the action.

Bremner proceeded to nobble Moore after the ball had gone, so blatantly that even David Coleman saw it. And when Hughes extracted more than ample revenge with a grossly late tackle, Billy Boy very nearly got to swing the right hook he had been threatening all afternoon. All this and Storey too ! Reader Martin Fitch supplies this graphic description of how Pete saved a dodgy moment in the England penalty area:

"With Moore and McFarland out of position and Bell in position but asleep, Storey had to cope with both Macari and Dalglish: in a flash he had the latter down with a throat arm-lock, then turned round to deliver a stunning head-butt to the former.'

So, slightly dazed, to the European finals. Liverpool were unexpectedly restrained in München-Gladbach, though Hughes did grace the notebook this time; Leeds got all they deserved against one lot of dirty Italians (see Review of the Season), and another lot failed to intimidate Ajax quite so successfully. The thigh-high effort by Juventus' Furino on Cruyff was not so much a tackle, more an amputation, and only the most spectacular of a number of attempts to put the frail Johann out of the game.

It was in fact less effective than the crippling of Causio ten minutes after the interval, out of sight of the cameras and, inevitably, the commentators. He had been the one Juventus player capable of initiating any attacking moves, and the half-time message was obviously that he had to be stopped.

As for the slippery Poles, Bob Wilson surely spoke for every decent upstanding Briton when he slammed their filthy play-acting - Lubanski refusing to get up when he'd merely had the stitches ripped out of his knee..the goalkeeper limping around as if Bell and Clarke had really crunched him... It took Bob's team-mates Ball and Storey to show us once again how the game should be played. But what can you expect from amateurs ?

No. 9   June 1973

Spot · The · Ball

No.1 ~ JELLYMEAT PUSKAS

No. 10   September 1973

Poets' Corner

once
i loved you deeply enough
to spend a saturday afternoon
when chelsea were at home
shopping in the kings road
with you

I was irritated by the bustling fans
because they reminded me
there might have been
somewhere else
I would rather have been

but i loved you deeply enough
to suppress such blasphemy

yet it took less
than a football season
to realise
that really
i hated you

almost as much
as I HATE TOTTENHAM

Malcolm Peltu

No. 12   November 1973

WARNING! These books are packed with dynamite!

HE WAS the man they hated to read. People said they didn't know what he was on about. Perhaps Don Revie was right when he ignored completely this man's warnings. Only time will tell. But now YOU, in the privacy and quiet of your own home, can be party to the words and thoughts that sing in every line of mighty intellect allied with classical education, a combination that can truly mean only one name . . . GLANVILLE.

GLANVILLE . . . 'In the country of the blind, the one-eyed man is king' wrote Joyce, another spokesman of his age, and no more fitting epitaph can be spread about the memory of this lank-haired prophet, the seer who foresaw soccer's death-rattle a generation before the rest. Now you can share this vision for less than a quid.

Too beautiful for words...

DEAD DUCK BOOKS

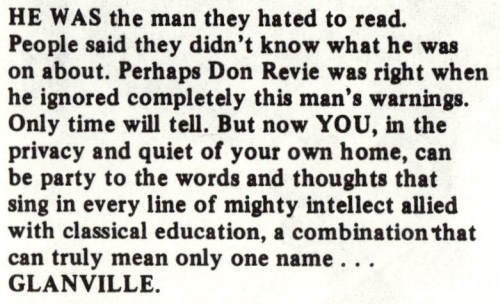

Strange Power

JUST WHAT strange power did this man wield? With a turn of his quicksilver tongue he could lay bare and raw Bob Wilson's

empty bonhomie, Alan Ball's falsetto burble. And champion football's unlauded and deserving at the same time! One anecdote tells how once he bitterly belittled the Arsenal machine and heaped praise on plucky Orient, all in the same piece. That very week 56,000 saw the Cup-tie at Highbury, while less than a dozen miles away 4,000 made the pilgrimage to Brisbane Road and brighter football. Such was the influence of the Sunday supremo.

Grecian 2000

AND REVIE! Tales of the duo's ideological tussles are legend. Wagging tongues said that Glanville fawned round the England boss at press receptions and then went away and wrote nasty pieces about him. These are the same malicious spirits wno said that every mention of 'Catenaccio' and 'Total' earned him another gallon of free petrol for his Fiat. Such meanness exists around the truly great. Was it not Boswell, another inimitable chronicler, who remarked 'Fate never wounds more deep the gen'rous heart, Than when a block-head's insult points the dart'? For the story of the true relationship between these two Titans, send off now.

Misunderstood . . . abused . . . unread . . . inchoate . . . Perhaps. But as the man himself might have said – Finito La Commedia!

WHEN THE PRESS BOX ROARED

SOME PEOPLE WILL tell you that sportswriters are different, somehow, but quite honestly I don't reckon that's true. I'm Harry Bates, and you'll know me as Britain's Number One Voice of Sport. That's what my paper, the *Sunday Rabble,* calls me at any rate. But it's not so long ago that I was a kid going along to the match on a Saturday afternoon just like anyone else. Even then I had a favourite spot, though — just up behind the press box, where I could hear everything going on, and feel like I was really part of it.

Brentwich United was my team — and still is, even though I've seen all there is to see, and could travel in the coach with any top-class club in the country. It's a small ground, is Brentwich, and you were so close to these geezers with their notebooks and telephones that you could really imagine you were in the box there with them, timing the goals, calling newspapers in parts of the country I'd never even heard of, and asking each other who'd scored just then.

In fact that was how I got my first big chance. I forget which match it was now, but it had only just kicked off, and half the press hadn't turned up yet, or were still talking and looking at their programmes. And we went and scored — Sid Fenchurch got it out on the left to Terry Bogie, Terry crossed it to Dennis Kremlin, who nodded it in. But you should have heard them in the box! They didn't have a clue! They finally decided they'd all say it was an own goal from a Fenchurch free kick. Well, I couldn't keep quiet any longer. "Following a Brentwich build-up engineered by United skipper Sid Fenchurch in the fourth minute," I said, "Bogie made space down the wing to cross to KREMLIN, who headed into the top left-hand corner of the net."

There was a bit of a silence, then they all started scribbling and making phone calls like mad. Someone even shouted "Well done, the youngster!" I got a cup of tea at half time for that, and the biscuit with jam on that no one wanted. And at the end, this bloke in a big coat with binoculars, who it later turns out is from one of the posh Sundays, buys me a bottle of pop and some crisps and gives me a lift home in his flash car! Not only that, on the way he was asking these questions, you know — did I want to be a football reporter, was I at the match every Saturday, what hobbies had I got, did I go out much with lads my own age, had I got a regular girlfriend — all the way to Snaresbrook.

Well, I didn't think much more about this until about ten days later, just before my seventeenth birthday. I got this phone call at the bottling plant (I used to ride my old bike to work in Dagenham every day, going via Ilford and Wanstead). It was from Slaytor's, the big sports agency. Would I come in and have a chat with them, and maybe do a trial match report that Saturday? Naturally I jumped at it. In fact I was so chuffed I went into town on the tube that lunchtime, and didn't half get a rollicking from the foreman that afternoon for being half an hour late! But I didn't care, because I'd seen Ted Slaytor himself — 'Uncle Ted' or 'The Boss' as I was soon calling him — and we'd agreed terms: 50p a thousand words, shilling a goal, notebook thrown in, watch my language, and no word to be more than nine letters long.

They were all dead nice to me in the box, too, that first day. One bloke in particular, Bert Palmer I think his name was. He reckoned he'd been working forty years for Slaytor's, though I couldn't remember ever seeing his name anywhere. He taught me a lot, did Bert, about the different kinds of writers I'd come across, and the way most of them had their own superstitions, like not leaving before the end and so on. He also gave me lots of practical tips — how to have two cups of tea at half-time and still manage to snaffle half-a-dozen sausage rolls, how to write a couple of paragraphs while the ball was bouncing on the stand roof, and how to get as many facts in as possible. For instance, I'd written "Redknapp fouled Brench, the dirty arab." Bert showed me that by filling it out to read "With the score still 0-0, United had their best chance shortly after the restart to open their account when awarded a free-kick after transfer-seeking Trevor Brench was adjudged by Chester referee Jeems to have been unfairly tackled by Stan Redknapp, today making his 173rd consecutive appearance as centre-half for the promotion chasing Lancashire side." I could save myself a lot of time when it came to doing the final report, and earn myself a bit more money into the bargain.

So I packed in my job at the bottling plant, and started writing full-time. Though the old man didn't like it at first, he soon changed his tune when I bought him a packet of his favourite Wrigley's out of my first wages — glowing with pride, he was, I can tell you, as he went off to tell his mates on the night shift. He reckoned, what I hardly dared hope, that this was just the beginning. I needn't tell you what happened the next few years — how I started to get by-lines here and there, how one day my mates went with me up the West End to buy my first sheepskin coat, how I went abroad and stayed in this hotel, and was the only English bloke in a press box full of Greeks — you must have heard it all before. What you can't know, what's special to each of us, feature writers, ghosts, stringers, is the feeling you get when that first goal goes in.

Mine was at Brentwich, as it happens, a big local derby against Borough. The score was 0-0 with about two minutes to go. I was reporting for the *Borough Surveyor,* and suddenly I knew someone was going to score — I didn't know who, which side even, just that there was a goal coming. I grabbed a Slaytor's phone and dialled the *Surveyor* number without taking my eyes of the play. "Get me late sports copy — quick! Please keep this line open. Brentwich vs. Borough — ready?" I thought this is it. "Then in the dying seconds of the match, Borough/Brentwich took the lead and eased their relegation problems/made promotion a racing certainty — sort that out later — when" .. here we go. . . "Ptashko, making his debut for Borough, dribbled past Fenchurch and punted a long ball across the Brentwich area to SCOLLAY, who gave goalkeeper Ironmonger no chance with his first-time shot from twenty yards. This was the last kick of the match, as referee . . . er . . . Trench blew immediately for time."

There! We'd lost, but I didn't care. I'd done it, that was all that mattered. Holding back my excitement, I listened to the copy read back to me, okayed the names, put the phone down, and sat back. And the press box roared. ●

FOUL'S
REVIEW OF THE SEASON

NOT for fifteen years have so many people decided that they don't want to watch football matches. The drop in attendances this year has been a staggering 3,400,000. Which is not much more than the total figure in £sd spent on signing star attractions.

This is the single most important trend in a season which has nevertheless produced more incident for the sensation-craving public than any other; a season in which soccer has moved off its traditional spot on the back pages and into the areas of news,fashion,business and sex.

Is it all FOUL's fault? In the last edition of our first season we examine this paradox and conclude that no sector of professional soccer has reacted positively to this disastrous drop in demand for the product.

1 HAVE CLUBS SERIOUSLY TRIED TO MAKE ENTERTAINMENT AS IMPORTANT AS WINNING?

Brian Clough and Bill Nicholson were the only managers to talk much about the entertainment value of their teams. Even after Spurs had won the League Cup, Nicholson expressed immediate disappointment at the poor value his team gave the 100,000 bored Wembley fans. Was it a coincidence that their respective clubs played the most memorable match of the season? ...a freak in a season in which predictability was more sought after than spontaneity.

To look at the question the other way round,and to assume that winning equals entertainment is to miss the point that the way a match is won is more important than the actual winning; the gut-reaction entertainment of seeing the home side maul the opposition is not the same as being prepared to be entertained by the opposition - which is essentially the difference between the spirit at Highbury and the spirit at Anfield. The most hopeful signs this season have come from sides who in away matches have managed to win friends as well as points - QPR,Burnley and West Ham (at last).

It is no surprise that the most exciting players to emerge were from this sort of team - Roger Davies,Brooking, Leighton James,Stan Bowles. Their personalities have been brought out by their clubs' not bothering too much about week-to-week consistency,and complementing them with the more reliable (if unsung) Hector,Bonds,Dobson and Givens respectively.

On the other hand,Arsenal made a deliberate choice between entertaining and winning when they removed Marinello, Charlie George and George Graham from the team and bored everyone to death. Although fans were walking out in increasing numbers as the season went on, there is no evidence that more than a few managers made the obvious connection as to what was driving them away.

"I will not have cloggers in my side at Derby. I would not have fielded Sir Alf Ramsey's sides that played Germany or Scotland.They were brutal,violent games"

— BRIAN CLOUGH

"If they knee me,I butt them"

— CHARLIE GEORGE

"I make a habit of never butting anyone 'cos I cut so easily"

— WYN DAVIES

No. 9   June 1973

2 DID ANYONE GET THEIR JUST DESERTS?

As with Tesco wine, the final sip is always the bitterest. Norman Hunter left it until the last club game of his season before getting himself sent off (for retaliating to the sort of foul that he himself had been guilty of all season). Leeds also got what had been coming to them since August, losing the FA Cup Final to a team who enjoyed their football more than Leeds did, and losing the Cup Winners' Cup Final to a team whose cynicism dwarfed even theirs.

Some of the teams who put the emphasis on entertainment made it pay off (see above) but since the First Division was once again dominated by the relentless professionalism of Liverpool, Arsenal and Leeds, it was elsewhere that enterprise was most tangibly rewarded - three of the teams promoted from Division Four showed that by consciously rejecting the laws of the jungle they could win out...but we mustn't be too rude about Hereford in their first season.

Equally gratifying was the fact that West Brom after embracing the Arsenal philosophy in the shape of manager Don Howe were relegated, after surviving for years with their former happy-go-lucky ways. And Crystal Palace proved that it simply wasn't enough to flash a cheque-book and buy First Division security. This meant unfortunately that Norwich escaped justice (but see this column in twelve months' time). Manchester City's transformation from a footballing into a kicking side brought them as little success as did Sir Alf Ramsey's transformation of England from a kicking side in September into a kicking side with ten men in June.

3 HAS THERE BEEN A DECREASE IN VIOLENCE ON THE FIELD?

The number of bookings and sendings-off was higher than ever before. But this says as much about referees as it does about players - figures alone are no evidence that soccer is getting dirtier. What is clear is that referees are still booking the trivial offences, sending players off for a word out of place, while ignoring the kicking and punching, especially if it goes on off the ball. Refs are still reluctant to book anyone in the first five minutes, and to send off straight away for violent fouls.

Players have not mended their ways, because the attitude of their managers has remained as cynical as ever. Only Brian Clough is known actually to fine players for dirty play, the approach of most other managers being that a goal saved by a professional (sic) foul is worth a booking, especially when the club is prepared to pay any resulting fine. It is these managers who have evolved the concept of the first team squad, which is designed to cover not only players maimed by their opponents' retaliation, but also frequent suspension of members of the first X1.

4 HAS THERE BEEN A DECREASE IN VIOLENCE OFF THE FIELD ?

"Hooliganism" is the most convenient scapegoat for the falling crowds, because it draws a veil over the unsatisfactory nature of the football actually played. In fact, hooliganism has declined during the season and may now be at an all-time low, in spite of League, FA and media attempts to prove the opposite.

Typical was the totally inconclusive opinion poll done by the London Evening Standard in collusion with the Football League, which purported to show that hooliganism was the main factor in keeping people away from soccer. Terrace violence tended to make the headlines only when it was a quiet week for bookings and transfer sensations.

The attitude of Authority has reflected only paranoia and fatuous thinking like that of Denis Follows, who suggested banning everyone under 18 from the terraces. Alan Hardaker, true to form, denies that there is a problem. The only reaction of the League and British Rail has been the League-Liner, a souped-up special that young fans can't of course afford. The truth is that the boot is on the other foot in that it is violence on the field which is alienating the 18-24 age group, the real "hooligans" of a few years ago.

No. 9   June 1973

5 HAS THE PRESS TAKEN ITS RESPONSIBILITIES MORE SERIOUSLY?

Quite the opposite. This season has seen a proliferation of ghost-written banalities, prompting the annual NUJ conference to a resolution to ban the lot which has obviously induced panic in those Fleet Street offices where the "sports-writers" can write nothing else. It remains to be seen whether this ban will come into effect, but what is certain to continue is the trivialisation of soccer on other pages.

We thought we had seen the nadir when David Webb put on a kaftan and beads in the Express last year, but this season has produced some even more grotesque gimmicks. The Sun had Malcolm Allison and his City team in the bath all over the centre pages, and used players like Cyril Knowles as clothes-horses. Talking of horses, McLintock starred as a cowboy Daily Male, while Osgood modelled Mafia gear - which was perhaps more appropriate. Trivialisation intensified in coverage of the sport itself, not only in the popular papers, but more seriously in the Sunday Times, where "creative" ad agencies began to get more space than James and Glanville and Willie Morgan's change of hairstyle merited a half-page; so that running radical pieces

like Chris Lightbown's appeared (rightly or wrongly) to be just another trendy gimmick. The only sportswriter to make a really strong stand was David Miller, but he pays the penalty in that Revie will not speak to him, and Giles is talking of sueing.

The only paper which does not compromise itself by fraternising with the clubs is the Morning Star - and it shows. David Meek's outspoken coverage of the upheavals at Man. Utd. resulted in his being banned from official contact with the players; the way the rest of the Press behaved over the Best affair made it clear that despite all the soft-edged bonhomie between journalists and football management, all the Press was really after once again was the chance to nail a story and sell more copies, regardless of the harm done to the individual - in this case Best himself. Using his emotional crises to put more pressure on him, their hypocrisy was matched only by their lack of understanding.

The prospect of the Press improving its coverage of soccer is bleak, unless readers get as bored with the endless pages of tat as they appear to be with the sport itself.

6 IS TELEVISION COVERAGE DOING ANY LESS DAMAGE TO THE GAME?

Obviously there is still too much football on TV, both in terms of the number of games shown and of duplication. But the bad effects have not so much hit attendances directly as indirectly moulded standards and values. Soccer is still presented as an endlessly attractive affair, involving supermen creating and scoring goals of scarcely imaginable beauty. With this sort of showbiz background, how can we expect anyone to react to a goal-less draw in the third division in the rain? Faced by two loosely-connected forms of entertainment, the newcomer would examine the real thing by the criteria of the manufactured version and go back to the Wrestling.

Because TV removes all sense of the breadth and rhythm of the game, goals are

all it has to offer. There is no sign that TV this season has come to terms with the nature of the problem. Swapping Jimmy Hill is the most original idea either channel has come up with all season, and bracketing him with the BBC's bunch of toothless yes-men will restrict his freedom to criticise still further. And nothing will change if ITV simply look for another Hill, with the same obligations to be an entertainer.

The Football League are to discuss the new contracts in August; it is their responsibility to see that these take football's interests more seriously than audience ratings. But of course we know they won't.

four

7 ARE THE NECESSARY LEAGUE REFORMS MATERIALISING?

This was the season that produced three-up and three-down. That was all it produced; and it was hailed as "revolutionary" and "a routing of the reactionaries". The League have so little faith in the proposals made at the secret January crisis meeting that they appeared delighted to have squeezed this compromise through.

This short-sightedness is not limited to the management committee or even the League clubs: at a time when the Third and Fourth Divisions should be regionalised the leading non-league clubs produce a suicidal plan for a national non-league. In a season when Oxford,Hereford and Cambridge all got higher than ever before,it is ridiculous that no new clubs should have been elected. David Frost's TV show should not have been enough to save Darlington, and wouldn't have been if <u>one</u> nor-league club had been proposed as a replacement.

At a time when one of the main reasons for declining attendances was the burgeoning of fatuous sponsored competitions it is typical of the League's interest in short-term financial gain (cf the piddling Pools deal) to have taken no steps to ban any of them.

8 ARE CLUBS RESPONDING TO THE FEELINGS OF THEIR SUPPORTERS?

Now that supporters are getting fewer, the clubs' cavalier attitude towards those who remain is no longer good enough. It is now ten years since Coventry showed how a club could identify itself with its community,yet there have been few signs this season that the lesson has been learnt.

Chelsea appeared genuinely interested in community involvement for a short time, but produced concrete plans for only squash-courts and a bowling green. Other clubs continued to introduce Vice-Presidents' Clubs for those who could afford them,but most still obstinately refuse to recognise their responsibilities locally: indeed,Charlton Athletic are prepared to move away from their supporters altogether and show no signs of responding to the virulent campaign led by lifelong supporter Les Comer,who has been fighting a lone battle against a management whose only response to slumping gates is to blame the supporters.

Although clubs take little notice of what supporters say,they are not averse to packing them in through the turnstiles when there is a big attraction,risking another Ibrox disaster, as in the Arsenal/Chelsea Cup replay at Highbury,in order to squeeze the last penny out of the event. The same attitudes can be detected in QPR's extortionate new season ticket prices,now that they have gained promotion.

What we would like to see next year is less airy-fairy talk about £4m sports centres and more concrete means whereby supporters can have a direct say in the affairs of the club. The kind of attitude needed to bring supporters back into active and enthusiastic involvement with clubs is the kind of attitude that will narrow the gap between "champers and all the trimmings" in the boardroom and the state of the public lavatories on the terraces.

No. 9   June 1973

"FOUL has yet to come to terms with its own contradictions, to overcome its carping whine against all authority."

LLEW GARDNER, THE LISTENER

2 Who runs the people's game?

The passing of time inevitably adds irony to apparently innocuous statements. In the following chapter we learn that Charlton "look enviously at Selhurst Park"; that if Southport were re-elected in 1975–76, "things would go from strength to strength" (they finished 23rd in both of the next two seasons and lost their League place); more damagingly, that "football hooliganism is all but over". No magazine is perfect, of course, but Chris Lightbown's 'Look-I-know-these-kids' pontificating on terrace violence, wildly inaccurate in retrospect, was not something which *FOUL* could look back on with much pride.

On the other hand, contradictions between different writers can be a sign of strength, not weakness. Calling for "multiple sackings" of managers (issue 13) and then complaining about the "managerial merry-go-round" (issue 23) is one example of how *FOUL* was always a collection of diverse, and perhaps equally valid viewpoints, and never a monolith. It could not be expected to produce a single coherent argument on every subject, and would have been much more boring if it had. The point was to raise the issues at all.

FOUL's attacks on football's structure, highlighted here, is today even more relevant than when they wrote it. While power may have shifted from the Hardakers and the Westwoods to the likes of Ken Bates and Ron Noades, it has predictably stayed well and truly over the heads of the supporters. The chairmen have learnt to speak up for themselves, and the signs are that, at long last, the supporters are constructing themselves an alternative to "voting with their feet", through the Football Supporters Association. *FOUL* recognized that the "pork butchers and scrap-metal merchants" would only drive football further and further into the mire, and so they have done.

The incompetence and narrow-mindedness of so many football club chairmen and directors has been a major reason for football's utter failure to adapt to external change. The state to which they drove many clubs left them prey to wealthier, more ambitious, and in some cases even more unscrupulous men, whose influence has grown enormously since *FOUL*'s day. However, this, if anything, *increases* the validity of *FOUL*'s argument – that democracy in football is worth the effort, not just because it is intrinsically just, but also because through giving supporters a genuine stake in their club, it can be a major part of the solution to football's ills.

FOUL's analysis and conclusions were miles ahead of its time, for although football was demonstrably in serious decline in the 70s, it wasn't until more recent and tragic events that its complacent masters were finally forced to consider radical change in its structure. Inevitably, they came to the wrong conclusions even then, and the Football League still remain "unconvinced of the merits of democracy". When will they listen?

FOUL

Football's Alternative Paper!

12p ONLY

Number 23
November 1974

LEAGUE CHAIRMAN IN PARROT POWER SHOCK

DEMOCRACY IN ACTION

FIFTY years after universal suffrage was finally introduced in this country, the Football League remains unconvinced about the merits of democracy. At next month's League AGM, the 44 First and Second Division clubs will each have a vote on the particularly crucial issues before them; the 46 Third and Fourth Division clubs will have just four votes between them.

Given the fact that the wise men of Lytham often appear to be half a century behind the times, it is an appropriate occasion to demand the end of this anachronistic farce. The principle of one man/one vote may be as abhorrent to the League's reactionaries as it is to Messrs Vorster and Ian Smith, but the evils of ignoring it are equally plain. For as the gulf between football's rich and poor yawns wider, the 'property qualification' of First or Second Division membership is used simply to protect the interests of those who possess it.

There are one or two courageous exceptions. A few years ago, Crystal Palace and Manchester United suggested that the derisory 4% of gate receipts which is eventually shared out among all 92 League clubs — what amounts to a direct subsidy — should be increased; predictably, the richer clubs used their vote to throw out the proposal. The fate of the four-up and four-down plan, first introduced in the 'thirties, is similar testimony to this policy of 'what we have we hold'. If one vote per club is desirable, who is to effect it? The First and Second Division clubs will need a lot of persuading that the interests of football may be at variance with their own vested ones; the League Management Committee, dominated by chairmen of these same clubs, can half-heartedly make the proposal and then claim, as in the past, that it was turned down by "the clubs".

Where are football's pressure groups, representing the people who genuinely have the game's interests at heart? The players? PFA chairman Derek Dougan is known to be in favour of a vote for all, but when was the last time his union campaigned for anything except an increase in the fee for international appearances? The supporters? What channels do they have for expressing dissatisfaction, apart from voting with their feet? And what of the many managers, coaches and ex-players, who having been through it all, could apply some informed experience to problems on and off the field?

For the Management Committee to be persuaded that these new-fangled democratic principles might be worth a try and have the courage to introduce them, is only a very small though essential step towards a radical democrat- and socialisation of the game. It scarcely needs saying that the clubs are even more undemocratic and elitist than the League itself, and for the same reasons — because they have lost sight of football as a game, a form of entertainment and community service, and instead hide behind fatuous comparisons with Big Business, where chairmen and directors are the men who count, the men of destiny.

Football's whole financial structure needs to be changed.

19th century men using 19th century methods to control the game will eventually mean that football stadiums become the Methodist chapels and Victorian railway stations of the next century — open to offers.

Meanwhile, the interests of 2000 players and 750,000 spectators are ignored, and a handful of rich businessmen, having bought up the requisite lump of their local club, sit down to decide the game's future — these same Powermen who were invited to the League's little get-together in January, when not even the Press were allowed to find out what they were up to.

This is how the greatest game in the world is being run. It is no surprise that people are staying away from it.

No. 8 May 1973

THE HUNTING SEASON

The soccer publishing sensation of the 70s, "The Glory Game", has not been received too well at the football club it is supposed to be about.

In fact Hunter Davies, the chic author of the book has been told never to show his face at White Hart Lane again. He was called to a Spurs board meeting a little before the book was published and informed of the ban. The board were reasonably polite. He was just asked to fuck off and stay away forever.

Other members of the EUFA cup-winning organisation are not so restrained. Asst manager Eddie Baily, who emerges from Davies' golden pages as a cross between Alf Garnett and General Amin, requires only the slightest prompting to describe exactly what he would like to do to friendly old Hunter should he ever lay hands on him.

The problem is that the book is only too accurate. Time and again it underlines the essential lack of intelligence common to nearly all the human machines whose job it is either to play, coach, or manage for money. Davies seems hurt that none of the people he admired so much as footballers, in reality turn out to be his equal in mundane things like conversation, wit, or even reading the Sunday Times.

But telling people they're stupid does not go down too well; not that Spurs didn't lay themselves open to it. Chairman Sid Wale as the book points out, is bitterly jealous of North London neighbours Arsenal. A certain way to earn Chairman Sid's hate was to comment on all the publicity that Arsenal got in the year following the Double. Further aggravation is caused by the aristocratic air of Arsenal Chairman Denis Hill-Wood. Lots of football folk had heard of him — and he went to Eton to boot, Nobody knows Sidney Wale. Something had to be done to put Spurs back into the heavy publicity ranks.

Meanwhile, Hunter Davies, anxious for a follow-up to his money-spinning Beatles book (which also won him the undying dislike of at least three of the Beatles because of its excessive concentration on their foibles as humans rather than their prowess as music-makers), had asked Chelsea if he could spend a year with them to write an intimate book on a football club. Chelsea said no, so Hunter turned to Spurs.

Chairman Sid Wale had him checked out, learned he was a respected features writer with the conservative Sunday Times, which never embarrasses football clubs, unlike the daily papers, and signed him on. Sid could only see respectful paragraphs about Spurs' dynamic Chairman filling the pages of the ST. Manager Nicholson was more perceptive but Wale had his way, and Hunter settled down with the club for a year.

Apart from the unsympathetic picture that appears, one of the training staff, for example, laboriously fills in a form, asking all the time for spelling help, many football reporters are seriously questioning Davies' accuracy. Nearly all the national reporters who went with Spurs on their EUFA Cup away games are finding it difficult to remember all the incidents Davies describes. He never took notes, and the feeling is, that he highlighted or compressed statements or events, so that they appeared more dramatic than they actually were.

There is nothing new in the book to anyone who has spent time at a football club. But what is worrying London reporters is that at a time when they had gradually earned Bill Nicholson's confidence as journalists who were worthy of it, Davies' minute details of club gossip and personality clashed will kill Nicholson's interest in talking to the press (and thus to the public) stone dead.

Possibly the press have got off lucky. Davies has not included a long chapter he wrote on what the footballers think of the press. Apparently it isn't too complimentary and although the official reason for its suppression is that there wasn't room in the book, it is obvious that in future years Hunter would have to drink with the journalists ripped off in the unpublished chapter.

Unfortunately the book looks like rebounding in Davies' face. Reaction in the football world is a massive "so what?", combined with sympathy that so much dirty washing should be laid out in public. Reaction in the board rooms is a wide smile that vain Sid Wale has been caught out. And reaction from everyone mentioned in the book is a feeling of pity for the next group of people Hunter decides to write about.

"THE GLORY GAME", by Hunter Davies, was published on October 26 (Weidenfeld and Nicolson) price £2.95

FOUL MOUTH

The story opposite is in the same vein as the outspoken remarks of Mssrs Wooldridge and Batt on "The Glory Game". But while prepared to print it, we cannot support this attitude to Hunter Davies' book. For once, somebody has cut across the usual platitudes and evasion and has actually tried to portray Football as it is lived. It is fair comment on the football world that footballers and press have closed their ranks in order to protect their cosy mutual aid society.

Of course the Press are angry. Hunter Davies has queered their well-tended pitch. Of course Tottenham are angry. The Happy Family image carefully built up in successive editions of the "Spurs Football Book" and the like, is not enhanced by eyewitness accounts of blazing rows between Nicholson and Chivers, or schoolboy pranks in French shops. Equally galling for the club, Davies is mortalising the Demi-gods whose public-relations value depends so much on their being considered a race apart.

It is in the Media's interest, too, to perpetuate this myth. Star pix, and star columns sell papers. If there are no stars, they have to be created. So Chairman Wale was entitled to expect another sycophantic PR job. Instead Davies told the truth; and must now face the consequences.

There is indeed "nothing new in the book to anyone who has spent time at a football club". So why should it have taken someone so long to tell it like it is?

***

No. 2 November 1972

Spot The Foul

+++ GAME: INTRIGUING ALL-NORTHERN FIXTURE BETWEEN TWO TOP 1st DIVISION SIDES ++ WEATHER MILD FOR TIME OF YR + WIND EAST/WEST +++ TEMPERS: RISING ++ BALL: NOWHERE ++ TIME: 1 MIN AFTER KICKOFF

40 CROSSES 25P

No. 14 January 1974

HARDAKER: HARD FACTS

It isn't often that a paid official can move the headquarters of one of the world's great sporting institutions from one town to another just to suit his own domestic happiness. But that's just what Alan Hardaker, Secretary to our own Football League did in 1961.

Students of last-minute transfer stories can describe in cartographic detail how the appropriate forms are rushed to an obscure seaside town in Lancashire called Lytham St Annes for registration.What nobody questions is why the League offices are there.The answer- Alan Hardaker lives there.When he became Secretary in 1957,sadly for the family Hardaker, the offices were in Preston,a long daily trip for our Alan,who had bought a very nice house in Lytham and felt that the bracing sea air of his own town would be more conducive to the decisions of English soccer than the pollution of Preston. So,in 1961,with no-one taking a great deal of notice,Hardaker moved his office and hence the Football League to Lytham.And there it remains to this day.

The revealed chapters of Mr Hardaker's life before 1957 are few.The only wage-earning posts he filled were also in the secretarial field.He was secretary to the Lord Mayors of Hull and Portsmouth;a Lord Mayor's Secretary is the chap who talks smoothly to the Press,keeps an eye on the office,and makes sure the Lord Mayor is correctly attired.No doubt the management committee of the League thought they had done well to capture such a specimen of quiet,punctilious efficiency when they appointed the ex-amateur footballer from Yorkshire.Hardaker had different ideas and now,16 years on,you would be lucky to find a press-man who could give you the name of a member of the Management Committee,in theory the body that runs football.But everybody,just everybody who knows which way to kick a football knows of Alan Hardaker.How did he do it?

A quick answer is by getting his name in the papers.For all his avowed dislike of pressmen - he once told a crowded press conference that he never believed anything he read in the newspapers - Hardaker has always been available to reporters when it counted.His press-cuttings book is as fat as any top manager's and even his denials and 'no comments' have been violent and,at times,abusive enough to ensure headline treatment.He also proved an articulate mouthpiece for the League management committee.Pork-butchers, scrap-metal dealers,and the other seedy entrepreneurs who run English football like to see themselves on the back page of the national press but have no idea of how to get there. Hardaker showed them.And although in his early days he ensured some public mention of the amiable,if elderly Chairman,Joe Richards,since his retirement,Hardaker has managed the task of getting the Committee's decisions into press stories,whilst ensuring that the only name actually to appear is his own.

His most durable reason for fame is his pig-headed stupidity on most of the big soccer controversies of the last ten years.He has continually hated European soccer,fought like a drowning rat against the removal of the maximum wage,and totally misunderstands the role of television in British soccer.

On Europe,there is surely some reason rooted in some bizarre personal disaster abroad for Hardaker's hatred.One of his first acts as the newly appointed secretary was to issue a statement saying he wanted to discourage visits from European clubs.It took brave individual decisions by Busby and Stan Cullis to take Man.Utd and the Wolves into Europe in the teeth of Hardaker's disapproval. It would be pleasant to report that Hardaker - "World Cups,European Cups - you can live without them" - is against extra football per se;that he disliked the extravagance of one third of div I hawking itself round Europe because of the wear and tear it caused our players,devaluing the League Championship and the FA Cup. But the ludicrous overcrowding of our fixture-list is the direct result of Hardaker's insane attempt to erect an alternative set of competitions to those embracing the top teams in Europe.Thanks to him,we must now endure the Petrol (texaco) Beer (watney)-and Spaghetti (anglo-italian) competitions;and even the people's Cup,so-called,the Football League Cup,normally the 3rd division chance to prove that it too can clog its way to fame,has been progressively reduced to a footnote to the real purpose of the affair,which is to provide ITV with their ridiculous penalty-prize competition.

For a man who only 12 months ago predicted that the high wage-structure of modern football would soon collapse,Mr Hardaker has ensured that if it does,he will have had his share of what has been going. His last negotiated salary was about £10,000 p.a.,about right for one of the top six managers,and a shade below what Martin Chivers would earn in a goodish year.   Still he disliked and continues to dislike the notion of players earning a lot of money.The amateur ethic just will not lie down.In 1964 he announced that a basic wage will have to be forced on clubs because of "ridiculous demands by players.";in 1966 he told a pressman that players' wages should be brought under control.In 1967 he said that incentive payments should be limited;last year he forecast the collapse of the present wage structure.And he wouldn't dream of admitting that matches get fixed.

Overall,Hardaker's sense of the economic value of football is strange. He has just sold the Football League fixture list to Littlewoods Pools Company for £2 million,when a more realistic figure would be £1 million per division,a scandalous undervaluation when so many of the smaller clubs are on the verge of bankruptcy,and the Pools firms make a multi-million pound profit,none of which goes back into soccer-except insofar as Littlewoods involvement with Everton provides money for misguided Goodison purchases.

If Hardaker's track record as an administrator has been such an odyssey of disaster,despite occasional PR attempts by the League to portray him as football's best friend,why hasn't he been sacked? Apart from the docility of the Management Committee and the controlling chairmen, Hardaker impresses by always having something up his sleeve.He is constantly announcing new disciplinary measures,attacking magistrates courts for lenient sentences,accusing players of cheating,suggesting that the first div. should be retitled the 'Premier' division,claiming there is no crisis, as gates plummet,inventing the fourth div,announcing a new 4 up, 4 down plan,telling the world that he "wouldn't hang a dog on the word of a professional footballer".

Whatever it is,Hardaker is there saying it.And to the unsophisticated minds of his employers,he's doing just fine.After all,someone has to speak up for the chairmen,and if they got rid of Hardaker,who on earth could do it as well?

Only two serious attempts have been made to get rid of him.In 1971,Arthur Wait of Crystal Palace called a special press conference to demand Hardaker's resignation after the mishandled introduction of the referees' clean-up;Wait spluttered and fumed,but now 18 months on,he has been ousted from Selhurst Park, while Hardaker still controls Lytham St Annes.In 1966,Stoke played a more cunning game,simply asking the League to prevent Hardaker from speaking to the Press,since he was damaging the image of the game.They lost that one,and the only gilt-edged chance of dropping Hardaker came a few months later when he was offered £11,000 p.a. to become Mr Soccer in the USA;but he didn't want to leave Lytham St Annes and we've had him ever since.

Despite all the news stories,allthe thoughts off the top of his head,Mr Hardaker has done just about nothing for soccer.His record is one of negative achievement hidden by a good deal of rhetorical publicity.In the end his excuse is that he is no worse than his masters.Football's problem, some might say tragedy,is that he is no better.

Anthony Hollis

No. 8   May 1973

O.K. ~ WHO RULES?

1:Gentlemen v Players

THERE are four elements in a football club, all of them indispensable. One element, the board, determines the financial and administrative policy: the same one, via its chairman, has the club's voice at the League's annual general meeting, which settles the destinies of all the other three elements — managers, players and supporters.

The reason generally given for the dictatorship is that the board is entitled to this power because it bears the financial burden. Certainly the board makes a contribution; but it is no more than the other three. *Yet it is these three groups which produce the income.*

The real reason why the board has so much say in most clubs is that right from the start the aim has been to establish power among a small group, and keep it there, unchallenged.

Directors lose, however, by their supremacy, because there is no effective channel by which the ideas of player, manager or supporter can be heard; their influence — on club or League policy — is advisory and quite without teeth. If any conflict arises, the chairman will always win, because he has the vote at the League AGM.

This is especially damaging in the case of managers. These are men with playing experience who have been sifted out for their ability to handle players and run a team. Their originality and practical experience has been put to the most gruelling test. The proof of their pudding is their survival. Having been on both sides of the touchline, they would seem to be the best counsellors the game has.

Yet not until October of this year did the FA see fit to bring them all together in London to seek their opinions on discipline and other matters: regional committees have been set up as a result, and a Secretaries and Managers Association is struggling for form and recognition. But still they are a body without a head; although directors certainly consult them on policy issues, they have no constitutional power.

These weaknesses are most apparent on the League Management Committee, the body which governs most of a club's life. Whatever view you take of its proposals, the narrowness of its representation is beyond dispute; both in who sits on it (basically club chairmen)and who votes at the AGM (basically first and second division club chairmen). It is the Gentlemen ruling the Players. Some way to bring other voices onto this governing body must be found.

The pitfalls in front of soccer are acknowledged by everyone to be dangerous; only with the widest consultation are they likely to be avoided. And those consulted must be given a vote as well as a hearing.

M.O'N.

No. 13   December 1973

TRUANTS!

FLEET STREET sub-editors had a field day earlier this month when within two hours of the BEST MISSING AGAIN headlines being churned out, news broke that two other Bad Boys,Osgood and Hudson, had been listed by Chelsea.

The common denominator they seized on was three persistent trouble-makers getting their noses dirty again. What was universally ignored was the idea that here were three people who despite all football's battery-farming and numbing conformity, have remained *individuals* on the field and off it. Even worse, Best was a man prepared to turn his back on the game and the people who had 'done so much for him' (like ghosting his columns and scarring his legs); Osgood and Hudson had dared to question Authority in the shape of a manager like Dave Sexton, and make the point that, like Sexton, they have some pride and dignity too.

Two years ago, Sexton transfer-listed Osgood for 'not trying', and briefly got away with his bluff to provoke the player into running up and down like everybody else for 90 minutes. This time, the public humiliation of being dropped and forced to train with the reserves didn't work. The bluff was called, and Sexton, being a proud man, couldn't give in.

So in the space of 16 months, at a time when everyone in the game is bemoaning the shortage of real talent and real stars, Chelsea have got rid of Osgood, Hudson and Cooke. It prompts the question of who the crowds are paying to see – players like these, or managers like Sexton, who find themselves quite unable to cope with anyone not fitting into their functional little systems?

As we've said before, though, the buck doesn't stop with the manager. Sexton,convinced that he had the Board's support, must have sweated a bit as the crucial Board meeting dragged on for six hours. But in the end, authoritarian principles and the lure of two fat transfer cheques swayed them. Bearing in mind the feudal notions of a player's role in the 'society' which is a football club, we could have expected little else.

There had been a similar case in London two months earlier when Millwall published in their match programme an astonishing diatribe (apparently written by manager Fenton) against Eamon Dunphy – a player brave enough to disregard the maxim that, on the real issues, footballers should be seen and not heard. The nasty impression was that the club couldn't wait to get shot of a player who'd dared to express his personality within the context of the club.

Meanwhile, the Press just re-inforce public disapproval of non-conformists, with no attempt to balance a picture of over-paid, over-dressed playboys. The vindictiveness of seasonal Best obituaries, the front-page stories of his taking a day off work because of personal problems, the snide implications of a court-case story . . . And at the same time, the cream of Fleet Street can completely ignore the crowd reaction at Stamford Bridge when, two days after the transfer-listings,Osgood's name was chanted before and even during the game, together with shouts from below the press-box of 'Osgood IN, Sexton OUT'.

Press and Board alike reinforce each other's attitudes, hardly surprising when they see so much of each other over the rims of their well-filled glasses. Keep an eye on Chelsea's attendance figures for a more accurate reflection of 'public opinion'.●

No. 15   February 1974

Dear *FOUL*,

Southern soccer fans have loved it. After ten years of being forced to acclaim the Leeds Utd success story, the chance to jeer has come at last. You'd better get on with it. But don't try going any further, such as the boardroom. The soccer establishment has taken enough recently with all the talk of 'player power', without the fans getting in on the scene.

Not that a few thousand fans stampeding along the carpeted corridors of Elland Road would achieve much either. Chairman Manny Cussins and his cronies have never been ones for taking advice, however blunt. The nearest they got to it was the day Don Revie left. They actually asked for his opinion as to who the next manager should be. He recommended John Giles, keep it in the family.

This advice, of course, went unheeded. Why? Because the Board *own* Leeds Utd, so of course they know better than anyone else. If you take the leaving manager's advice, it's only a stone's throw from taking the players' advice, and from there you might as well let in the groundstaff, charladies, or any other Tom Dick or Harry who pay their minimum 60p every fortnight.

So the Leeds board, to perpetuate the myth of their own fallibility, appointed showbiz whizz-kid Brian Clough. This drew in the crowds once to take a peep — at the Birmingham City game, for instance, excited fathers were pointing him out to their children. But like all gimmicks it soon wore thin.

We all know the result of Clough's reign at Leeds. A player on the Board here, a representative of the Supporters there, and we'd have been saved all the bother (and this letter). It's not as if this is a new idea. Industry has known about it for years — it's called worker participation. You, the workers, help the company keep its profits up.

The 44 day fall (he never rose) of Brian Clough has been attributed by the press to the following factors. 1) He spent too much time on the telly. 2) The Board never gave him a chance. 3) In the words of David Miller, *Daily Express*, 'the Board was stampeded by that menacing trend in the game, Player Power.'

None got to grips with what really happened. The events at Elland Road the other week, were one more signal for the end of the football structure as we know it. The old system where a group of rich gentlemen run everything to do with a club is showing its cracks. Soccer is being dragged kicking and screaming into the 20th century.

Yours,
Gordon Wilson,
Leeds Other Paper,
Leeds 6.

No. 23   November 1974

SPOT THE BRAWL

No. 31   December 1975

THE GAME is an attractive tussle between two top North of England sides who have been in the forefront of the honours race in recent seasons. (Clue: Many famous and respected internationals play for both teams, and several of them are in this picture. And one of the sides, in the words of a Scottish international forward, is "playing its best football for ten years").

ALL YOU HAVE TO DO is put an 'X' where you think the next fist will land.

Entries to *FOUL* House, please.

Why John is cross at Cross

By DAVE BERRESFORD
Coventry 3, Sheffield U 1

The Sun

No. 14   January 1974

JOHN CONNAUGHTON stood in the swish main entrance at Coventry and took off his shirt to show the evidence which rubbed the glitter from Coventry's two-goal hero David Cross.

The evidence? Three stud marks on the Sheffield goalkeeper's chest the result of a foul by Cross.

It was bad enough to have got him sent off

Afterwards he admitted: "I did him.

MoM: *David Cross* (Coventry).

WHAT has happened to Bill Nicholson and Ron Greenwood proves how dangerous modern players can be if they're not controlled

Jimmy Hill, ex-chairman of Players' Union, News of the World 1/9/74.

No. 22   October 1974

'Jeffo'

BIGGEST INFLUENCE ON CAREER: *Uncle Tommy.*
BIGGEST THRILL IN SOCCER: *A good 50-50 tackle.*
IF YOU WEREN'T A FOOTBALLER WHAT WOULD YOU HAVE BEEN: *Something to do with animals.*

Wolves' 1974 League Cup brochure

Unietd started to get a firmer grip on the game and it took a brilliant save from ex-Manchester City goalkeeper Mulhearn to keep out a rocket of a shit from Greenhalgh as the game entered its last quarter.

The drama-drenched game exploded in an incredible three minute spell in which United

from The Cambridge Evening News

PART OF THE UNION

Or, The Mill - Owners' Charter

EAMONN DUNPHY, of Millwall and Eire, on the role of the players' union.

THE IMAGE of the Professional Footballer as a glamorous show-business type, surrounded by pretty girls and flash cars, is firmly implanted in most-people's minds. I know him more accurately as the deeply insecure family man or the tearful, failed Apprentice. Getting that image across is what the Professional Footballers Association, the players union, should be all about.

And while it is often said that the Trade Union movement in Britain is too powerful, the equation between Union and power in football contains an element of black comedy.

The PFA is a small organisation comprising two fulltime officials and fifteen hundred largely apathetic members. We have in fact, practically no say in the games' decision-making process, there is no consultation process, and very little consideration of the players' point of view. It is a situation no normal Trade Union or professional body would tolerate for a moment.

Consequently, our conditions of employment are such that a reincarnated 19th century mill owner would be gratified to see that restrictive practices so dear to his heart are alive and well in football.

Men can still be bought and sold in the market place, apprentices (sic), are callously dismissed on completion of their apprenticeship, and the possibility of retirement through injury, without compensation, looms over every game — an additional tension in an already high-risk profession.

The existence of such conditions could be regarded as a massive indictment of the PFA. However, this would be an oversimplification. The unenviable task of securing civilised working conditions falls almost wholly on Cliff Lloyd, the Union secretary. He brings to the job of negotiating with soccer's abrasive bosses a rare dedication, allied to a keep concern with the plight of his members, particularly those in the lower divisions.

He is, however, badly handicapped by the apathy that exists among the superstars employed by the wealthier First Division clubs, most of whom do not bother to attend the AGM, the annual gathering that attempts to gauge the players feelings in order to develop a coherent policy.

It is ironic that those who are the main beneficiaries of the one significant gain achieved by Union militancy, the abolition of the maximum wage, should now cripple the organisation that served their interests so well, by lack of interest. The removal of the maximum wage was only achieved after a long and bitter struggle with soccers' administrators. It took the inspired leadership of Lloyd and Jimmy Hill to overcome the apathetic membership and relentless bosses. Since Hill, no one else has emerged with the character to unite the Union behind any of its demands.

That was over a decade ago — since then the rate of progress has been painfully slow. The slave mentality still exists among professional footballers. Despite the powerful weapons at our disposal, among them the Government sponsored Chester Report, which bitterly attacked the terms of employment in football, we have failed to mount the militant campaign necessary to achieve real freedom. Given the nature of many of the game's administrators, progress will only be made as a result of sustained pressure.

The PFA cannot move in that direction without the support of all its members, particularly the game's star players. If any of these stars doubt the need for action they should look more closely at the situation in their own clubs. Wealthy clubs are frequently the most ruthless exploiters of players, particularly youngsters who sign on as apprentices. Their economic strength allows them to employ the full quota of 15 boys in the freely admitted hope of finding perhaps a couple with First Division potential. What happens to the remaining dozen in terms of education and opportunity should provide food for thought for even the most irresponsible superstar.

In their treatment of older and more established players, these clubs also leave a lot to be desired. Competent professionals are often retained in reserve teams, for instance, thus being denied the opportunity to seek more fulfilling employment in a lower division.

Obviously, there is no cause for complacency at any level of football. And it is the job of the PFA to combat apathy where it exists, in any form. I believe this can be done by raising the issues wherever the opportunity occurs.

There must be more discussion of the problems among players, perhaps through Regional Councils. Players' easy, and constant access to the media should be used to present a more realistic picture to the fans who may understandably mistake the high living excesses of the few as typical of the footballer generally. 🌐

DOOG PUTS THE BOOT IN

The Players' Union Chairman replies to Eamonn Dunphy

DEREK DOUGAN LTD., 120 WROTTESLEY ROAD, TETTENHALL, WOLVERHAMPTON

Dear Eamonn

This is an open letter (though I prefer closed letters as a rule) about some scathing things you had to say concerning the P.F.A. in the September issue of FOUL. To say that I am exasperated and frustrated by a few P.F.A. dissenters is an understatement. You give the impression that the P.F.A. committee does absolutely nothing but sit around and idle away the time.

It does not take much research to discover that committee members devote considerable time and energy to improving the welfare and fundamental rights of players. I agree with you that big-name stars are not noted for their active interest in the Association and its affairs. Few of them attend the annual meetings. This is a regrettable example to younger, less celebrated members. But even before the maximum wage was abolished the situation was the same. Perhaps the stars think they don't need the P.F.A. — a short-sighted view.

But for the magnificent team that assists and advises the P.F.A. committee — that is, Cliff Lloyd (Secretary), Miss Hardman, and George Davies (Legal Adviser) — the Association would not be able to operate.

What dismays me about your article is its absence of information about the achievements of the P.F.A. You seem to be under the impression that we are ineffective if not, indeed, wholly impotent.

But since 1961 we have won the George Eastham case, got a percentage of transfer fees for players, and obtained independent tribunals to adjudicate in disputes involving players' contracts. To me this is even more important than the lifting of the maximum wage, which was inevitable anyway.

We fought and won the John Cook case in March, 1972, establishing the right of a player to be re-registered by the F.A. when he returns to England after fulfilling a contract abroad. The Ernie Machin case was won, though it could not have been foreseen that the decision would be reversed on appeal. Having followed that case minutely, I am still baffled by the reversal.

A new disciplinary procedure was introduced a year ago, with a further right of appeal should a case go against a player. This surely was a major step forward.

Two years ago the P.F.A. appointed Bob Kerry as Education Officer, and in a short space of time we are now seeing remarkable progress, because of the response by the vast majority of our members. I must point out that not all the response is coming from the lower divisions. No one can point an accusing finger at the P.F.A. and say that they are not offering to players the opportunity to add another string to their bow.

I would like to point out that in the P.F.A. there are 2,500 members and four not two full-time officers, as you mistakenly say. In the eight years I have been on the committee it has always been P.F.A. policy to treat all members as equal. You know as well as anyone that our professional organisation is different from any other. You should also know that there are many issues regarding players' welfare and rights with which the P.F.A. has dealt. Here obviously I can only mention a few of the more important.

The P.F.A. has not been dragging its feet, as you are trying to make out. The way it is at the moment constituted means that the committee is severely handicapped. What I look forward to is, freedom of contract, and the implementation of a pension scheme for all members of the P.F.A. Then we shall have given you and everyone else a Utopian Association!

I welcome criticism from members if it is constructive and well informed. But I cannot accept you, Eamonn, as a member. Your subscription has lapsed and you appear, therefore, to have disqualified yourself from present membership, and also from the role of critic. I am sure, however, that Cliff Lloyd will be delighted to receive back dues.

Yours sincerely,
Derek Dougan
10th September 1973

No. 11   October 1973

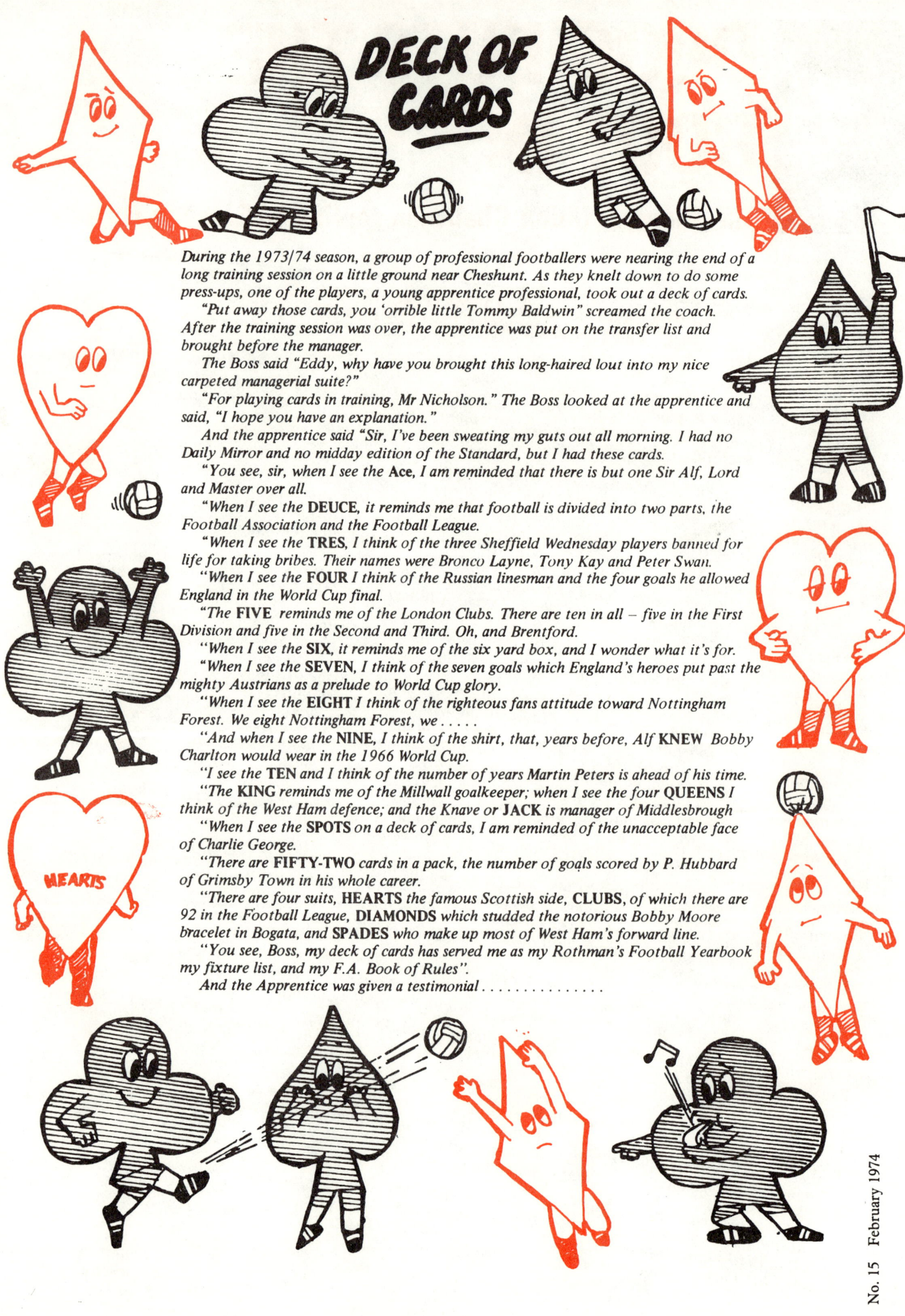

DECK OF CARDS

During the 1973/74 season, a group of professional footballers were nearing the end of a long training session on a little ground near Cheshunt. As they knelt down to do some press-ups, one of the players, a young apprentice professional, took out a deck of cards.

"Put away those cards, you 'orrible little Tommy Baldwin" screamed the coach. After the training session was over, the apprentice was put on the transfer list and brought before the manager.

The Boss said "Eddy, why have you brought this long-haired lout into my nice carpeted managerial suite?"

"For playing cards in training, Mr Nicholson." The Boss looked at the apprentice and said, "I hope you have an explanation."

And the apprentice said "Sir, I've been sweating my guts out all morning. I had no Daily Mirror and no midday edition of the Standard, but I had these cards.

"You see, sir, when I see the Ace, I am reminded that there is but one Sir Alf, Lord and Master over all.

"When I see the DEUCE, it reminds me that football is divided into two parts, the Football Association and the Football League.

"When I see the TRES, I think of the three Sheffield Wednesday players banned for life for taking bribes. Their names were Bronco Layne, Tony Kay and Peter Swan.

"When I see the FOUR I think of the Russian linesman and the four goals he allowed England in the World Cup final.

"The FIVE reminds me of the London Clubs. There are ten in all – five in the First Division and five in the Second and Third. Oh, and Brentford.

"When I see the SIX, it reminds me of the six yard box, and I wonder what it's for.

"When I see the SEVEN, I think of the seven goals which England's heroes put past the mighty Austrians as a prelude to World Cup glory.

"When I see the EIGHT I think of the righteous fans attitude toward Nottingham Forest. We eight Nottingham Forest, we . . . . .

"And when I see the NINE, I think of the shirt, that, years before, Alf KNEW Bobby Charlton would wear in the 1966 World Cup.

"I see the TEN and I think of the number of years Martin Peters is ahead of his time.

"The KING reminds me of the Millwall goalkeeper; when I see the four QUEENS I think of the West Ham defence; and the Knave or JACK is manager of Middlesbrough

"When I see the SPOTS on a deck of cards, I am reminded of the unacceptable face of Charlie George.

"There are FIFTY-TWO cards in a pack, the number of goals scored by P. Hubbard of Grimsby Town in his whole career.

"There are four suits, HEARTS the famous Scottish side, CLUBS, of which there are 92 in the Football League, DIAMONDS which studded the notorious Bobby Moore bracelet in Bogata, and SPADES who make up most of West Ham's forward line.

"You see, Boss, my deck of cards has served me as my Rothman's Football Yearbook my fixture list, and my F.A. Book of Rules".

And the Apprentice was given a testimonial . . . .

WORLD CUP DRAW
CARVE~UP!

SCOTLAND in the same group as Brazil was the obvious peg for British journalists to hang their reports of the World Cup draw on. What nobody mentioned was the inevitability of it.

There was in fact a 50 per cent chance of the teams getting drawn together, so contrived has the 'draw' become.

In 1970, the draw was allegedly an 'open' one, with all the balls drawn out of one bag. So we were asked to accept as coincidence that Brazil, Peru, Mexico and Uruguay avoided each other in the qualifying groups, and that Rumania, Bulgaria, and the Soviet Union did likewise.

This time, FIFA decided that credibility might become just a little strained. They therefore admitted to dividing the countries into four sections as follows:

Had the draw been anything but a convenient arrangement, that is in fact how the groups would have worked out (reading vertically). The only difference to what was actually "drawn" is that South American paranoia has again been pandered to, with Argentina pointedly moved out of Brazil's group and into Italy's. It was possible to use the four sections above, taking one team from each for each group: but there was no legitimate way that South American teams could be kept apart from each other as well, unless the little choirboy pulling the names out was under fairly careful instructions as to what he was supposed to do.

What happened was that the four seeds were despatched to their various groups, and given a number (2,6,10 and 14 respectively), the purpose of which was to determine the order of their fixtures – ie. the first 'round', is 1 v 2, 3 v 4 etc through to 15 v 16. Next to be allocated was the Western Europe/South American section. Chile conveniently came out first, which put them in Group 1, avoiding Brazil and Uruguay. The next team out should have gone into Group 2. But to the embarrassment of all, our choirboy produced Argentina. With admirable pragmatism, he was guided not to the bowl with Group 2's numbers in it (5,7 and 8) but to Group 4's (13, 15 and 16); put in his thumb and pulled out a 16. Result – everybody happy.

The controller of the draw didn't question this. When Scotland came out, he looked round for help and mumbled something about a wrong number. But he needn't have worried. With the final team in this section, Holland, left to slot into Uruguay's group, the job had been done beautifully.

And the rest proceeded in an orderly enough fashion. The Eastern European block emerged East Germany, Yugoslavia/Spain, Bulgaria, Poland in that order, and went into groups 1,2,3 and 4 in *that* order. Likewise the also-rans.

So there was just one surprise: that East Germany should be allowed into West Germany's group. Another little slip? Or is choirboy Detlef pushing Willy Brandt's detente?●

1. Seeds	W. Germany	Brazil	Uruguay	Italy
2. Eastern Europe	E. Germany	Yugoslavia/ Spain	Bulgaria	Poland
3. Western Europe/ Sth America	Chile	Argentina	Scotland	Holland
4. Also-rans	Australia	Zaire	Sweden	Haiti

No. 15   February 1974

Third World last ?

FRANK TAYLOR's Postbag must have bulged with indignant mail once the full horror of the Leopards, the Socceroos and Haitian voodoo had sunk in. Here was Mick Channon cooling his heels prior to a stern season in the toughest Second Division in the world, and there were these nobodies, Bournemouth and Boscombe rejects, rain-priests and goodness knows what else, wasting peak-hour viewing time with their gaudy shirts and olde-worlde 4-2-4 formations. Where's the justice in that? And when Billy's brave boys got sent home on account of not wanting to spoil the party for the fellows in their first World Cup match — well, frankly, Frank, where will it all end?

Certainly the stickiest problem facing FIFA at present, stickier even than the China-Taiwan dispute, is the question of Third World soccer. For the developing nations to establish themselves on the world football scene,

they have to face regular competition from European and South American sides, and the World Cup is a convenient neo-colonialist excuse for such competition. But while Zaire and Haiti will have learned valuable lessons from their games — how best to pick the ball out of the net etc. — three defeats in a fortnight and the next flight to Kinshasa isn't much to build on.

Perhaps Joao Havelange, elected FIFA President on the Third World vote, will come up with a more satisfactory system for weaning African and Caribbean football than the present one, in which Africa, Asia and Central America have a maximum of three places to aim for. If the qualifying rounds were spread over a longer period, and Third World teams competed with European and South American countries instead of contesting the African championship and its equivalent, the World Cup would be a sterner test all round. It would guarantee greater involvement for the smaller footballing nations, and there would be more chance of finding the 16 or 20 best squads in the world at the Finals. And isn't that what we all want, panel?

No. 20   June 1974

No. 20   July 1974

THE latest moves by the League and FA ruling bodies in pursuing their uneasy seduction of companies who wish to inject money into football has brought the whole problem of sponsorship back into the sporting eye.

Football is obviously having increasing difficulty in maintaining standards and keeping the weakest from the wall. So any money which comes into the game, whether from television companies, pools firms, advertisers or local councils is much needed and theoretically welcome. The issue, however, is the terms on which the leeches are to be allowed into the bloodstream.

The problem is that football is already slipping into the mire at the hands of people who care little about the game, do not have its welfare at heart, and are only interested in using football as a 'product' to be exploited for what they can get out of it. But there are still some of us left who don't look on football as product, and are concerned about the increased vulgarisation of football at the hands of the Press, television and business interests who look on football as a soap opera or variety show which is there to be manipulated by anyone who can possibly cash in.

Before sponsorship of football's major competitions or clubs may be permitted, two things must be proved:
1)   That the game's administrators show themselves capable of handling all the wealth that this will bring into their jurisdiction, and
2)   That sponsors show that they care about the way they support football, and will not pull out at the first sign of slackening public interest.

On the first point, Alan Hardaker and his ilk have a wretched track record. The Texaco Cup and the Watney Cup have had a pernicious effect on an already bloated domestic programme. The current row over television only highlights the incompetence of the League management in the face of large commercial interests. Men with radical reputations like Tommy Trinder and Bob Lord are telling the League that what is damaging football is the quantity of televised soccer, and are asking for much more money. But what they seem incapable of realising is the disastrous effect of the quality of television's handling of football. For that is where the real damage lies. It is possible to visualise these men with their 19th century outlook quarreling with sponsors over cashflow and location of advertisements when they should be concerned with the image of football that is being presented to an increasingly cynical public. Can we really trust men like Hardaker and Shipman with an issue as contentious and vital as this?

For sponsorship will make football more vulnerable than ever before. The fact that the Texaco Cup and the Watney Cup have not been dropped, in the face of massive public apathy, shows how dependent the game could become on the income provided by sponsors. Once the sponsors come in, and they look like coming in on *their* terms, it will be practically impossible to get rid of them. Cricket's administrators know that a return to the County Championship, without the Gillette, and Benson and Hedges Cups, the John Player League, is unthinkable.

Also, sponsors inject money into a sport, because the press use their name, and on condition that the visual media photograph players performing against a background of their advertisements. This makes sponsored sports desperately dependent upon television coverage, and is bound to bind football even more completely to the baneful influence of television. A recent survey showed that without television fees, boxing promoters frequently cannot afford to mount title fights. Football must not be put in that position.

However, football resembles boxing in that it is a basically healthy sport which has suffered from mismanagement and from the activities of people trying to live off it. A recent disquieting trend has been the extension into football of the tentacles of organisations like those of Bagenal Harvey and Jarvis Astaire. Rather than giving them carte blanche to increase their stake in football, (one of the side-effects of sponsorship,) a way must be found to decrease their influence upon the way the game is run. And the fact that the FA's chief adviser on the commercial potential of football is none other than Jimmy Hill, employee of the BBC and for many years a client of the notorious Bagenal Harvey shows the blindness of the FA to things that are happening beneath its very nose.

The danger is that the current situation where sponsors are exploiting football will change to one where football is living off, and is entirely dependent upon the sponsors. Sponsorship is a miracle panacea, a charlatan's cure, which permits the disease to get worse without the patient noticing, until the condition is fatal. Both the League and the clubs must rationalise their affairs now, and begin to run themselves upon responsible, democratic lines. Sponsorship is the stage before rigor mortis.

No. 14   January 1974

COMMENT

DON'T kill the goose that laid the golden egg.

That, this morning, is the message from Mirror Sport to West Ham and Fulham, the Cockney Cup Finalists.

Have your pools, enjoy your perks.

But do it with dignity. Don't become infected by a desire to grab and grab.

Don't arrive at the big day having forgotten why you are even going to Wembley.

Daily Mirror 11/4/75

Daily Mirror 18/4/75

Bobby and Alan ham it up for the Cup
THE OLD CAMPAIGNERS

FOULM@!*!%!! UTH

THE possibility that within a few months Britain may have opted out of the EEC is no real excuse for the lack of debate recently about what we were once told was "the most important football issue of our time" (Bernard Joy, *London Evening Standard* 1/8/73).

Joy reported at that time that "A high-powered European committee, including Football League secretary Alan Hardaker and some lawyers, have been trying without much success to devise means of holding back free contracts and free movement between countries." They have clearly found no means, yet 18 months later, still don't need any. Because of the innate conservatism of League club directors, these illegal restrictions have yet to be tested.

Eamon Dunphy has put the case for freedom of contract (FOUL 25) in positive fashion, and if the PFA fail to achieve it, they have only themselves to blame. But despite public admissions from managers like Mee and Neill that the ban on foreign players without a two-year qualification is illegal under the Treaty of Rome (signed by Britain on 1/1/73), the timorous approach to FA regulations persists.

At the end of January, the High Court of the European Community even made a ruling about professional sportsmen. A Dutch cyclist won his case against the International Cycling Union for restricting the practice of his trade. The Court emphasised that this ruling applies to any other professional sportsman: so there is nothing to stop any English club from signing a player from another Common Market country, then winning a restraint of trade case if the FA were stupid enough to try and enforce their illegal rules.

The effects would, in theory, be immense. In the short-term, an influx of foreign players would create some interest, and reverse the graph of attendance figures. In the long-term, far more important, there could be a real move towards encouraging players with talent to express it, with a little less emphasis on "work-rate" and destruction. The schoolkids now modelling themselves on Alan Ball and Terry Yorath (Letters, page 2) would try to emulate some of the tricks of the continentals; teachers might encourage them, rather than showing them the professional foul.

Foreign players might also bring with them foreign coaches—if directors had the foresight and courage to offer them sums comparable with what they can earn on the continent. These men might at least try to change the stereotype English game, the long centres aimed at centre-forwards with concave foreheads, the mid-field men who can only pass five yards with any accuracy New ideas would be flowing through the game, ideas emphasising the skilful rather than the physical side of football.

That's the theory. In practice, numbers would almost certainly be small. "It would be a hell of a gamble for the clubs," says Cliff Lloyd of the PFA, "to bring Continental stars into the game where the commitments are so heavy. And very few Continentals would want those commitments." Commitments aside—up to 60 games a season, in rain and mud and ice—the prospect of playing against the likes of Bremner, Colquhoun or Waldron every week is not an incentive, even for very large sums of money and a free subscription to BUPA.

As for foreign coaches, even Ron Greenwood is depressing: "I don't think foreign coaches would have any great success here. They would never properly understand our ways. Apart from outstanding individuals, the influence of the coach cannot over-ride national characteristics. They will always come through in the end." And we all know what they are.

So who else is keen on the idea? Apart from the 750,000-odd who tend not to be consulted about these things. The attitude of the PFA is particularly confused. They don't want a large influx of Continental players reducing the opportunity of employment for British players: an understandable attitude in view of the vast number of redundancies expected at the end of April. On the other hand, they are committed to breaking the dead hand of the FA on the game, and to having the laws of the country, rather than of Lancaster Gate, determine what goes on: that means they stick by the Treaty of Rome. In addition, they are members of FIFPRO, the European federation of footballers' unions. They'd presumably be quite happy if equal numbers of British players were employed abroad. But who wants them? The days when players such as Greaves and Law and Gerry Hitchins were watched by hordes of Italian scouts are long past—most players have trouble getting people from the same town to come and watch them, never mind from across the Channel.

Since English football has become increasingly unattractive over the years, it's doubtful that foreigners could do the good now that they could have done even five years ago. But English managers using British players have shown, with half a dozen exceptions, that they can't make attractive football successful. Others should be encouraged to try.

No. 28   April 1975

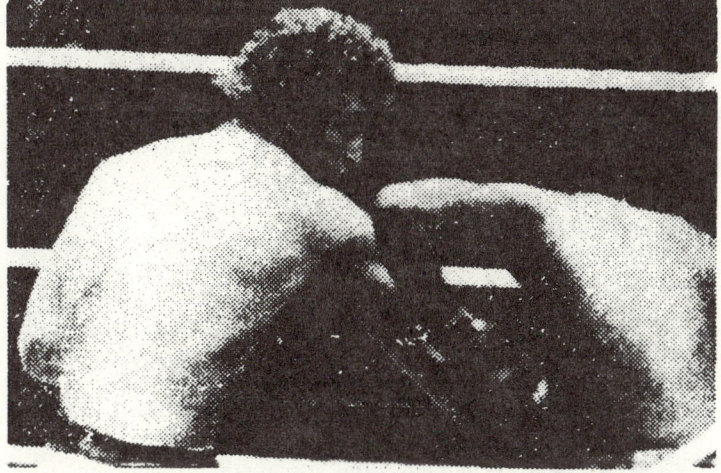

THE GROOM'S parents, Mr and Mrs Peter Phillips, arrive at Westminster Abbey.

London Evening Standard

'Euro fairies'

SWANSEA City manager Harry Gregg last night accused the football authorities of ruining the game by pandering to "a bunch of European fairies."

"I want to look at the practical side of football," he said. "People who are running football at the top are ruining the game.

"Manliness has been taken out of football and I believe we are now pandering to the demands of Europe and changing our game to that played on the Continent which, after all, is only being played by a bunch of fairies.

Western Mail

No. 26   February 1975

63

NOTHING TO BOVVER ABOUT

A recent survey in WHICH? on why people go, or don't go, to football revealed "second-rate play" and "poor facilities" as main deterrents. It also shattered the myth that fear of life and limb because of "Hooliganism" keeps vast numbers away.
CHRIS LIGHTBOWN, now retired after long and distinguished service on the North Bank, West Ham, traces the decline of Boot Power.

WHATEVER the Press may say, football hooliganism is all but over. And although it is possible to extract an ample dossier of incidents from provincial and far-Northern clubs, this phase has effectively ended in London and all the big city clubs that follow the capital's trends.

Any young person could start a fight on the flimsiest of excuses in 1968; in the early days of the Skinhead period it was literally considered provocative for any "normal" Lad to wear any colour but white, brown or black. Music tastes were kept similiarly basic, as Reggae —the simplest music available— was adopted.

This was the period of weapons crazes, bordering on the use of guns in some areas of London. Train wrecking was far more frequent, and consisted of far more than the heavily publicised total carriage wreckings; hardly a Football Special ended its Saturday without some wrecked lights, seating or windows.

The other thing that killed the violence, apart from the uni-sex movement, was the trend in young peoples' ideas; Skinhead-ism and social violence were a spent force by 1971, after an incredibly heady run from 1967. Just as the violence came into football because the youth movement was going through a violent phase, and not because of any inherent defect in the game itself, so it ended because violence stopped being the criterion for young people.

All youth phases, be it platform shoes or football violence, start in London, and spread themselves over the rest of the country in a period of some 2 years. Skinheads were a London export from 1968, and by 1971 Liverpool and Manchester Skinheads were making themselves a laughing stock to London lads who had long since grown their hair. The only thing stopping the same thing from happening to violence as a whole, now that it is at an all-time low in London, is repeated press ravings about the subject.

Football Authorities have missed their one chance truly to stop the violence; in the last couple of years, the age group that created the havoc of 4 years ago, finally hung up their boots. And there was a resultant 18 month gap before the younger kids started to fill the vacuum. There was literally a changing of the guard at 3 of the London clubs, where End leaders in their early 20s gave way to new leaders in their teens. Shortly after that, the new, but still very over-rated round of violence that we are hearing about now, started up.

The main violence was from 1968 until 1971, at the very latest. It was barely noticed by the media. Skinheads, for a youth group, were very under-publicised by the press. The mass publicity on football hooliganism only started when football attendances plummetted last year, — for which football hooligans were held responsible. Knowing the unoriginality of Football Officialdom, it might be fair to surmise that it was no coincidence that they picked on the one group of people in the game with no spokesman to defend them.

The scene is peaceful now because there was an inordinate amount of violence 4 years ago.

The very fact that football's authorities were utterly unable to take advantage of the lull — of course, they did not even know it existed — shows how out of touch they are with the situation. Their own constantly proffered remedy, "Stamping it out", is impossible, as with any subversive organisation. As long as the supporters involved in football violence — and they are a lot more than the ridiculous estimates of 2%, etc — have the tacit support of the rest of their generation, there is no way the movement can be stamped out. The most ordinary lad of 15 who goes to football matches, and who would *never dream* of getting involved in a fight, is interested in the Ends fighting, and what gang has done what recently.

The contrast with 1973 is unbelievable to anyone involved in the scene 4 years ago. The amount of goodwill around is enormous, and could only have followed the unremitting blood-letting of 4 years ago. The guy of 24 who was a prize football hooligan in 1968, is now wearing a droopy moustache, long well-groomed hair, listening to heavy pop music, and resolutely doing his own thing. These days, there is no happier atmosphere in London than in the pubs and discos of the football areas that supply the Ends. The big uncertainty is the younger generation, under 18, but on their showing so far, they hardly stand boot high compared to their predecessers.

Whatever the degree of violence, the structural basis is always the same, — a strong North-South mutual dislike, and a matrix of local derby hatreds.

Contrary to what media coverage suggests, most football hooligans differentiate between their club's opponents. Most of them have a second team, and although this is an entirely personal matter, some general tendencies can be seen. Liverpool are popular, Chelsea and Spurs have considerable out-of-town support, while West Ham come nearest to overcoming the rabid provincial dislike of London clubs. Both Rangers and Celtic are held in awe, as much for the antics of the supporters as for the prowess of the teams.

Basically, it is fair to say that every Club's supporters have a particular local rival, and then antipathy increases with distance. North hates South and vice versa, while the gang-riddled Midlands have dreams of mounting a holy crusade into London. The prospect of All Northern Cup Finals, too, always revives the Northern dream of sacking the Southern Babylon.

Even so, it is safe to predict that the fighting in the forseeable future will just be an acting out of what has come to be expected; the arrival of football hooliganism in Workington, just serves to show how truly finished the phase is.

The one imponderable that could upset all the calculations outlined above, is the generation coming up, under 18. They have grown up in a far more relaxed atmosphere than their elder brothers; if they become involved in football violence, then it will be because they find themselves expected to carry on the tradition, rather than any sort of revolt against their circumstances. That is really the ultimate tragedy of football violence. If only everyone had not been on their particular hobby-horse on this issue, it could have been settled for once and for all in the last 2 years. I personally think things will not get bad again, but this is no thanks to anyone in football, the media or any position of power.

RUPTURE
AND THE OAKTREE SKINS

Rupture and Willie are in dismay, Uniteds defeat has spoilt their day

Bill's chants are too much for our pair, Such untimely reminders cause deep despair

Bill Badger means to rub it in, But Rupture is going to do Bill in.

Nutwood United boot boy Rupture Bear and his sidekick Willie Mouse are in a black mood after Oaktree Rovers' shock local derby victory over Nutwood United.

Rupture was even more upset as he'd been hauled out of the crowd at half-time for roughing up a Rovers skin who'd strayed on to Spion Copse. That would mean Rupture would be up before the beak- Judge Owl-on Monday Morning.

So to keep their spirits up, The two pals busied themselves kicking a few trees and trampling the odd Dandelion on their way home.

Then the two Unitedites heard a voice drifting up through the trees – a happy chant of "We hate Nutwood Forest, we hate Underhill too – we hate Nutwood United, but Rovers we love you".

Rupture clenched his fists. "I'll bet that's that ugly Badger geezer" he glowered, and so it was.

Coming round the bend in the path was Bill Badger, Oaktree Rovers' suedehead leader. He was just about to launch into "We're gonna win the Acorn Cup again" when he saw the two pals blocking his way.

"Look 'oo it ain't" said Bill, "Bruno and his squirty mate" "Watch it, Badger" squeeked Will "Piss off, or I'll tie your tail into a knot" was Bill Badger's quick reply. "And look at you Bruno, still wearing those same old bleedin' yellow trousers you've had for years". Rupture seethed with rage. He hated the taunt of Bruno-especially from a Rovers skin. Bill was enjoying himself now, "Two-One" he began to chant and clap, "Two . . ." But he got no further, for in a flash Rupture's trusty boot swung high into Badgers cobblers and the suedehead crumpled to the floor with a groan. "An' that's why I'm called Rupture" growled our little bear.

O.K. – WHO RULES? ...(2)

Derby: shares and shares alike

THE Derby County Supporters Movement refuses to lie down and die. Its long-term objective, to get Brian Clough and Peter Taylor back, is still possible while results at Derby and Brighton remain equally bad (Clough apparently has a clause in his contract which will free him as soon as he wants to go): the short-term aim is to get chairman Longson and his sidekick Jack Kirkland off the Board and put Clough-sympathiser Sir Robertson King, the club president, back in the chair.

A meeting on December 11 resolved to press on with the aims, and to put the Movement on a proper financial footing, with subscriptions replacing haphazard collections. And as FOUL went to press, a turbulent Derby County AGM was due.

The supporters' problem is that what counts in football clubs is not people but money — ie, shares. Any vote carried at the AGM on a show of hands, which is unfavourable to the Board, can immediately be turned into a ballot, with one vote per share. Two years ago, this might have been a threat to the Board, but since then they have shrewdly built up their own little empires.

In 1971, Board members held only 501 shares. Within two years they had raised this to 10,789; passing the magic 50 per cent which enabled them, as long as they remained united, to do what they liked. Methods were dubious in the extreme: the excuse given for a "two-for-one" share issue, for instance, was that capital was needed for a mythical "new grandstand", which has never been heard of since.

"The real reason," says Mike Keeling, the director who resigned along with Clough and Taylor, "was simply to concentrate power", Keeling raised his holding by little more than the legitimate 100 per cent (35 to 91): other more ambitious parties took the opportunity to get in for everything they could lay hands on. Longson increased his holding from 110 to 1,325; vice-chairman Bradley from 156 to 1,372; Mr Innes and the recently deceased Bill Rudd, who were later to decide Clough's destiny, went from 10 shares each to over 1,200 each.

Most spectacular of all was the rise of Jack Kirkland, now emerging as the villain of the piece. In August 1972, he had no shares at all. By May 1973 he'd become a rabble-rouser who held 4,247 — easily the largest individual holding. Keeling, thinking it better to have him on the Board's side of the fence, sponsored him for a directorship — and now admits his disastrous mistake.

The real problem at this stage, however, was chairman Sam's increasing eccentricity. The public row about Clough's newspaper criticism of the Leeds' disciplinary fine blew over, but he was under FA pressure to curb his manager's outbursts, and reacted in bizarre fashion.

At the Birmingham away game he complained bitterly because a programme article depicted Clough as 'Man At The Helm': then accused Clough of financial fiddling; told fellow-directors that he wanted Clough/Taylor's contracts cancelled; and refused to sign their August pay-cheques.

One director proposed that a new chairman be appointed before any serious damage was done. Kirkland (fearing it might not be him?) talked him out of it, and proceeded to castigate Clough at Board level. Longson, finally admitting ill-health, briefly designated authority to vice-chairman Bradley, though demanding that Clough

broke off negotiations for Bobby Moore's transfer. But come the crucial board meeting, after Clough/Taylor had tended resignations, Uncle Sam was back in the chair, proposing acceptance. Sir Robertson King, who is in a weak position because he holds only 50 shares, promised Clough and Taylor a say at the meeting. Longson refused to let them in, and Kirkland seconded the proposal to accept resignations; it was carried 5-2, with Keeling and King against.

The crucial votes were those of Bradley, Rudd and Innes who voted, Keeling maintains "not with their hearts, but with the two major figures."

Sour grapes? Subsequent events suggest not, for within days, Rudd and Innes had summoned Keeling to discuss conditions under which Clough would come back. But before anything could be worked out (Clough seriously considered a public apology for the offending criticism of Leeds), the cynical appointment of Mackay had gone through. His acceptance embarrassed not only the players (McFarland had pleaded with him to turn it down) but another fringe figure, club secretary Stuart Webb, who, when Mackay's name was first mentioned had said "We're not having any second-raters here."

The story from then on became public knowledge, albeit through the eyes of a press which threw its full support behind the opportunistic Mackay, blanched at the idea of direct action from either supporters (the inevitable "militant minority") or players (horrors!) and refused to look beyond the time-honoured Board structure.

The basically pessimistic conclusions of FOUL 13 remain. But the worth of the cause becomes more and more apparent as new issues are raised, new investigations made and new malpractices discovered. A thorough look at the share system has shown how corrupt and anachronistic it is — a small group able to buy up all the power and influence; literally hundreds of shareholders untraceable; a local brewery, Bass Charrington, allowed to hold 3,000 shares and granted exclusive bar rights on the ground; and a secretary with a financial interest (since transferred to his father) in the firm giving free holidays as part of Derby's promotions drive, and organising club travel.

S.T.

No. 14   January 1974

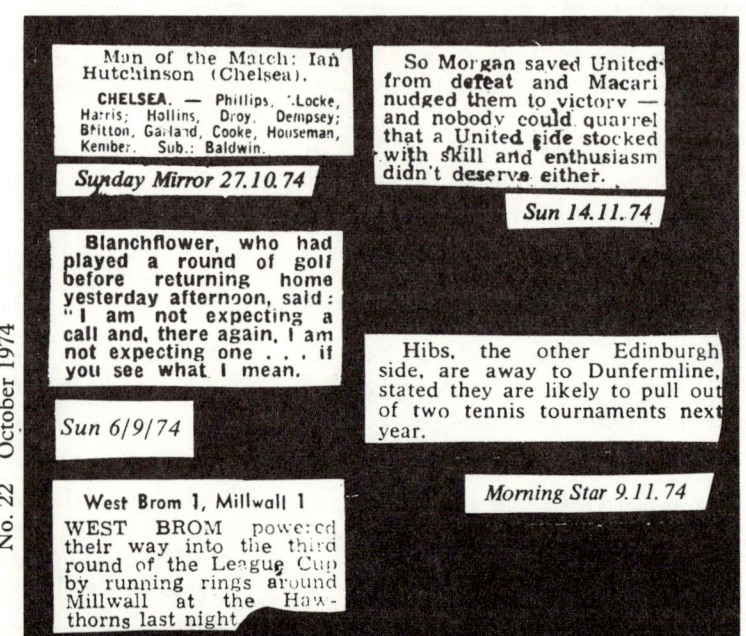

No. 22   October 1974

No. 24   December 1974

Man of the Match: Ian Hutchinson (Chelsea).

CHELSEA. — Phillips, Locke, Harris; Hollins, Droy, Dempsey; Britton, Garland, Cooke, Houseman, Kember. Sub.: Baldwin.

Sunday Mirror 27.10.74

So Morgan saved United from defeat and Macari nudged them to victory — and nobody could quarrel that a United side stocked with skill and enthusiasm didn't deserve either.

Sun 14.11.74

Blanchflower, who had played a round of golf before returning home yesterday afternoon, said: "I am not expecting a call and, there again, I am not expecting one . . . if you see what I mean.

Sun 6/9/74

Hibs, the other Edinburgh side, are away to Dunfermline, stated they are likely to pull out of two tennis tournaments next year.

Morning Star 9.11.74

West Brom 1, Millwall 1

WEST BROM powered their way into the third round of the League Cup by running rings around Millwall at the Hawthorns last night

Playing football on Sundays

From the Bishop of Norwich

Sir, I believe there are four clear grounds of objection to professional Sunday football, which are not fully drawn out in your leader last Saturday.

1 Family. Sunday draws many families together, at Church, at Sunday lunch and through family visits, "The family that prays together, stays together", and certainly Sunday lunches and 2 pm kick-offs are mutually exclusive! Your own leader and the BBC comment on Scottish football make the point that many footballers are against Sunday football and the strains on their family life should not be extended.

2 Social. Professional football is big business today, and Sunday football would seriously jeopardize the good social patterns of the day. Sunday excursion trains would be needed for away matches, with extra rail and coach transport for home games. More police, officials, caterers, and football staff would have to be on Sunday duty, and other major sports would soon be vying with each other for a financial cut of the commercial Sunday cake, and the breathless Continental and American Sunday would increase the already large amount of transport on the roads on a normal Sunday.

3 National. Doctor Dillistone's perceptive article on the same day as your leader, suggests that in England, social ethics and revealed Christian religion are less related than in earlier days in England. I believe Sunday is a vividly clear illustration of this. God created His world to work well, and from the start provided a rest or Sabbath Day, for the good of mankind, which is not narrowly restrictive, but is given by God as a day of rest, worship, refreshment, and family happiness. Above all, it is a Holy day, in which all men can remember their Creator, and in the words of one of my predecessors, Bishop Reynolds of Norwich, can thank Him "for our creation, preservation, and all the blessings of this life".

I believe that what appears to be a comparatively small issue, ie professional football on Sunday, does, in fact, point to the need of a fresh discovery of the law and love of God in days when many people are realizing the instability of the old material world, and the need of finding spiritual resources in Christ, to face with energy, courage, imagination and unselfishness, the tasks that lie ahead of us.

Yours sincerely,
MAURICE NORVIC:
The Bishop's House, Norwich.
January 28.

THE TIMES

FEBRUARY 2 1974

Come Off It, Your Holiness! says THE POPE

HONESTLY, the way some people talk, you'd think they'd invented Sunday! So when I read that the Bishop of Norwich, no less (or Norvic Kiltie Extra-Wide Fit, as we used to call him) has been putting his holy oar in, I just had to swallow the wafer-thin mint I was eating and sit down to tell you what Old Red Socks himself thinks of the whole schemozzle.

So 'the family that prays together, stays together', does it? Jesus Mary and Joseph! If that sort of talk got around I'd be out of a job tomorrow! Sure, 'God created His world to work well, and from the start provided a rest or

what-I-say-goes type of fiat. Right here in Roma you'll find the happiest workers in the world, bar none. Six days at work producing a great little motor, followed by a rest-day dividing nicely into Mass in the morning and goals after lunch. You can't beat it. And what's Britain got to offer? Fords of Dagenham and West Ham? Don't make me laugh!

Which brings me to my seasonal message. Now out of my personal trinity of favourites Everton and Celtic are doing very nicely thank you (thank You), but I think most would agree

THE BIG NAMES ARE ALWAYS IN FOUL

Sabbath Day'. But let me ask one question — do I hear the Bishop of Coventry complaining about commercialisation and the 'instability of the old material world'? Do I hell as like! Because his Sky Blues aren't bottom of the table, are they?

Y'see, all the good bishop's pious talk about 'rest, worship, refreshment and family happiness' sounds to me like so much sour grapes. So let me clear up one or two misconceptions. The family that PLAYS together stays together. Look at the Charlton Brothers. Don't let your lads go into soccer, Mrs Worthington? Ha! Look at George and Clyde Best. And when I hear Norwich bleat about 'Sunday football would seriously jeopardise the good social patterns of the day', then I'm afraid I just fall about. Look at Fiat — and when I say that I don't mean the

that the Old Trafford lambs are going astray a bit. Well I was on the phone to them the other day (that's right, The Pope talks to The Doc!) and I spelt it out chapter and verse — if United go down, my name's Ian Paisley. I told Matt and the team as much on their visit to Vatican City last year, and it seemed to do the trick. So I'll say it again — Man. Utd. Know Thyself. Face the tasks that lie ahead of you with energy, courage, imagination and unselfishness, and it'll all come right in the end — some other heathen bastards will go down.

Oh, and if my old mate Brian Glanville's reading this, many thanks for the black pudding, caro, we can't get it round here like we used to. Your corrected page-proofs are in the post. C'WAY THE BLUES!

Interview by: PETER LORENZO

SUNDAY IS POPE DAY

SOCCER REBEL

"THERE SHOULDN'T be any need for a Union in football. The mere fact that the PFA exists at all is evidence of bad management. The entire purpose of the Professional Footballers Association should be to dissolve itself."

The words are not those of Bob Lord, Denis Hill Wood, or Alan Hardaker. They are the words of Jimmy Guthrie, a self-confessed Soccer Rebel, a man who feels that the continued existence of the Footballers Union shows only how badly Derek Dougan, Cliff Lloyd etc are failing. Guthrie should know. He was the first chairman of the PFA when it reformed after the war, and held the post for 12 years. And as another season opens, with even the feeble Freedom of Contract compromise still as far from ratification as ever, Guthrie is a bitter man.

"The Football Players and Trainers Union was formed in 1907 with only two aims. First to fight for the removal of the maximum wage. Second, to abolish the Retain and Transfer system. That's all. Right from the start, footballers wanted the basic freedoms that every other worker has. To be free to earn as much as they could, and to work for whom they wanted. And what has happened? We got the removal of the maximum wage, oh yes, but freedom of contract? We are still waiting. I pick up my paper and read about Duncan McKenzie and the bloody wonderful time he is having over in Anderlecht, and what he is getting paid. Well, he should be able to have it here. But what has the PFA been doing for players like McKenzie? As far as he is concerned, his Union might as well not exist."

Guthrie may be right, but his feelings must be put into context. He was no mean player himself, and captained the Portsmouth team that won the Cup in 1939, thereby giving an answer to the most asked programme poser of them all — which club has held the FA Cup for the longest period this century? He lost his best playing years in the war, and after a spell coaching Crystal Palace (then, as now, a demanding task), joined the FPTU when it reformed, as their paid chairman.

The Union organisation was virtually non-existent in 1945, but Guthrie gradually pulled it together, gaining a series of minor victories over payments for televised games, and floodlit matches, establishing the Provident Fund, accident insurance for players, and the principle of a minimum wage. He hung around Fleet Street, always quick off the mark with a good quote, held meetings with leading barristers and lobbied Lord Monckton, the Minister of Labour. In his own words: "I did all the talking, the shouting, the bawling, the tub-thumping."

In spite of all the noise, he had by 1957 made little progress on the two major aims of the Union, although he did get nearly all his members to sign a petition demanding freedom of contract and an end to the maximum wage. These signatures now lie in his Chiswick flat on tattered, yellowing paper — an autograph hunter's El Dorado. But then a funny thing happened. The Committee decided that because he was not a registered player or trainer, he could no longer be chairman of the Union. He still hasn't got over the shock, and records that Cliff Lloyd and Jimmy Hill "just sat there like ventriloquists' dolls". Jimmy Hill replaced him as chairman: and you can draw your own conclusions from that as to who was behind the plot.

Guthrie, however, doesn't blame Hill. "I think the committee were got at by the League and the FA. They thought I was too dangerous, and they leaned on the players to get rid of me."

But this primitive conspiracy theory doesn't hold much water since the next six years saw the abolition of the maximum wage and the George Eastham case in the High Court. Nevertheless, Guthrie does have a point when he asks: "What the hell has the Union

Continued

F.O.C. off

"I WOULDN'T pay £300,000 for any player in the world at the moment, not with freedom of contract coming up. Peter Taylor may not find any English club coming for him at Palace's price."

The words are those of Tommy Docherty, and they tell us a lot about what has been happening in the transfer market this season.

It has been a depressing picture, the quietest season for transfers since the abolition of the maximum wage. It's more than a pity. There is nothing better to galvanise the waning interest of supporters whose team is losing matches, than a brave plunge into the transfer market. There is nothing more fascinating than watching an established, big name signing working his way into the machinery of a new team. And the prospect of a new and famous face in the side is something to keep you going through a long winter on the terraces, something to give you hope as you down a pint after the game. It's no surprise to me that with scarcely any big transfers this season, gates have slumped again.

What we have seen has been enough to make anyone despair. Rodney Marsh hung around for three months without getting an acceptable offer from an English club, before reluctantly crossing the Atlantic. Peter Anderson couldn't find any club willing to pay even £80,000 for him, and he too went abroad. Stanley Bowles has been on and off the list without a single offer. No English manager has raised the courage to sign Scotland's Willie Pettigrew, although they all complain about there being no good goalscorers around.

And at the time of writing, the position seems to be that Leeds United will either sell Duncan McKenzie to Anderlecht to raise the money for Peter Taylor, or they will hang on to McKenzie and Taylor will go to Anderlecht himself. How long will it be before Tony Currie or Kevin Keegan play their last game in England?

The message is obvious. Ramseyitis has seeped very deep into the English game. What all the players mentioned above have in common is a very high degree of skill, and slightly suspect temperament and workrate. When players like Marsh and Anderson have to go abroad before they can find a club who will employ them, in spite of their obvious crowd appeal, the reason is not that managers are scared of the prospect of freedom of contract. They are scared of the risk of the gamble of signing a highly skilled but individualistic player, just as Ramsey wouldn't pick Greaves for England.

It is absurd for managers and chairmen to use freedom of contract (which will not come in till 1978-79 at this rate, if at all) as the reason for not buying new players. They say there is nothing they can do if an expensive new signing walks out on them — they won't get anything for him if he goes and plays for someone else. But that's quite wrong. First, if a player wishes to leave a club while he is still under contract to them, then they can ask whatever they like for him, just like now. Second, if the club cannot reach agreement with a player at the end of a contract (and it is almost always because they are trying to get away with not paying him what he is worth) then they would receive a fee for him based on an agreed table . And anyway clubs on the Continent that are operating freedom of contract are not finding any difficulty in signing players. If they were, they wouldn't be over here trying to get McKenzie, Jordan, Pettigrew and the rest.

The truth of the matter is that managers like Docherty and Tony Waddington have been crying Wolf so loudly that other managers, who can't work out what freedom of contract would really mean, have believed them. Docherty says this sort of thing for a reason. He knows that if the rich clubs like Manchester United can convince the smaller, poorer clubs that there is no market for their best players, then he will be able to get the players he wants cheaper. Much cheaper. This year he picked up Steve Coppell and Gordon Hill for £130,000 the pair, whereas three years ago Southend asked, and got, £110,000 for Taylor. Other clubs have not been slow to spot the bargains. Liverpool paid Northampton £60,000 for Phil Neal, who was in the England team within months. Millwall (again) only got £57,000 for Bryan King from Coventry, even though they had turned down offers of £150,000 for him before.

Continued

done since then? What is there for them to do, except to make footballers free; and if they are not doing that, then, they don't deserve to continue. They said I was stirring up trouble, making players unhappy, causing unrest. Some clubs banned me from their grounds. But tell me – which clubs has Dougan been banned from for agitating?"

Even now, Guthrie does what he can: "I wrote to McKenzie at Leeds and told him he should take his difficulties to court – I wrote to Macdonald when he said he wanted to leave Newcastle and said that now was the moment to claim his contract for himself and hire himself out to the highest bidder like Best and Marsh have done." But Guthrie is a forgotten man, and neither McKenzie or Macdonald replied. The forces of conformity that prompted Tom Finney, when sharing a platform with Guthrie, to stand up and say he was quite happy with his £15 a week maximum, are clearly still as strong as ever.

He has written about his time at the PFA in *Soccer Rebel* (Pentagon Books, £3.50). The affairs of the PFA do not make very fascinating reading, even coming from somebody as committed as Guthrie. But the book serves to remind the present smug and apathetic leadership of the PFA that the Union did once have a more radical chairman, and that the ideal of winning the war in order to disband the army is not one to be despised.

Alan Stewart

No. 34 October 1976

It's bargain time in the Football League.

This time last year I wrote that we had seen the last of the £350,000 Bob Latchford deals, and that it wasn't a bad thing. Now I am not quite so sure. Derby County found £300,000 to keep Leighton James here, and now we are desperately hoping that other managers will find the cash to do the same for Currie, Taylor and McKenzie. There's one ray of hope in all this gloom. Easily the most successful deal this year was Charlie George's signing for Derby. There is the proof for anyone to see that if you treat a player right, he will play for you regardless of his supposed temperament.

It's now time for managers of unexciting, unadventurous teams to stop giving us all that cant about how great a value they put on individual skill and flair. It's time for them to start putting their money where their mouth is. Otherwise the answer to the question: "Where are all the Bests, Laws and Charltons of today, Daddy?" will be – "Playing on the Continent, son."

Alan Stewart

No. 33 May/June 1976

Help us find the Footballer of the Month

THE FOUL AWARD

YES, it's back! Kerrrrunch! *FOUL* is ready to erase the memory of that lilywhite Cup Final that shamed Wembley . . . by bringing back the award that every player wanted to win last year—THE FOUL AWARD.

English Soccer under Don Revie is entering the era of the Iron Man. Entertainment and Excitement and Hospital Treatment is promised. We aim to play our part by making sure that what the camera doesn't see is not forgotten either.

The other face of football—happily brought to light when Billy Bremner and Kevin Keegan became the first British players ever to be sent off at Wembley—will be rewarded. We will again be looking for the players worth putting on a pedestal. Our search, each and every month, will range through all five divisions of the Football League.

Pedestal

Brutality, retaliation, the sort of selfish genius that wins matches. These are the qualities that make a *FOUL* Award-winner. Derek Dougan, unanimously recommended by YOU, the fans, as deserving an honorary award last season, said modestly, "Oh shit".

And when collecting his Novelist of the Year cheque he added: "It means nothing. None of them—FA Cup, Texaco Cup . . . Nothing. Give me the *FOUL* Award. It's the only one that matters and The Big One as far as yours truly is concerned".

There are thousands like him. *FOUL* wants to find them. It wants YOU the fans to help us. In this way we—and you—can contribute to football's better and brighter side. Look out for more about the award that is guaranteed to be a winner.

BOBBY MOORE, England's captain and most capped player: "It's a great idea. No matter how many honours a man wins in the game, an award of this nature would give a great thrill to the winner. "So many good professionals never have a chance of winning any honours. This monthly contest gives them that chance and will create a lot of interest in the good things of football."

No. 21 September 1974

HALT AT MAINE ROAD AHEAD

The Angel of Death showed up on time again at Maine Road. Two Passovers ago he brought Rodney Marsh and two disastrous defeats that cost Manchester City the Championship. Last year he came for Malcolm Allison and this time it has been cuddly Ron Saunders. Just to prove conclusively that he has left Egypt for Manchester, those who say prayers for George Poyser will remember that he too forgot the sacrificial lamb nine years ago.

The events of the last three crises have been all of a piece, because what happened that stormy Thursday two weeks ago had its origins in the disastrous Easter of 1971-72. After it, the side that had taken 16 out of the previous 20 points dropped 5 of the next vital 10. In 1968 City had won their last four crucial games to take the Championship from behind. Why the last minute stumble this time? Simply a failure of nerve on the part of Malcolm Allison — a failure of nerve that is still evident in the club.

Three weeks before Easter 1972, after five years of trying, Allison bought Rodney Marsh. A few people wondered where the money was coming from but there was hardly a voice then that doubted the wisdom of the purchase. Unfortunately, Marsh's arrival coincided with City's fatal decline. He was incapable of blending his skills with those of Lee and Bell — a fact that gained in significance when rumours of dressing room rows between Lee and Marsh quickly surfaced.

After the team's title chances were finally laid to rest at Ipswich, Mercer bailed out thankfully to Coventry and Allison was left with an exhausted team — literally — and Lee dropped out of the Home Internationals for this reason. Likely Championship winners in August 1973, the end of October found City in 21st place, playing like Allison's robots.

Frightened into defensive, indeed violent, tactics, Allison stifled the remnants of his players' skill and failed to inspire that self-confidence that had previously been his hall-mark. Meanwhile, on television, a new Allison was emerging. In 1967-70 he was making outrageous, tongue-in-cheek claims for his team. After the popularity of the ITV panel was established in 1970, Allison in his public appearances neatly divorced himself from the side to whose performance he was indebted.

One of the humiliating home defeats suffered by City in the last few weeks before Allison's departure for South London was at the hands of Coventry, whose general manager was given a standing ovation by the Maine Road crowd, while Allison looked on stonily. How ironic that when Palace came to Maine Road for the last match of the season, already doomed to relegation (and also duly beat City), Allison was accorded a large raspberry by his former worshippers. Allison, who lived by his public image died at its hands that day even though he, not Mercer, had been mainly responsible for City's triumphs.

Thereafter the club slipped into the mediocrity already apparent the other side of town. Whatever could be said about United's desperation on the field, to the outside world the boardroom presented a united face. At Maine Road the years of triumph had seen nothing but division and vicious in-fighting. Three times Allison had been on the verge of leaving (twice to join Cantwell at Coventry, once to go to Italy), once he was fired only to be reinstated when Mercer threatened to resign. The boardroom struggle resembled a cross between *Mogul* and *Coronation Street,* as Vice Chairman Frank Johnston's crucial shares wavered between the various factions, landing up in the High Court.

Eventually Allison's backers won, only to see their raison d'etre first fail and then resign. The chairman, Peter J. Swales, in his mercifully few public utterances makes Sooty seem like Albert Einstein. Appearing on Granada's *Kick Off* programme,

the night of Allison's departure, Swales gave an interview of such outstanding incomprehension that even the urbane Gerald Sinstadt, who is used to talking to Jim Holton et al, looked puzzled.

The past few months have been a grisly melodrama. Johnny Hart suffered cardiac trouble and retired. The players sent a polite note to the board asking for the appointment of Tony Book. No reply could have been ruder than the arrival of Ron Saunders, who tried to instill into a skilful but childish team a surly aggressiveness better suited to the ice hockey rink. The swapping of Towers for the unspeakable Horswill and the threatened transfer of Summerbee to Leeds for £75,000 all added to the dismay below stairs. Eventually the players simply decided to stop playing and achieve instant relegation. The Board's hand was forced. Saunders was asked to resign and sensibly refused thereby making sure that his inevitable sacking would be accompanied by a large financial settlement.

Tony Book had been an inspiring captain, but he was greatly under Allison's influence. In the short term the City team (average age 29) will fight for him. In the long term Book has to build an entirely new side with few youngsters and a large overdraft. How well he succeeds we may judge from the situation next Easter Monday. ●

Colin Shindler

EDWARD74

No. 18   May 1974

AllisonWonderland

ALLISON LOOKED ABOUT him as he fell down the well. First Division, Second Division – would it never end? He came down, splash! into a pool of salt water – the tears of thousands of men who appeared to be attendants at a vast palace made of glass at the water's edge. As he emerged from the water he spied a bottle labelled "Drink me!", so he did – and at once shrank to a height of six inches. Facing him was a door marked "Bored Room". He went in.

Inside was a large table at which the March Hare and the Mad Grocer were having a tea-party; a Dormouse was asleep between them. The Grocer wore a top-hat with a ticket in it saying "Shop at Bloye's". The March Hare was saying: "I represent the Supporters' Club."

"He must be even madder than I thought," said the Grocer.

"That's right," said the Dormouse, "club the supporters!. . ."

"We'll support the club through sick and sin," cried the Hare.

"You mean 'thick and thin' " said Allison.

"I know what I mean," said the Hare.

"Come, my dear fellow," interrupted the Grocer, "have one of my best biscuits." Allison took a bite.

"Look," said the March Hare, "his head's even bigger than it was before!" And so it was. Then suddenly a loud voice behind him called: "Off with his head!"

"Who are you?"

"I am the Queen. This is the palace, isn't it? Off with his head!"

"He certainly won't miss that," said the Grocer.

"No," said the Queen, "I have a better idea. Shall we dance?"

"Yes," said the Grocer, "Let's line up all the players and have a Transfer Quadrille."

So they danced solemnly round singing:

" 'Will you play a little harder?' said the trainer to his men,
" 'Or we'll put you on the transfer-list at twenty-two pounds ten.'
" 'Will you, won't you, will you, won't you, will you join the Orient? . . . ' "

No. 19   June 1974

FLASHMAN

NOT a bad do then, was it? I was getting £25 minimum for a £6 stand ticket from the moment the Liverpool boys passed them on to me. By the Friday before the game, I was charging £90 the pair, and getting it most times. I even got more than £20 for a standing one pounder, and that'll keep me in woolly underwear for a week or two. The main reason was, supplies was short. Stupid decision to give the finalists an extra 5000 tickets each. Too many of the real fans got them at cost price, and that's not good for business. But short supply brings higher prices on what's left, so I'm not broke.

My usual clubs weren't very helpful. Sheffield Wednesday lost 8-0 to Middlesbrough on the weekend I usually move in. The result was that everyone in the club was too scared to sell me their tickets. They let the directors have all they wanted, just so they would keep their jobs. Nottingham Forest was a bad scene too. The players didn't get enough tickets, and complaining to the board didn't help. After that, the only thing for sale there was Bob Chapman. Arsenal were tight as usual, but Chelsea and Leicester came across with a few.

The worst moment of the game was being offered £150 for a pair of tickets and not having any left to sell. The best moment was on the Monday morning after the game when Leslie Grade got four tickets in the post.
By the way, who won?

Hard~Up?

No. 34   October 1976

AN INTERESTING item from the annual accounts of The Football League Ltd., Lytham St Anne's. In 1975, one (unnamed) employee 'earned' between £12,500 and £15,000. By 1976 this salary was clearly not sufficient to support him in acceptable style, and, pay code notwithstanding, was raised to between £15,000 and £17,500. It is believed that the identity of this lucky chap may not be dissimilar to that of the man who once said that removing the £20 maximum wage would be the death of football.

FOCUS ON FACT

No. 34   October 1976

"When I was with Crystal Palace I couldn't spend any money. . ."
– Malcolm Allison on 'The Big Match'

The Manager as Superstar

THE mere fact that Tony Pawson could write a book entitled simply *The Football Managers'* shows that they have reached a position of unparalleled, and unmerited eminence in the ranks of present-day football. Big Mal pontificates upon the shortcomings of others from his position at the bottom of div 2; Cloughy is walking on, and out of, the sea at Brighton; the Doc's prescriptions are being swallowed at Old Trafford; and the myth that 'Svengali' Stokoe has performed miracles at Roker goes utterly uncontested. We have entered the era of the Manager as Superstar.

The book is descriptive, rather than analytical, and is concerned almost exclusively with Managership, and how it is interpreted today. One or two of the quotes leave a rather bitter taste; Herbert Chapman asked 'Can it be believed that the Arsenal, in order to produce results, would cultivate a style that did not appeal to the crowd?'. Pat Saward says: 'I will take Brighton to the First Division, then move out of football within ten years' (the second proved easier to achieve than the first). And Pawson notes without comment in a piece about 'Godfather' Revie how in 1962, Leeds had only 26 points with but 6 games left, 4 of them away from home, and that they saved themselves with 10 points from those last 6 desperate matches. Without doubt that kind of activity is required of the ambitious, modern Manager.

But it is where Pawson deals with the history of Managership that he is most interesting. 'In the early years, the clubs were run by Chairmen, and as often as not the captain was in practice nearest to the modern track-suit Manager. He would work out the formation and tactics of the team , and organise such training as there was. Management was concerned mainly with the buying of players, with the finances and administration of the club'. Herbert Chapman changed all that, and he was so successful that he altered irrevocably the development of the Manager in these islands.

Ever since then, the Manager has increasingly centralised the functions of the Club upon himself, until in the last resort the Club becomes, as at Derby, a battlefield for the warring egos of Manager and Chairman. English football is currently in the grip of the desperate plight where the Manager is more important then the Club that employs him. This is essentially why the F A do not dare sack Ramsey. They do not know how they could cope without him.

During the last two decades, Matt Busby became so indispensable to Manchester United that his belated 'retirement' resulted in three successors in four years; and while an ocean of ink has been spilt on this catastrophe, it is often ignored that Glasgow Rangers are on their third manager since the Demise of Scot Symon at about the same time. What are Tottenham or Liverpool or Celtic to do after Nicholson, Shankly and Stein go? All these men, who have built team after team in their own image, will leave a terrible legacy to their unfortunate successors; the crown will not lie easily on the brows of the pretenders to their thrones.

It is now almost December, and a third of the season has passed. Just three Managers have been sacked; and English football is in the throes of tactical paralysis. These two facts are directly connected. Ramsey's fund of innovation had been drained by 1968; Nicholson's by 1964; Shankly's by 1967 when Ajax beat them 5-0 and he said "you canna play fitba against these defensive sides" — the recent humiliation at the hands of Red Star is just a replay of that, but six years on. But these men still cling to their jobs. What is needed is not greater security for Managers, but multiple sackings. No wonder nobody has any new thoughts, or fresh tactical ideas; unsackability leads to complacency, security of tenure leads to total atrophy and decay.

Because the Managers have become greater than the teams they serve, they have been demanding, like Dave Mackay, four-year contracts and more. Sacking the inept O'Farrell and sidekick Musgrove cost United nearly £50,000, and Bert Head is still not working, in order to avoid paying tax on his golden handshake from Palace. Many clubs simply cannot afford to sack their Managers, something which is paralysing the natural and healthy evolution of the game.

This problem would not occur if Managers were put on one-year contracts, as at many Continental clubs.

Only by reducing the influence of the Manager can the balance be restored to self-expression by the team. As Danny Blanchflower asked (FOUL 1), who can remember who managed Real Madrid when they won five consecutive European Cups? Who cares? What really mattered was the on-field leadership of Di Stefano, Puskas, del Sol. Likewise Ajax, who have just completed a hat-trick of wins in the same competition; a third Manager has succeeded Rinus Michels and Stefan Kovacs, but the philosophy behind their football has remained, independent of these changes.

Brazil changed their Manager a few weeks before the 1970 World Cup, but still won it; just imagine the disorienting effect upon the brainwashed England crew had Ramsey been removed at the same time. Here, the style of the team is moulded by the Manager; abroad the style of the team evolves naturally, and if the Manager does not fit in, he leaves at the end of the season. This is more akin to the English pattern before Chapman than the English pattern today.

English football is not likely to emerge from its current depression until clubs begin to regard the Manager as a dispensable employee responsible to, and appointed by, the players and supporters of the club who provide the cash for his salary. Books such as this one only encourage delusions of grandeur.

('The Football Managers' by Tony Pawson is published by Eyre Methuen £2.50)

No. 13   December 1973

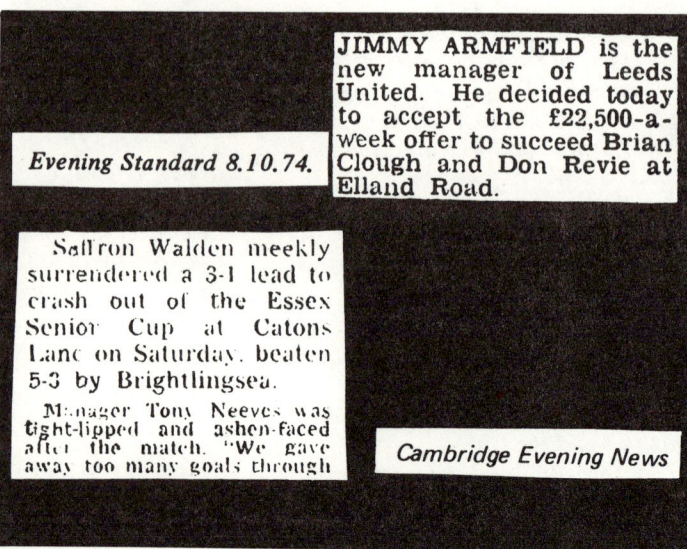

Evening Standard 8.10.74.

JIMMY ARMFIELD is the new manager of Leeds United. He decided today to accept the £22,500-a-week offer to succeed Brian Clough and Don Revie at Elland Road.

Saffron Walden meekly surrendered a 3-1 lead to crash out of the Essex Senior Cup at Catons Lane on Saturday, beaten 5-3 by Brightlingsea. Manager Tony Neeves was tight-lipped and ashen-faced after the match. "We gave away too many goals through

Cambridge Evening News

No. 32   April 1976

Keep an Eye on Albert

IT WOULD be easier to shed tears about the catastrophic season at Southport FC if the history of the club over the last couple of years were not so bizarre. Enough ludicrous tales have come from Haig Avenue to indicate that inane management is more the cause of the current crisis than inept play. Money, of course, is the problem: how to make it, how to save it.

Knocked out of the FA Cup in the first round by Spennymoor (an appropriately absurd conqueror), Southport's hope of cutting back their deficit of over £100,000 has rested firmly on League attendances. But these have been sinking rapidly (an all-time low of 870 was recorded this season) and those few remaining faithful are further disenchanted and alienated by such decisions as the playing of their home League Cup tie against Newcastle United at St James's Park. A hard core of dedicated supporters run a Special Events Committee to raise money, but early last year it was felt that this sturdy band was not enough. Southport needed the professional touch — a commercial manager. Send for Albert.

Albert Dunlop had shown less ability at handling money for various clubs than he had shown handling the ball as Everton goalkeeper in the pre-Gordon West days, and the bankruptcy of his sports equipment business should not have inspired confidence in what he could do for Southport. His selection as commercial manager was thus an odd, if not a highly irresponsible decision of the Board. But the machinations of the Southport Board about that time had not been distinguished by much sense or openness in personnel matters. Why for so long did the directors tolerate Alan Ball (Senior) maintaining a lucrative coaching appointment in Sweden when as Southport manager he had plenty to occupy him at Haig Avenue? Why did Ball's appointment occasion three resignations from the Board? Why was the dismissal of coach Matt Woods so hushed up? And was it no more than coincidence that Jimmy Melia (not long sacked from Crewe) was on hand to take over the job? Why did Alun Evans not go on loan from Aston Villa to Southport, after the probability of his moving had been announced at the 1974 AGM to placate disillusioned shareholders?

A former vice-chairman of the club was quoted as stating that the blame for the situation fell not on the directors but on the local authority, but the boardroom shemozzle would hardly achieve the support which the directors sought, and the appointment of Albert was a characteristically terrible blunder. Shortly after his appearance at the club, Albert had been indicted at Liverpool on a charge of gross indecency: this is of course incidental to his commercial record at the club, which has an indecency of its own. Functions were arranged, money was raised, bills were left unpaid, and whoever was reaping the benefit, it was not the club. Albert's final fling was a pop concert in July, with the bill topped by the group Showaddywaddy. Albert anticipated an attendance of 10,000, the largest crowd at Haig Avenue since Red Rum put in an appearance there in 1973. But only a few hundred people turned up for the concert, and Showaddywaddy did not, on account of some eleventh-hour contractual difficulty probably not unconnected with Albert's inability to pay the group any advance. The concert was a total flop, causing the club heavy loss, and in a rare moment of understanding the Board suspended and then removed Albert. The whole matter of what happened to the money raised during Albert's reign as commercial manager is currently the subject of a court action.

The Albert Dunlop farce was a symptom of the bungling way in which the club was being controlled, and the rapidly waning confidence of the remaining supporters was not helped by the comings and goings of managers and directors. When Alan Ball failed to show up at Haig Avenue for the beginning of this season, he was replaced by Melia. After a month Melia removed to the Middle East, and from September until January the club had no manager, the caretaker role being assumed by player Duncan Welbourne. The lucky man now at the helm is Allan Brown, and the improvement which Brown has wrought in the results strongly suggests that had he been appointed on Melia's departure the club might now be a good deal further along the road to safety. And then there was the meteoric rise and decline of chairman Tom Robinson, erstwhile off-screen amour of Coronation Street's Bet Lynch. Robinson was confirmed as a director in December 1974 and became chairman the following month. In February 1975 he blithely proclaimed that "I know we will get promotion next season and go up as Champions" — so why did he hold only the minimum possible number of shares for a director? When, in December, Robinson's fellow directors passed a vote of no confidence in him, they were not so much looking for a scapegoat as admitting that in making him chairman the Board had made yet another crass mistake. Robinson had some money and less commitment, and the club had need of a great deal more of both than he could part with. After his resignation last December he stated that he had been offered a seat on the board of other Lancashire clubs, but whereever he goes he will have to learn that being a director of a club in the lower divisions is a thankless and expensive task.

Desperate remedies: the idea of a door-to-door collection was turned down because the club was not a registered charity; when local coach firms refused to carry the team until bills were paid, the club took advantage of British Rail cut-price fares; and, craziest of all, Romark was called in to hypnotise the team into a winning state of mind — they lost the next game. When an exit gate had to be repaired in order to meet safety requirements for the first game of the season, the club could not afford to have the work done, and the bill was met by a supporters' organisation.

Yet still they struggle on, and since the arrival of Allan Brown and the departure of Robinson, the spirit of optimism is growing stronger. Southport are still a certainty to apply for re-election (if they have not shut up shop when the time comes), but at least their points total will be more respectable than at one time seemed likely — it should not be forgotten that they did not win this season until 6 December.

Re-election itself, however, is less certain. Nearby Wigan Athletic have good claims to take Southport's place on the grounds of stronger support, and the recent Haig Avenue happenings will not impress the League with the credentials of the management for running a League club. With Liverpool and Manchester so close, Southport will never be able to attract the support necessary to raise themselves out of the lower divisions (they went straight back to the Fourth in 1974 after winning promotion in a canter in 1973). The best they can hope for at the moment is survival. The first requirement for that is a minimum attendance of 2,500 at each home game, and currently they are managing about half that number. With weekly expenses at around £1,000, and income from home games something worse than nothing (as in the game against Cambridge, when out of the gate receipts of £392, £400 had to be guaranteed to the visiting team, for a start), the directors cannot finance the club indefinitely, and for Southport FC the writing is well and truly sprayed on the wall.

If they are re-elected, things will go from strength to strength, and the misery of this season will not be repeated: the present buoyant mood leaves no doubt of that. But if the club does sink, the verdict must not be accidental death. It was suicide, while the balance of the mind was disturbed.

Sean Magee

FOUL AWARD

***** Nobody clogs a *FOUL* correspondent and gets away without due recognition. We're delighted to award the first-ever five-star award to young STEVE PIPER, Brighton defender, whose "tackle" put your very own Eamon Dunphy not only off the pitch but out of football for five weeks.

Piper arrived quite some time after the ball had gone. . . his foot was just below knee-high. . . both Dunphy and the club doctor thought his leg was fractured. But referee Powell (Stourport)'s priority was to dump the injured man on the touchline and get on with the game — without a word to the assailant. When Peter Taylor, one of the men who pays the Piper, was tapped interrogatively on the shoulder by Dunphy's crutch afterwards he suggested that "He went for the ball".

"About the lamest response ever," says our Eamon — not intending the pun.

*** Reader "Bluenose" of Salford puts the case for ex-Celt BOBBY MURDOCH, now showing the studs for Jack Charlton's Boro: "Having crudely bowled over Donachie, he thrust his studs into the prostrate City defender's chest." Bye, bye Bobby, you might have thought — he'd just been booked for a handling offence. But referee Baker, mindful perhaps of another pitch invasion in the North-East, gave nothing more than a free-kick: and shortly afterwards it was DONACHIE who was sent to turn the showers on when he threw a punch at Foggon. Sad day for the lad altogether — it missed.

**** We hope "Bluenose" wasn't present at the City-Chelsea set-to ("a savage backstreet brawl" — *S. Express*) which put his team at the bottom of the Fair-Play League. Two sent off (HARTFORD for chopping Hollins in the throat, and KEMBER for felling Bell) and two carried off was the scoreline. A four-star show.

** In the QPR-Newcastle League Cup match (sic), an early 0-3 deficit, together with the patent lack of support from his colleagues, led STAN BOWLES to other distractions to make the second half tolerable. He spent the rest of the game niggling the opposition and Cassidy, Hibbitt and Macdonald were all 'Bowlesed over' before CLEMENT decided to join in. He scored with a neat head-butt on the unfortunate Hibbitt, who was knocked out and carried off — and the ref missed it too.

* At Highbury four days later, Bowles and a few million TV viewers were given a lesson in subtlety from the old master P. STOREY, whose trip on Stanley was so deft that Bowles thought

FAIR-PLAY LEAGUE

Deductions: Free-kicks (exc. offside) 1pt; Penalties 5pts; Bookings 10pts; Sendings-off 25pts.

IN FIVE matches since our last issue, Manchester City, those consistent entertainers, have managed 98 free-kicks, 5 bookings and two sending-offs: a total of 198 Trident points and a remarkable plummet to the bottom of the table.

Chelsea, with Eddie McCreadie putting some new steel into them as first-team coach now lead London's challenge — their match at Maine Road cost them a record 61 points (1 off, 2 booked, 16 free-kicks).

Stoke's fall from grace has been quiet but spectacular. But credit where credit's due. . . Liverpool conceded a new record low of three free-kicks against Middlesborough, and but for Emlyn Hughes' bookings would be even higher. So would the unexceptionable Leicester but for a tendency to give away penalties.

MOST FREE KICKS: Ipswich v Everton 44 (20-24)

FEWEST FREE KICKS: Luton v Liverpool 14 (6-8)
Liverpool v Middlesborough 12 (3-11)

INDIVIDUAL BEST: Liverpool 26 (v Man. City)

INDIVIDUAL FEWEST: Liverpool 3 (v Middlesborough)

		P	F/K	Pens	Bkgs	Off	Pts	Pos.
1	Newcastle	11	141	1	1	0	156	—
2	Carlisle	12	159	2	1	0	179	+1
3	Liverpool	12	119	0	6	0	179	+2
4	Tottenham	11	135	2	3	1	200	-2
5	Middlesborough	11	159	2	3	1	209	+6
6	Leicester City	11	159	4	4	0	209	+10
7	Wolves	12	165	1	5	0	220	-3
8	Coventry	12	169	2	5	0	229	+4
9	Luton	12	171	2	5	0	231	-1
10	Derby	12	162	2	6	0	232	-3
11	QPR	12	180	1	5	0	235	+4
12	Birmingham	12	150	1	8	1	260	-2
13	Everton	12	169	2	9	0	269	+1
14	Leeds	11	174	2	6	1	269	+5
15	Sheffield	12	128	2	12	1	283	-9
16	West Ham	12	198	3	7	0	283	+4
17	Arsenal	11	173	1	11	0	288	+4
18	Ipswich	12	210	0	8	0	290	-5
19	Stoke	12	162	2	10	1	297	+10
20	Chelsea	12	180	1	10	1	310	-2
21	Burnley	12	182	3	11	1	332	-1
22	Man. City	12	207	0	10	2	357	-5

centre-half Powling had done it. A few stars to referee Gordon Hill for spotting it and giving Stan a penalty goal. All those hoping he would actually stick one on ALAN 'THE NIGGLE' BALL either during the match or in the TV studio the next day were sadly disappointed. There they were, about as hatefully antagonistic as Roy Race and Blackie Gray. The only consolation was Ball's revelation of his footballing philosophies. . . "Players like that, you have to needle 'em, give 'em a good whack, put 'em off their game. . ." Can't wait till he becomes a manager.

No. 23 November 1974

The Road to Accrington

FOR A leading member of the Greater London Council to be talking about the municipalisation of football clubs, or even just increased cooperation between clubs and local councils is a small step forward. . . even if the GLC has no money to spend on such projects, and would need to divert it from the annual £4 million budget for the Arts in London.

One or two clubs have expressed a cautious interest in the idea. Meanwhile, Chelsea, Portsmouth, Luton and others are actually struggling to stay alive. A club which won the European Cup Winners' Cup five years ago is begging supporters to contribute a few pence for each goal scored, while Mr Deacon frantically denies that Portsmouth wage cheques have bounced, or that players are owed money, even though his own manager says it is so.

Fortunately the football public is wising up and would, we hope, insist that any ratepayers' money used to shore up the local club should not also support that club's prevailing power structure.

The Deacons and the Ray Bloyes of this world are failing now, even by their own dubious standards. "I have been successful in business, I intend to be as successful in football," said Bloye. Deacon does not even accept the standard business ethic that the buck stops with the chairman, and says that he is "very annoyed" by the suggestion that the club's present position is any fault of his; and this summer's Department of Trade report on the Vehicle & General crash (which originally caused Luton Town's troubles) has cast former club chairman Tony Hunt in an unfavourable light.

Mr Deacon, through his massive shareholding, will clean up if and when Fratton Park is chosen as the new site for Portsmouth Airport. Even if the club went bust, Deacon's investment is secure, since Superior Properties (only directors: John Deacon and his son, David) now own 74% of the shares in Portsmouth and would, after deducting the money owed to the bank, be able to keep about £1 million of the £2 million that Fratton Park would fetch.

Mr Bloye's recent manoeuvres included one of his own companies, Matthews Holdings, loaning £275,000 to Crystal Palace, who have released a four acre car park which Matthews can re-develop at any time. Should the car park fall below Palace's valuation of it, Matthews have the option of buying Selhurst Park itself. This from the man who told the world: "I wear two hats and keep them separate".

Yet the reaction of many people to all this machination and mismanagement is to turn from the hidden sponsorship of clubs by firms like Matthews Holdings or Superior Properties to the more overt sponsorship of cigarette, razor-blade or tyre manufacturers. They ignore the pattern, say, of Real Madrid, with its 40,000 subscription-paying members for whom the club is a centre of social life, preferring to follow the example of Bayern 'Adidas' Munich or SV 'Hitachi' Hamburg, selling their soul and shirts to sponsors who, as many minor sports have found out to their cost, can pull out as easily as they dropped in.

Arguably, such firms have even less commitment to football than the Bloye-boys, and the England team-manager, in taking up their cause as opposed to that of the local authorities', is helping us all further on down the road to Accrington.

No. 34 October 1976

Bennyfentons or Benefactors?

THE DIRECTORS of professional football clubs have changed little in attitude to their players and clubs since the early days of the professional game in the 1880s. To them must fall the burden of responsibility for the archaic industrial relations, autocratic control, unbending administration and generally narrow vision which characterises the game to this day.

Originally directors were vital in the evolution of the professional game, for their enterprise and money (generally acquired through a lifetime's commitment to the Victorian virtues of self-help), provided the expanding demand for football with a framework of professional clubs and organisations. Even before mass crowds gave the clubs the financial security to employ professional footballers, interested local businessmen had been able to secure players for local teams by offering them work in their concerns. Later, in the 1890s, when clubs became Ltd Companies, directors continued their financial support — often in the form of assistance in building the new stadiums.

While it is easy to see how much directors pumped into clubs it is more difficult to assess what they gained. For local businessmen, politicians, lawyers and doctors, to be known locally as a benefactor of the local club undoubtedly brought benefits. Politicians (in an era when universal manhood suffrage forced them to cultivate votes) could establish their name and reputation by patronising a club and thereby attract the votes of the working-class fans. Businessmen benefitted in innumerable ways from the prominence they acquired through football (a factor which still applies today). Manufacturers, merchants, entrepreneurs and newspaper proprietors rapidly established themselves as benefactors, but less obviously as beneficiaries of the football clubs.

These historical roots of football directorships go a long way to explain the continuing nature and dominance which the directors exercise over professional football. Directors, often nurtured in the unremitting schools of Dickensian business, were accustomed in their business and private lives to obedience and unquestioning industry from below.

Naturally enough, they came to expect professional footballers to fall into the same category; to be grateful for the opportunities offered, for a short while, of extricating themselves from poor working-class circumstances, and to play and to live as directed. Managers, though technically in charge of the players, were subjected to similar restraints from directors. In the intervening years, as industrial and personal relations have changed, and as the players' union has been able to squeeze better conditions of work from the game, the tone of football's directors has changed little.

Directors were led, from their seats of power in the clubs, into the councils and committees of the League and FA where they have succeeded in transplanting their narrowness of vision and antiquated opinions. Consequently on all the major progressive matters concerning the game (broadcasting, TV, wages, international and European games, transfers, discipline and freedom of speech among the players) the League's hostility has stemmed largely from the director-inspired mentality. Indeed many directors continue to speak of the liberation of the modern footballer, particularly since the abolition of the maximum wage, in the way the Duke of Wellington spoke about the first Reform Act.

Directors still have a useful function (and have legal obligations to their companies). But on the whole they form a self-perpetuating oligarchy whose influence is excessive, whose involvement is not always as disinterested as it appears. Their role was created and defined a century ago — but that role is badly in need of revision to make them more responsive to the needs of the game in general and their fans and players in particular.

James Walvin

No. 14 January 1974

NEWS

Valley of death

It is rare that a football club alienates its supporters so much that it is sued by them. But that is exactly what happened following an extraordinary sequence of events at **Charlton Athletic.**

The Valley Away Club was founded some four years ago to support the club in away matches. Officially recognised by Charlton, it changed its name to the Valley Supporters Club, and by the time it went on the excursion train to Rochdale on 16 March, it had grown into the biggest body of supporters that the club possessed. It says a lot about the present plight of Charlton that its total membership is just 150. There was a certain amount of rowdy behaviour on the train that day, and the match was played in a morgue-like atmosphere with some 800 hardy souls in attendance. The frustration of the Charlton support welled up at half-time, and they stood in front of the directors' box, chanting for the resignation of Charlton directors **Jenner** and **Wheeler,** and general manager **Rodney Stone.**

The following Monday, the Valley Away Club was informed by Stone that Charlton had withdrawn official recognition from it, and a note in the programme the following Saturday explained why. "We cannot countenance, in a train of Charlton supporters, young people arriving in Manchester before mid-day under the definite and obvious influence of alcohol. . . We cannot recognise any organisation that may, *even quite innocently,* be associated with conduct likely to bring the game and its followers into disrepute." Mick Walker, Chairman of the VA, is under no illusions that the drunken behaviour, with which he can prove no member of the VA was involved, was just a pretext for punishing a pressure-group of supporters who had dared be critical of the management of the club, and considers the Charlton statement libellous.

Accordingly an embarrassed Charlton Athletic received a letter from Simpkins Partnership, who were acting for the Valley Away, who told them: "Your statement. . . is very damaging to our clients, as it clearly has the meaning that our clients were so incapable of running an orderly and well-behaved club, that it was necessary for you to withdraw recognition. Your comment is therefore defamatory of our client, and we have advised them that you are liable to substantial damages."

This is just the climax of a long series of rows between Charlton, and dis-affected groups of supporters. In the past Stone has frequently criticised the local people and the community for not providing the club with more backing, and the club now intends to switch to Friday evening football next season because, as he put it, "the players get upset at the large gaps on the terraces, and under floodlights they won't notice so much." But in fairness to him, his ambitious plans for redeveloping the Valley in partnership with Greenwich Council were turned down in circumstances that reflect no credit at all on the Councillors.

Nevertheless, the supporters feel that the club is slowly dying, and that the present Board are doing nothing about it. They look enviously at Selhurst Park, which at least sees excitement, rather than genteel decay. But Chairman Mike Gliksten refuses to allow aggressive new wealthy blood on to the Board. And what Gliksten says goes, because of the 20,000 shares; he owns 10,000 of them, and his brother Dave who long ago lost interest in the affairs of Charlton and now farms peacefully in the South of Ireland, owns the other 10,000. The Charlton support feel that unless those shares are shifted into more dynamic hands soon, then there will be no club left to control.

OK: Who Should Rule?

OVER THE past three seasons, a motley bunch of club chairmen have figured in these pages. In the beginning there was *Ray Bloye (FOUL 3)*, who bought a controlling interest in Crystal Palace for £36,000 and led them to the third division and debts of almost a million. There followed *Arthur Page*, then of Orient, who banned a life-long supporter from the ground *(FOUL 11)*, had to re-instate him and was then exiled for swapping punches with his successor to the chair; *Sam Longson*, master of Derby, who tried to address a wrathful audience by putting a microphone to his ear *(FOUL 15)*; *Bob Lord*, the Burnley butcher, whose Utopia is a club without any supporters *(FOUL 16)*; *Harold Walker*, securing his position at Bournemouth by doing without a manager *(FOUL 18)*; arch-diplomat *Lord Westwood (FOUL 28)*, and many others, including those who've sat in the chair at Brentford.

This month, two extremes: *Dragan Lukic* of Stockport County, a dictator absolutely, with so much capital and personal prestige tied up in the survival of the club that he cannot afford any sort of challenge to his authority - from players, manager, supporters, aspiring directors or whoever. And Manchester City's *Peter Swales*, the liberal, the conciliator, wanting to do something for football; young, dynamic, he even admits mistakes. Ron Saunders? Well . . .

Swales is moving in the right direction, but the fact is that even he is unacceptable. The structure of club management which supports all the abuses and absurdities chronicled over the last 28 issues is rotten, and must be replaced by a democratic and representative one, which can nevertheless find room for financial and administrative ability (where it exists).

It is impossible to do this with the present system of limited companies run by moneyed directors, who hold a majority of shares and represent nobody's interest but their own. The alternative operates in thousands of smaller sports clubs throughout the country, a representative, elected committee - a principle which is also effective, in bastard form, at Nottingham Forest, the only non-limited company in the League. Forest's committee men are too similar to directors because they need to make

financial guarantees, and are elected by an exclusive 'membership' of only 250 people. The system works far more democratically abroad, where anybody with an interest in the local sports club joins it, availing himself of all its facilities and the right to decide who runs it; the 1966 P.E.P. report on Professional Football showed how a club like Benfica has 44,000 members involved in this process. Equally important, they contribute up to 40% of the annual income. The broadening of the base is an integral step to communal involvement and the development of community sports centres. And for a £1 or £2 annual subscription, people must be given some control over what they are joining.

The next fundamental principle is who rules: who actually sits on these club committees, and by extension, who joins the F.A. Council, and the League Management Committee (whose reform will follow as a matter of course)? Obviously representatives of the members/supporters, who even in clubs with a respectable supporters organisation are at present denied any say at all. This is something which both the P.E.P. and the Chester Reports - neither of them particularly radical in political terms- strongly recommended, and could be introduced tomorrow without any real restructuring at all, if the will to reform is there.

The players must also be represented, rather than consulted and then ignored (Swales and Saunders) or not even consulted (Leeds and Clough). And here is also an ideal opportunity to bring in the experience of all those former players and managers and coaches currently wasting their time and their talent, often in absurd circumstances: Shankly spends hours at Everton so he can't be accused of interfering at Liverpool; Everton's own man Harry Catterick, with a contract to run until 1977, does nothing at all; just across the water from them, Tranmere's Ron Yeats is sacked because he's been forced to play master instead of apprentice. Elsewhere, Mercer, Greenwood, Suart, John Harris are pushed into middle-management, still without any executive power. There should be room for at least two such figures on any club committee without crowding the manager and coach unduly; and how better qualified they are than the

businessmen to hire-and-fire, deal with players and even assess the merits of buying a new winger as opposed to a new w. c.

Enter Mr Swales. Our committee still needs expert professional advice on finance, contractual problems, basically on *business* matters. Businessmen can offer their services, in an advisory capacity or on a financial committee. This is a little different from the philosophy of Denis Hill-Wood: 'If you are going to run a biggish business like Arsenal, the more businessmen the better'.

The problem of finance may not be as difficult as it looks. At genuinely run-down clubs like Swansea City, Peterborough, and probably Stockport, the local authority should step in and offer financial support in return for the democratisation and development of the club. With shares as such nonexistent, and personal loans unnecessary, Dragan Lukic would no longer have any hold. If its true, as Man City and Spurs maintain, that directors of bigger clubs need not dip into their pockets, but only make guarantees, then the philanthropy which they all claim to have in abundance will still encourage them to support their neighbourhood club. One seat on the committee may be deserved. Otherwise the club membership, including the pools, social clubs, and development funds, will prove financially adequate.

Other anomalies, like the inheritance of football clubs (the Wales at Tottenham, the Mears' at Chelsea) will be avoided: in fact, once this sort of reform starts, there's no end to it. It's comparatively easy to build up a pyramid of football government, with one representative from each club or area or divisional committees, whose reps sit on *one* national body. With the distinction between League and F.A. abolished, one management team would control the game, run the international team, run the football pools, etc etc.

For the moment, we suggest for discussion: club committees of 5 people, comprising 1 supporter's rep, 1 players' rep, one fund manager or financial rep and two men of football experience committed to the club - one of whom can act as executive manager if necessary. A pre-requisite of which is the conversion of clubs to non limited companies, with as broad a membership as possible. Discuss□

REVIEW OF THE

So if we're relegated again, don't look at me! I'll have a nice little job lined up with Sutton Basket-Ball Team!

September 1973

SEASON

● THE FOOTBALL

THE FIRST DIVISION still dominated by the Leeds/Liverpool axis (although the third cog in that wheel, Arsenal, had a satisfyingly poor season); with the exception of Middlesborough, a series of mediocre sides fought hard to avoid promotion in the second. It sounds a bleak situation.

But in fact, it wasn't that bad at all. Leeds, after all, dominated the first half of the season by playing the football we had all been hoping they would for the last three or four years. And if Liverpool ground inexorably on, their style showed signs of developing more than one had expected. If, as Bill Shankly said, he doesn't know what 'flair' and 'skill' mean, his team had by the end of the season begun to ally a high degree of sophistication to their running. They atill aren't a side to take one's breath away with flashes of brilliance, but they have become more thoughtful, less frenetic in their approach. The lessons of Red Star obviously sunk home to some degree.

Even more heartening though was what was happening elsewhere. If England's success in '66 was a disaster for our football, their failure this year was, at least symbolically, a tonic. That, and the decline of Arsenal, gave an apt illustration that the state of the game is beginning to change. Ipswich, QPR, and Burnley especially represented a change for the better.

Ipswich look two years away from being the most dominating side in the game. And if they make it, and establish this domination, it will represent a complete turn of the tide back to skilful football rather than the negativity which has been prevalent since the mid-sixties. Unlike one or two false dawns – notably West Ham and possibly Leicester too – Ipswich's football has not disregarded defence and physical effort chasing after a chimera of elegance. Rangers and Burnley too both established themselves in the first division with great elan. With Adamson and Jago both espousing pure attacking football, and

with Leeds and Liverpool developing, there have been signs of change. And change for the better.

In the lower divisions, too, there have been signs of the same change, which is even more significant. The second division may have been disappointingly mediocre. But it was still significant that Luton and Orient, two very limited sides, but sides with a real commitment to attack rather than sterile defence should be so successful; the other side of the coin was the failure of Villa, who purchased Hockey the midfield killer, and Sammy Morgan, the big long ball chaser, to prepare for their push for promotion. All they achieved was a victory over their first division mirror-image in the Cup. And lower down the signs were even more encouraging. The success of Peterborough and Gillingham demolished the rule that you kick your way out of the lower divisions. And the third division sides in the top six showed a desire to play football rather than kick-and-run. As Red Star and other sides showed, English football still has a long way to go. But there were strong signs that we are finally emerging from the Ramsey-ite gloom. For that our thanks to Gordon Jago, Bobby Robson, Jimmy Adamson, Noel Cantwell, Andy Nelson, and about a dozen other managers in all divisions.

Peter Ball

No. 19   June 1974

TRANSFERS

LIKE inflation, big transfer deals feed on themselves. It took nearly seven years to get from £100,000 to £200,000, but just 17 months separated £250,000 from £350,000. And if big Bob is worth that amount, then what price Keegan or Channon?

The question becomes purely academic, because the season has seen a major change in the way the transfer market operates. Transfers have taken an irrevocable step away from cash. Soon, players will be like buildings, their values will only be paper values. The figure of £350,000 for Bob was a purely arbitrary one, arrived at by guesswork; his *value* was KendallplusStylesplus £80,000, but the actual figure could be anywhere between £200, and £400,000. (Indeed, if there were not %s to be taken off it for various people, then there would be no need to work it out at all.) This system of transferring players is commonplace in Europe and has been for years. It is not only on the field that we learn from the Continent.

The change heralded by the Latchford deal will penetrate the entire football system. It reinforces the concept of the first team squad, for a club must have players it does not actually need in order to be able to offer them in job-lots. It works the other way round, too. In order to buy Tueart, you must agree to buy Horswill too, and then stick him in the reserves till you have a chance to offload him to someone else.

But it is felt most at the bottom end of the scale. Morton sold Neil McNab to Spurs for £50,000; McNab was 16 at the time. You can't expect to get players of even that tender age without paying for them these days. And once you have gambled on their talent, you simply cannot afford to let the unfortunate boy develop nasty character traits like thinking for himself; Spurs will not make the same mistake they did over Graeme Souness, whom they lost not because they thought he was no good, but because he hated Tottenham.

Where, then, does this leave the players? Increasingly victims of the spiral which will bring them increased wealth without the independence to enjoy it. As evidence for this we need look no further than the "revolts" at Chelsea, Manchester City and Derby. Who led the players there? At Chelsea it was home-grown lads like Hudson and Osgood; at Derby it certainly was not the expensive Todd or Nish; and at City, Saunders was seen off not by expensive imports Tueart, McCrae or Marsh, but by the old lags of the forward-line. The pattern is emerging — the more a player costs, the more he has to lose by opening his mouth. As transfer fees are doubling the silence is becoming deafening.

Alan Stewart

PARTICIPATION(1)

1973-4 will go down as the Season that the lads started coming onto the pitch. The response from everyone was the standard response to juvenile delinquency of any sort; easy indignant headlines, particularly in the papers that profess to have the interests of the working class at heart; the usual garbage solutions — what do *you* prefer — fencing 'em in, or giving 'em all identity cards to be confiscated the next time they do it? And of course, the usual horrified quotes from the people who write pompous introductions in the Cup Final programme, and then, thankfully, the end of the season — another season where fans' passions were shown to have no outlet in the game.

In fairness to the horrified elders of the game, who must have thought that in football they had found a final shelter from the real world, the phenomenon has nothing to do with football. Football is a release for all the problems outside it, and has probably stopped more violence than it has created.

To assert otherwise is quite lunatic; the kids who are wasting their time in schools, and doing manly jobs like being clerks and messengerboys are not going to suddenly change the moment they come through the turnstiles. They are going to bring those problems with them, and wring

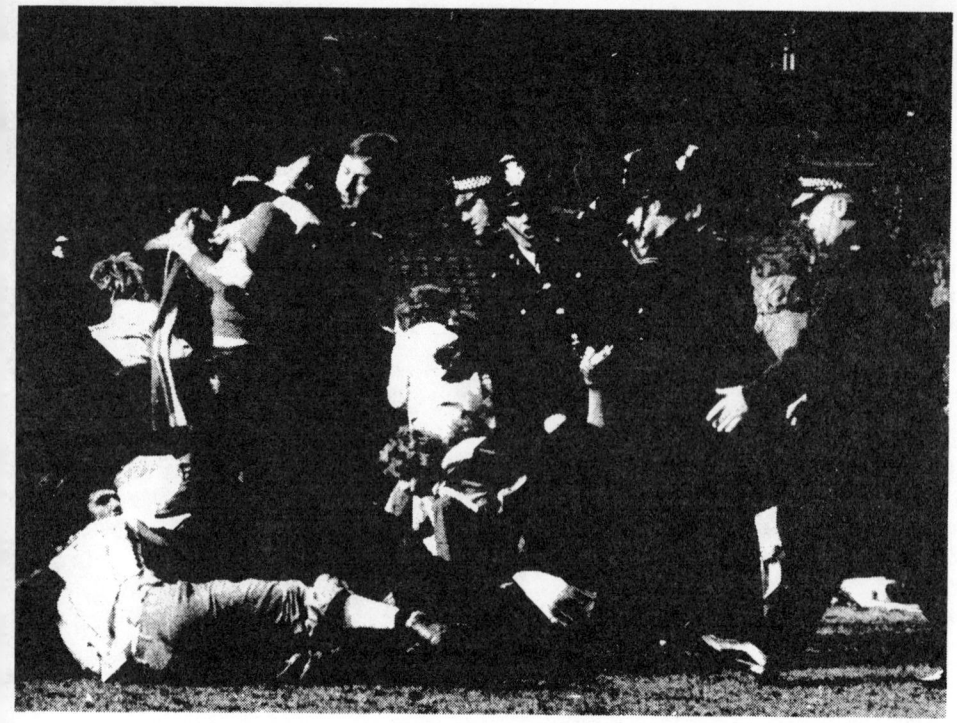

bloody havoc as soon as they catch sight of an activity that has the elements that turn them on — danger, passion and loyalty. Being a football supporter if you are 18 has all those things, so the kids' violence is in football. If Ten Pin Bowling had those elements, then they would be in that instead.

The idea of invading the pitch to get the result changed, has been in the air ever since the Rangers boys did it at Newcastle in 1969. With the later drabness of football from the spectators' point of view, it has since only happened in emotionally extra-ordinary situations like Manchester United's relegation, or with particularly ludicrous refereeing decisions like in West Brom's victory at Leeds in 1971.

The atmosphere in the city of Manchester the day they were relegated was much like the sort of beleaguered hysteria that gripped South East London in 1972 as Milwall failed to come up. The numbed disbelief of watching United fall must have been like one of those nightmares where your legs freeze as you go to run away from some horror. Football as it is structured now just does not allow for a supporter's reaction to those sort of events.

The solution has got to be bigger than football; its got to be a social one for all the social problems that have

come to rest in the game. Which is what true community involvement would be about. Football must not make the mistake of community centres and just set up the obvious things like Play groups and coffee mornings. It must get straight to the kids and give them some mentally stimulating and physically dangerous activity before they destroy the game. Otherwise, football involvement is going to go the way of Youth Clubs in the last 5 years and become a sanctuary for table tennis freaks and sullen guitar strummers.

It's not the kids who are letting

football down, it's the other way around. On the one hand, too much of the football played this season was drab — which is a betrayal; and on the other hand, situations occured which were exceptionally emotionally charged so there was no way for fans to work out their feelings without resorting to damaging means — which is another betrayal. THAT is the remoteness of football from its community that we keep talking about in FOUL and elsewhere.

No picture has annoyed me as much in 1974 as the Daily Mail's of some baby-faced 17 year old South London punk on his way to see United's last League game at Stoke, after being fined for invading the pitch in the City game. He, and the other kids now, are a lot softer than the kids of 4 years ago whose violence went largely unreported. These kids now are imitators, they are carrying on a tradition, and I suspect they have a lot less love of the game than their predecessors of 4 and 5 years ago. Wankers like that who strive to live up to a reputation garnered by others, are the most dangerous sort of all.

This is the Maggie May generation, the kids that got so fed up with school that they just walked out, with truancy rates of 30 and 40%. These kids have lost the fear of authority, and there is no barrier that they won't walk through. The pitch was sacrosanct to my generation, whatever we did off it, but to these kids, invading the pitch is peanuts.

Chris Lightbown

No. 19   June 1974

PARTICIPATION(2)

FOR supporters who wanted something more than bingo, stag nights and beauty queen contests from their club, it was a season of running up against harsh realities; of realising exactly who ran football clubs, and for whom.

The most celebrated example was at Derby County, where the Supporters Movement showed the way as an autonomous and militant body prepared to stand up for itself where the original Supporters Club had tamely submitted to Mr Longson's whims. Its aim was always a narrow one — to get Brian Clough and Peter Taylor back — and its tactics were confused. But the spirit and support emphasised that this was the way supporters must move as an effective pressure group.

Peterborough's supporters caught some of the spirit and threatened a sit-in when the club showed its gratitude by trying to evict them from their premises. But affairs at Brentford were more typical, and had a more typical result — a sense of helpless bewilderment at the way a club was being played with by the men who owned sixty per cent of it. Most of the 500 supporters who turned up one evening in February to hear the lurid details of the boardroom coup clearly had no idea at how little say they had, whether shareholders or not. And from their own Supporters Club officials they got nothing more than repetition of the debased motto of the National Supporters Federation — "To help, not to hinder".

Members of Charlton's 'Valley Away' group — the sort of people who follow their team to meaningless third division matches at Tranmere and Rochdale — managed some sort of response when "official recognition" of their efforts was withdrawn. But damages in a law court, even if they get them, are not what they really want.

And elsewhere, impotence and frustration showed up in more publicised incidents — pitch invasion, impromptu demos calling for the manager's head.

Derby was one instance of a militant spirit spreading to the players, who got predictably little change from the media, the directors, their new manager or — more damagingly — their Union. Perhaps the lessons of this open revolt were taken in at Maine Road, where the team simply stopped playing, forcing the instatement of the manager they had always wanted as relegation became a real threat.

The City players' achievement in getting rid of a manager who was appointed against their wishes might even prove a turning point. If Dave Sexton leaves Stamford Bridge before the remainder of the Chelsea first-team squad, the season will not have been a complete waste.

Steve Tongue

THE F.A.

THE hope that England's World Cup defeat might prompt some genuine soul-searching about our football has been partially fulfilled. Ramsey has gone, at last; more and more managers are talking about entertainment, and a few teams are even providing it. At Lancaster Gate, where the soul-searching was channelled into a committee, new-boy Ted Croker has publicly stated that there are too many old men clinging on to too much power — and slowly but surely the octogenarians are on the way out.

A State of Soccer Committee would obviously have been better in the hands of an independent body with some real authority, and no such animal exists. But to appoint the same reactionary old codgers who had doggedly refused to implement the key points of the Chester Report (an independent body with no authority at all) illustrated how terrified the FA is of outside influence, and possibly how hamstrung Croker is in trying to break down the Old Guard.

At the time of going to press, all we know about their six months of clandestine deliberation is that Ramsey has gone, and a young progressive is likely to replace him. This was the single most important event of the past 12 months, and the squeals from Ramsey apologists about ungentlemanly conduct and stabs in the back mustn't be allowed to obscure that fact. A useful side-effect was that many people were made more aware of how strong the FA bureaucracy still is — of how a man like Sir Harold Thompson doesn't just sit smoking cigars at the players' breakfast table, but exerts very real pressure and authority.

The Second Most Welcome Farewell of the season was that of Mr Len "Birch 'em" Shipman — an encouraging reminder that, like Thompson and his outdated Oxbridge ilk, old men get even older.

But whoever replaces the old guard — and that's another, vast, problem — will have to show a bit more tact, courage and sense of justice than we've seen this year on disciplinary matters.

While Leeds United received a derisory £3,000 suspended fine for years of violence, a fourth division club was fined £5,000 because they had only nine fit players, and doctors certificates to prove it. The effect on Exeter (see News page) was rather more drastic than on the Leeds players

GOOD LUCK SIR ALF!

IN YOUR NEW JOB!

October 1973

whom Revie maintained he was fining for every booking.

There must have been some poor men at Elland Road in the New Year once Leeds started to feel the pinch, and the FA should not merely lift the 'suspension' on their fine, but demand a sight more than one-sixth the revenue of a single Leeds home game.

The fumbling of the Newcastle affair, and of amateurism (see News) the internal wrangling over Ramsey, increasing public contempt for the old men at the top, lack of a firm lead on sponsorship and even television — none of these helped promote the brave new world of Mr Croker.

Derrick Winch

"The upshot is a strong vein of sanctimoniousness, which sits oddly with the paper's effortfully iconoclastic posture."
TIMES LITERARY SUPPLEMENT

3 Men who mattered

What the game needs, or so we are told, is 'characters'. Here, in the following pages are some 'characters', most of whom football would be all too pleased to see the back of. Doug Ellis, "in disgrace" in 1976; more than a decade later, it hasn't stopped him being chairman of Aston Villa again. Mr Bates has turned up again, like a bad penny. Dragan Lukic was last heard of in early 1987, a prime mover in trying to transfer Blackpool Borough Rugby League Club to Wigan. Jimmy Hill, eleven years on, was *still* trying to find out who is going to build what on Craven Cottage. Plus ça change . . . Others, like Willie Ormond and Don Revie are now simply part of football's history. Without Bob Lord, Burnley have nearly succeeded in achieving one part of his dream by getting rid of all their spectators.

Football people, especially on the non-playing side, tend to have a tremendously inflated sense of their own importance. Because it didn't take *itself* too seriously, *FOUL* was in an excellent position to puncture the egos and reveal the incompetence and arrogance of those who make their living from the game without necessarily contributing much to it. It was not, as some critics claimed, purely destructive and negative, but properly sceptical about motives which otherwise would have gone unchallenged. Equally, heroes were not acclaimed uncritically.

FOUL was sparing in its praise for individuals, though almost always fair. For every sympathetic profile of a player, there would be five chairmen getting their just desserts – which is how it should be. Football has shallow eulogies coming out of its ears (not that *FOUL* ever indulged in that), but intelligent and critical pieces are always at a premium. It is to *FOUL*'s credit in this respect that their profiles of individuals were well-enough researched and written (mainly thanks to Alan Stewart and Mark O'Neill) to nail the villains without resorting to crude abuse. It's only a shame that so many of their subjects are still with us.

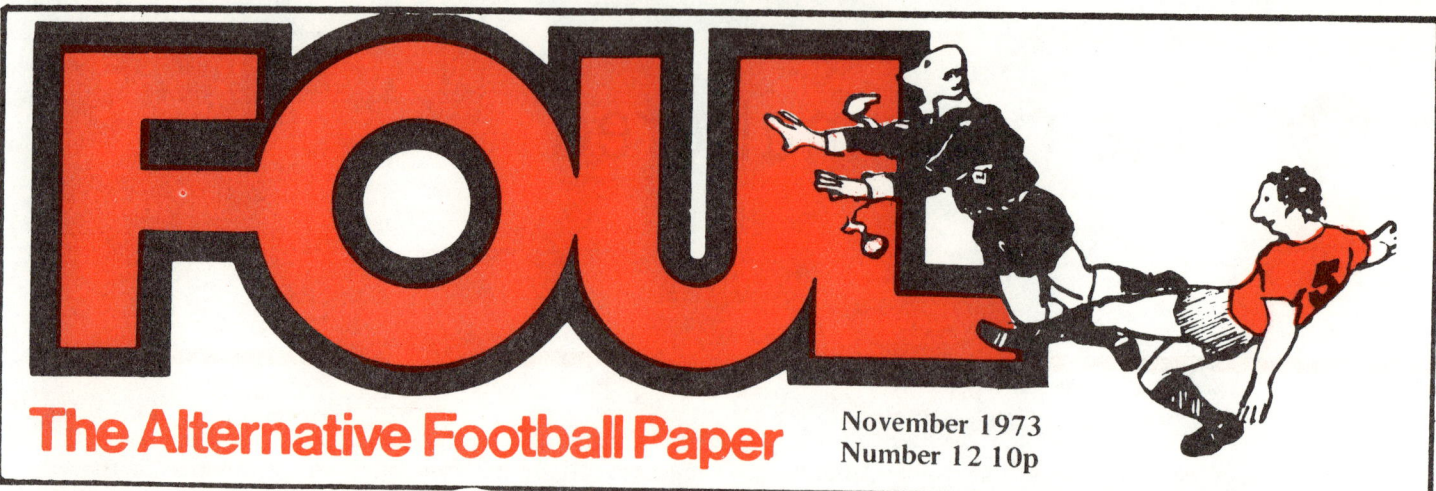

FOUL

The Alternative Football Paper

November 1973
Number 12 10p

CLOUGH SIGNS FOR US!

"I AM DELIGHTED TO JOIN FOUL MAGAZINE ON A FULL-TIME BASIS. THE EDITORS ARE BIG ENOUGH MEN TO EXPECT MY "ALTERNATIVE" FOOTBALL COVERAGE TO INCLUDE THE ALI-FRAZIER FIGHT IN NEW YORK, AND ENGLAND'S TOUR OF THE WEST INDIES, ON EXPENSES IF THEY DON'T LIKE THAT THEY KNOW WHAT THEY CAN DO".

Brian Clough

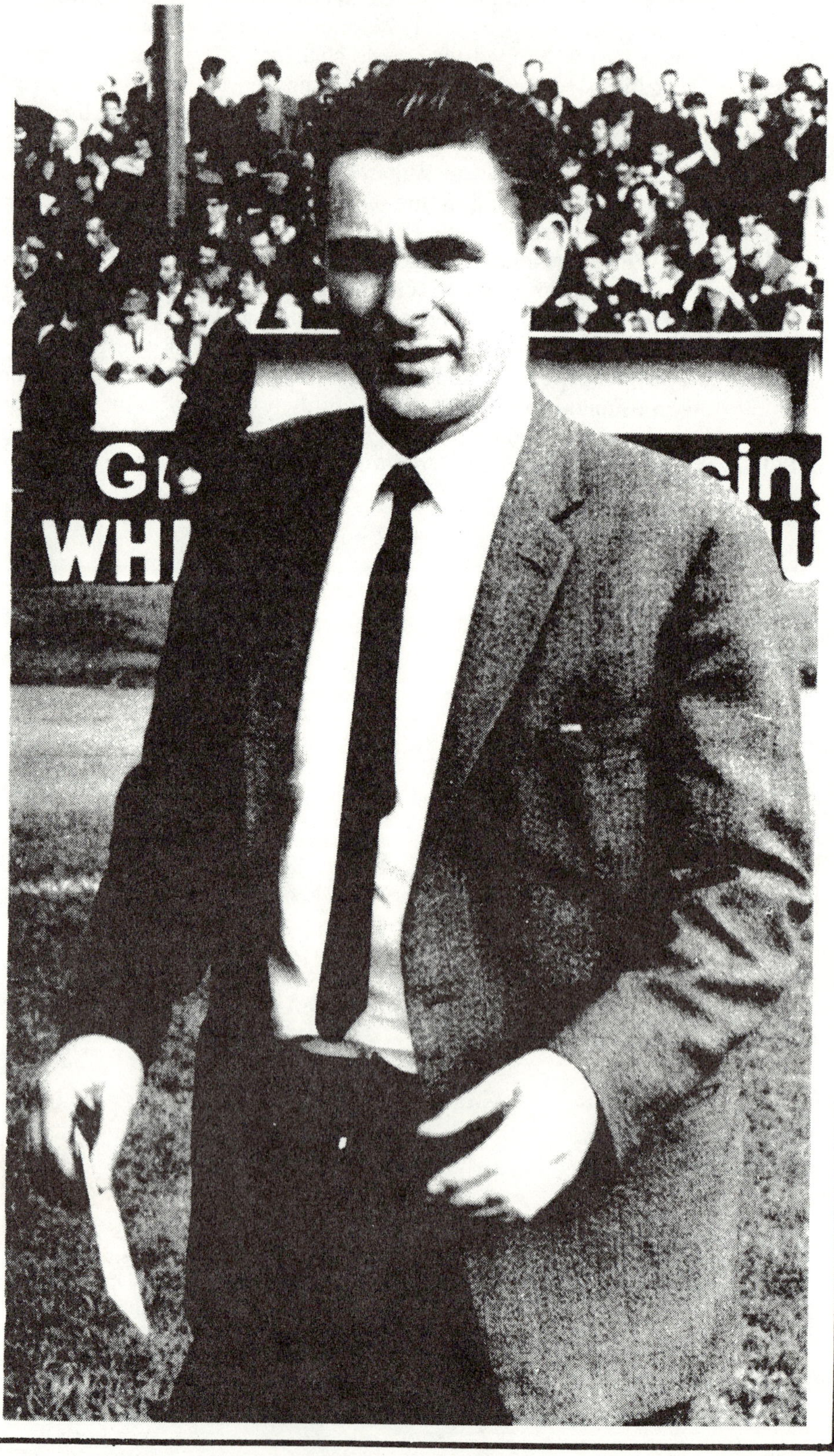

No. 12 November 1973

Clough

PART 97

I'm a loudmouthed bigot. Right. I'm boss of the greatest club in soccer history. Correct. I make errors of judgement. Right again. Hundreds of managers would give their right arms to stab me in the back. Too true.

But I think I know a bit about football; which is why I'm forking out half a million quid to put Sacha Distel in the Derby County goal. Why waste valuable recording time on vocal paraplegics like Gordon Banks, Jackie Charlton and choirboy-with-a-machine-gun Norman Hunter? Sacha will put Derby County on top of the Hit Parade. Just as not very long ago Derby County were on top of the Football League.

"There he goes again," you say. "That Brian Clough! What does he know besides football? I'll tell you. I know about success. And I'll shoot my mouth off about any job I think I could do better. Here for instance is my choice of a World Cricket XI which would lick Mars any day of the week:

Batters: Ian Buxton (capt), Sir Denis Bradman, Frank Sinatra, Colin Todd, Roy McFarland.
Wicket-keeper: Swadlincote's Jack Bodell.
Bowlers: Lillee. Colley. Massie. Millie. Lassie.

A lot of people wondered why I gave England so much stick in the Home Internationals. I'll spell it out.

Ramsey. The greatest compliment ever paid to him was on television when I called him the biggest bugger since Oscar Wilde. England will be a tinpot side as long as Alf lets decisions be taken for him by a gang of bodyguards, osteopaths, and brain surgeons.

I haven't been knighted by Her Majesty. But if and when that happens, it'll be for my services to football. Because my finger is on the Derby County pulse. I know what I want from them, and they do what I want. Even down to their strict diet of All-Brian.

It may not make for popularity. But I'm paid to win matches, not friends. And the flair and foresight that mark good management are not usually recognised till much, much later. Like the end of the season. When the Derby Countys are sitting on top of the League and the old men have taken a one-way ride to Palookaville.

Last Saturday night the entire team and staff came into my office and begged me to consider an offer to manage 1998 World Cup hopefuls Formosa. "Put down those bottles, lads," I told them. "I'll let you all know in good time." Then I did what I always do — went and asked Peter Taylor what I should do. Fair-minded as ever, Peter said it was my decision entirely, but that it was very nice there at this time of year.

The choice between Formosa and the Baseball Ground was agonising: Football's No. 1 manager, a respected citizen with money in the bank   or a potential TV audience 20 times the size of Britain's. It may surprise those who know me as the honest Socialist I am that I chose to walk the former lonely path.

But that's me all over. Unpredictable. Always doing the **unexpected. Putting my foot in it like as not.** At the start of the season I said I'd take a cut in salary every time Derby County lost. Today I'm on the dole. So what?

I've never been afraid of mucking in. When I managed Hartlepool I used to drive the team bus — but don't forget that's how Matt Monro started. (Matt and I are close friends, and he's on my short list if the Sacha Distel deal falls through.)

Meanwhile, not being one to let the grass grow under my big feet, I'm recording 'I remember it well', made famous by a frog called Chevalier. The lyrics are taken from some of my quotes and articles. Peter?

"Not much progress, I'm afraid, Brian. You could do the first lines and I'd put in the replies, something like:

'How about this for a back four?
(So far they've let in thirty eight)
And what a side we'd be with Storey-Moore,
(You were a day and a forged signature too late)
Ah yes, I remember eet well. . .'

"And so on. As for the rest, all I can find for 'With Derby County's supporters behind us we can win the Double' is some sort of line ending in 'rabble'; and 'David Nish' could go with what you said about 'a quarter of a million poundsworth of rubbish' — but then I need a rhyme for 'Costly failure'. . ."

Okay. That's enough. Get out, Taylor.

"I think you may have got it there, Brian."

NEXT WEEK: I PUT ICELAND RIGHT ABOUT COD FISHING.

FOULM@!*!@!!UTH

No. 9   June 1973

"OKAY THEN, IF I'M SUCH A DIRTY PLAYER, WHY HASN'T SIR ALF PICKED ME FOR ENGLAND, EH?"

THERE is no longer any question of whether Sir Alf Ramsey should go, only of when. It is clearly too late in the current World Cup campaign to replace him: the silver lining if we still fail to qualify is that he will have to go immediately, instead of after Munich.

In this respect, the results in Poland, Russia and Italy , and whatever happens in the next 12 months, are an irrelevance. The damage has been done in the 10 years of his reign. If England should suddenly "come good", the effect would be as disastrous for world football as our 1966 win, because it would once again assert Ramsey's values as the ideal. Post '66, British club managers took this hint, and we still haven't recovered: indeed the massive decline in attendances this season is largely attributable to the very qualities which were so greatly admired at that time - emphasis on "work-rate", destructive mid-field players 'getting stuck in', suppression of wingers, the preference for Roger Hunts over Jimmy Greaves's etc., resulting in negativity and brutality on the field and boredom off it.

Ironically, Ramsey is now caught in a vicious circle of his own making. Having for 10 years dictated the climate of English football, the attitudes of managers and young players, he finds a dearth of the players and skills to get him out of his present predicament. The realisation in Czechoslovakia that our £200,000 superstars can't pass accurately when the ball is soft or the grass is long should surprise no-one: they have spent most of the past decade being trained to run for ever, not to develop individual ball-skills. And the plaintive cry that if wingers existed Ramsey would play them is sheer hypocrisy from a man who has done more than anybody to discourage youngsters from becoming wingers, and encourage those who intimidate ball-players.

The attempts to pacify an increasingly belligerent press and public are merely token gestures - he keeps Summerbee in the squad (Hinton presumably isn't tough enough), plays talented individuals like Osgood, Keegan, Currie, Ian Moore and Richards for one match and dumps them when they do not immediately blend in. But particular team selections are far less important than the philosophy behind them, which is what the persistently near-sighted press criticism fails to appreciate. The issue is not 'Madeley or Storey', 'Currie or Ball' but whether Ramsey is prepared continually to select dirty players and versatile work-horses. Patently, he is: and under that set-up an occasional "good" result is as worthless as the headlines which screamed "Dreadful !" the morning after the N.Ireland game, and "Brilliant !" the morning after the Wales game.

The whole underlying philosophy of Ramseyism must go when its founder does: the sooner the better.

Something special for Thompson

No. 30   June 1975

Terry Mancini, Arsenal and Eire's flamboyant defender, has promised "something special" for Jimmy Thompson's star-studded testimonial match at the Abbey Stadium tonight.

Terry Mancini, Arsenal and Eire's flamboyant defender, has promised "something special" for Jimmy Thompson's star-studded testimonial match at the Abbey tonight.

Mancini, one of soccer's clown princes, who bared far more than his soul to the

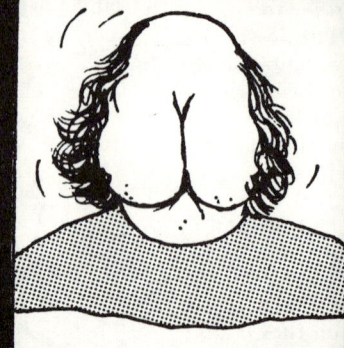

Terry Mancini

Cambridge Evening News 2/5/75

QUOTE OF THE MONTH

"The Czechoslovakia goal was a good one for them, and a bad one for us"
                    - Sir 'Alf Wit

Brian Drysdale (groin) and Cheesley (ankle) have been under treatment this week. And skipper Geoff Merrick only reported for training today for the first time after being in bed with a heavy cod and suspected food poisoning.

Bristol Evening Post 12/9/74

Christ Balderstone was a marked man but he was too good a footballer to be played out of the game by John Crags, or anyone else, and his pinpoint passes sparked off much of United's danger.

Newcastle Journal 21/8/74

No. 22   October 1974

THE KING IS GONE

Peter Ball mourns the end of an era

CHARLTON got cigarette boxes,TV coverage, presentations and miles of eulogy. He was the ideal professional. Quiet,modest, unassuming,brilliant,hard-working, a one-club man,and he refused to change in the same room as Best. He got 106 caps and scored 48 goals for England,played 604 games and scored 198 goals for United. He was one of the Four who made United synonymous with style and flair in the '60s.

But when one asks who was United's greatest footballer,it was either someone who walked out in disgust earlier in the season,or someone who was pleaced on the transfer list the day that Charlton made his final appearance before a capacity crowd and the cameras. Rumour has it that Best may return to Old Trafford. Docherty is reportedly making pacifying noises. And if Charlton's retirement means that the changing room will be friendlier towards Best,one may paraphrase a famous statement and say that nothing Charlton has done for United becomes him like his leaving it.

But where are the cigarette boxes and the cameras for Tony Dunne? He has been as great a servant to United as Charlton. And, more important,where are they for Denis? It's arguable whether it was he or Best that established the United style. Possibly Best was the more talented footballer; just possibly. But for those of us who have followed United for years,we admired Crerand, respected Charlton,marvelled at Best but,as the Stretford End proclaimed,'Denis Is The King'. I hope that United swallow their pride and persuade Best that there is still a place and a future for him at Old Trafford.

But the dismissal of Law,for that is what it is,says farewell to the era of United. He represented the style,the arrogance and the passion of United's football better than anyone else there. Charlton had the talent,and was an admirable player. But somewhere the flair and arrogance not of just being best,but thrusting it down scoffers' throats,was lacking. Best was the most brilliant. But somehow,somewhere, he didn't quite match Law. Not in our affections. Best had the balance,ball control and flair that even the next greatest footballer in Britain could only daydream about.

Yet somehow Law was the one who captured the imagination. Law the one who proclaimed that United were the champions, even when their leaky defence had conspired to place them in an average position. Law who strutted arrogantly around Anfield or Elland Road showing the pretenders just where they got off. Law who got involved in the fights when other lesser teams tried to make up for their deficiencies by kicking. Law,unfortunatley,who could be provoked into forgetting about the game and looking for some pig defender who wasn't really worth being on the same field. Law incorporated United in his very being. He had all their talents,and all their weaknesses. All to excess,as United had both their strengths and weaknesses to excess.

And in a way perhaps it is fitting that Law has been given a free transfer. No one could imagine Denis coming modestly onto the field,receiving a cigarette box modestly and then after modestly saying that he wasn't being put away in a home, modestly touching the ball three or four times in the whole game. It was a sad farewell; but it was Bobby's farewell. Denis couldn't have done that to us.

Instead of strolling round peripherally while Buchan and Holton swore at each other,Graham swore at both of them,and Docherty swore at Buchan (all audible on the other side of the ground),Law would have been joining in,and if ignored in the same way,would probably have provoked an incident by kicking Osgood or Droy,if he hadn't attracted attention by scoring a brilliant hat-trick.

But if United are becoming small enough not to be able to live with Law's size,so that it's Bobby's retirement which receives all the publicity (because it's safe),the fans know that it was Denis who represented United. And if he is not receiving the tributes which are his due, it's because the contrast with United's present insignificance would be too great.

No. 9   June 1973

EVERTON: the Young Idea

THE MAGIC OF Goodison. So hard to put into words, especially today when John Hurst and Mick Lyons are dumping opposition forwards on the mortal sod. But even today there is some virtue, some quality all the same; they are bred of Alex Young and the Sixties team, gliding their way to the Championship, passing by the brutality of their opponents rather than repeating it. Clinical, lean, spare; an economy of style that left the ball and the opposition to do the running.

The Academy of Soccer the locals are calling it by 5.30; Billy Bingham compares Goodison Park to the Conservative Club in Liverpool; and chairman 'Little John' Moores tells his players off by saying "Everton don't play that sort of football." They all refer to it, the Idea, the image in their mind, stretching perhaps beyond Young to Davie Hickson, Dixie Dean and the Irish labour boats; a specialness obvious to those who know, mysterious to the outsider. Unknown to Shanks in the toilet to be sure. But they *know* what they mean.

If I may be so definite, the Idea of Everton is mainly the work of Harry Catterick, born 1920, late centre forward of the club, former manager of Crewe, Rochdale and Sheffield Wednesday and now gestating on a huge retainer in a golfing suburb of Southport. He treats the Idea with respect but distance: "*I was engaged to win trophies. We'd had 25 years of no success. But what we did was ultimately not in the best interests of football.*"

Which is quite an admission from a proud man. He defers to the Idea while falling short as a custodian of it. He admits there was a standard, an ideal he could not live up to (and which has probably disappeared for good now). So: what did he have to work with when he arrived in April '61, days after Johnny Carey got sacked in a taxi?

He found the most expensive team in Britain and a forward line of Bingham, Roy Vernon, Alex Young and Bobby Collins. Carey was a gentle man; when Brian Labone came, Carey had let him alone, so much so that Vernon had to tell him 'if you can get this boy centre half to knock himself about, he'll play for England'. Catterick had a

different method. '*It is a manager's responsibility to tell players to kick if necessary.*' John Moores was excluded from team talks. Catterick demanded single-mindedness and self-discipline. "*Professional footballers cannot move around socially as they would like; you must stick to the rules and I was quite severe with those who didn't.*" After one month as manager he sent Vernon home from New York for being 10 minutes late back to the hotel. This restraint extended to business as well as boozing: "*I don't like players having business interests; they get so involved in their finances that it puts them off their football. Granted, the tension may be less but I really prefer a man who gives me 100% of himself to football.*" — e.g. Labone, whose family plumbing and electrical firm nearly made him give up two years before he did.

His vision was a brigade of Spartans, of Marines selfless and professional, their skills sharpened by hours on Bellefield's shiny surface and marathons on the Southport sands. His best team he believes was the 69/70 Championship side; its only rival was the 50/51 Spurs team. Push and run, economical, efficient and surgical. What about the trio of Ball, Harvey, Kendall? '*A luxury*" he said; marvellous to have, but to rely on such a combination left too much to chance. No-one must be indispensable. A squad must be built to survive bad luck and heroes equally. "*You've got to have competition for places. The Press would say you've dropped Royle or Vernon or Young; he's not happy. I should say I'm glad. I should be worried if he's happy. I want him to be worried. That's good. Let's have a few more.*" Catterick's men were Dennis Stevens and Tony

Kay: Jimmy Gabriel, Colin Harvey, Ray Wilson. Everyone had to be an all-rounder.

What then about the Golden Vision Alex Young, whose rays drenched Goodison when Catterick arrived? Wisely, he kept his preferences under lock and key. Young and Vernon — both Carey men — were a venemous, if anachronistic pair. With them, Catterick took Everton to 4th, 1st and 3rd; the Parisian pair scored 116 times between them. They and no-one else were allowed to be lazy in training. But they felt increasingly out of place. The wingers were ordered to tackle back: Fred Pickering cast his giant shadow: 'Harry's principal concern was the state of his defence' (Vernon). Alex Young was '*afloat in a world far too rough for him*' (Catterick). Pickering, Joe Royle, David Johnson — they were the wave of the future. "*What we did was ultimately not in the best interests of football.*" Catterick has reservations about the system he created; he won't deny Young's contribution. Still, his comment is more epitath than remorse.

For his part, Young feels he was at the wrong club at the right time. His talent was not fully realised, his powers underused. By April '64 he was saying 'the doors have been closing against me'. He was in fact the prototype Non-Catterick, a man who needed personal attention under a manager who '*did not mix with players, in case anyone thought he had favourites*' (Vernon). The lute player and the brigadier. At team talks Catterick sang the praises of the opposition: "*It took me half an hour*" says Young "*to realise they were not as good as he said they were.*"

And Catterick blunted the national chances of his Scottish players, so

"WHEN YOU'RE BUYING KEENLY THE WORLD OVER YOU CAN'T AFFORD MISUNDERSTANDINGS," SAYS JOHN MOORES CBE, CHAIRMAN OF THE LITTLEWOODS ORGANISATION.

Continued

Young believes; he got just two caps out of his finest years and then only after Scottish manager John Prentice had seen him in the 1966 Cup Final on television. His portrait of the club is of a divided and fearful dressing room; the players hid in the loo when John Moores was on his way down. Their livelihood, their opportunity was dependant on a remote and introspective man who sent transfer-mongers to train with the apprentices and told the national team managers not to bother. His way of thinking was obscure and devious, his favour capricious but mortal; and his responsibility was to a board headed by the most successful man in England whose ambition outran Concorde. Why did Young stay? The pay was good and the crowd fantastic. Only once in 251 games was he barracked; against West Ham and for three minutes. They loved Scots and assaulted Harry Catterick in Blackpool when Young was dropped for Joe Royle's debut. Reflecting on it all, in the mess of a seaside hotel, Young had to say: "was it all real? Was it a dream?"

For Young then the Idea existed more in spite of the manager than because of him. If Everton was something extraordinary, the chemistry took place on the field, when Dennis thumped, Alex flicked and Roy ran, when they forgot what they had been told in the team talk. Vernon's view is more sanguine: *"Catterick had a good understanding of human nature, he knew the score."* For example, when Bobby Collins left after a row with the chairman, Vernon was made captain. Vernon? A Carey man and one whom Catterick had disciplined conspicuously and who did not like training? But Catterick knew what he lacked as a manager, and Vernon was made captain because of his accessibility.

And Vernon excuses Catterick's methods because of the pressure on him from elsewhere. He praised even the training: *"You pushed your body till you thought you could do anything. I was never so fit again."* Was Tony Waddington different after the transfer to Stoke? *"If you're in jail and you shout for water and no-one comes, you stop shouting. But if someone comes, you go on."* Vernon needed Catterick as Alex Young needed Waddington. Vernon admires Moores too: *"He liked our company, for him it was a change from big business."* So though he did not like it, Vernon excuses Catterick's adoption of the modern system. He did the best he could, within his limitations.

For all this gossip, though, the Idea will persist. Catterick, Young and Vernon become figures in the canvas, faces pointed to lovingly in the corridors of the Everton Supporters Club while the Idea has been passed on to other hands. And whatever the finished article on the field, what it was (or ought to be) shall never be forgotten. So much for the braying of the Kop.

Mark O'Neill

EVERTON, as any journalist knows, must be leading contenders for the honorary title of Most Miserable Club in the League, using miserable in the sense of parsimony, bloody-mindedness and non-cooperation.

They once refused to give their public relations manager's home phone number to an inquiring writer, because "it is not the policy of this club to divulge personal information".

Now they have perpetrated another example of niggardliness, over the memorial service to the late Bob Prole, former sports editor of the Liverpool Echo.

Mr Prole covered Liverpool and Everton affairs for more than a quarter of a century, and gained a reputation on Merseyside and further afield. Even though he retired as long ago as 1958, he is still remembered with great affection, as the turnout for his memorial indicated.

Liverpool sent a delegation headed by the Big Four at Anfield — manager Bob Paisley, chairman John Smith, secretary Peter Robinson, and president T.V. Williams, who ignored the miserable weather, and his 80-odd years, to pay his last respects.

Everton's representation consisted of one: Bob Gamble, the press box steward. The service was held at St Luke's Church. . . which adjoins Goodison Park.

4.25 Sooty
4.50 Magpie: A visit to Liverpool Football Club and a look at the ways in which animals have been used throughout the ages.
5.20 p.m. Wait 'Til Your

East Anglia Daily Times

No. 29 May 1975

SOCCER-LOVING M.P. Walter Johnson last night tried to kick Alan Ball out of his new job as England skipper.
He described the fiery Arsenal captain's appointment for tonight's match against West Germany as "a **bloody** disgrace."
In a withering attack, the Labour M.P. for Derby South said: "We don't want a footballer who swears and misbehaves.

Daily Express 12/3/75

Revie will obviously now h a v e to experiment in this department —and though he wasn't giving away any private thoughts y e s - terday I w o u l d be surprised if Gerry Francis of QPR and A l a n Hudson of Stoke aren't given the chance to challenge as a trio.

Daily Mirror 30/1/75

Four minutes later they took the lead when North- ampton's goalkeeper, Star- ling, collided with his own defender John Gregory; leaving Gordon Cattrell to fire home from six yards. Darlington dictated a crap- py first half but Northamp- ton's Paul Stratford missed two good chances from 12 yards out.
Half-time: Darlington 1, Northampton 0.

Cambridge Evening News

■ TOMMY CARBERRY: I had a great ride — with just one anxious moment. I hit the one after Becher's first time round and nearly went.
■ KEN WHITE, who fell at the second on Junior Partner: He hit the fence hard and came down. Paul Futcher was sent off.

News of the World 6/4/75

No. 29 May 1975

But in the 57th minute a sudden lapse gave Birmingham their chance. Gary Pendrey's centre slipped between Moore and John Lacy for Joe Gallagher to find himself with an open road to goal.
He did not strike the ball cleanly and it was easy to imagine the sheer desperation coursing through Mellor's mind as he groped away to his right ball.

Sunday Express

No. 30 June 1975

Profile of Lord Westwood

William, second Baron Westwood of Gosforth, Justice of the Peace and President of the Football League lists his occupation in Who's Who as 'company director'. It's fair enough; he is a director of 29 companies including Newcastle United Football Club. But he's more than that. The man with the silver hair and eyepatch is one of that rare breed of men, the professional chairman, a natural conciliator, born to preside over everything he surveys. A man who can mollify the most stubborn reactionary and defuse the most ardent reformer. Radical he is not.

They say that the most patriotic men are immigrants. It's certainly true of the aristocracy if Westwood is anything to go by. Although his father gained the title as recently as 1944 and was a Trade Union official before that, Westwood has nothing to learn from more established barons about the sophisticated ways a title may be used. Football is ideal territory for him to operate in. Club chairmen, who are on the whole wealthy local businessmen, are desperate for outward signs of respectability. Westwood has got his title, his trade union origins and the fact that he is an exceedingly wealthy man in his own right all going for him. In the country of the blind, the one-eyed man is king.

The Westwoods are not a Geordie family. They came originally from Dundee where William's father served an apprenticeship in shipbuilding. However the family talent for conciliation soon showed itself, and he moved to the Clyde to become Supervisor of the Shipconstructors' and Shipwrights' Association. He also made waves in politics and in 1917 became chairman of the Scottish council of the Labour Party.

"My father was never a Socialist, but on the right wing of the Labour party. I see myself as a left-wing Tory; there's not much difference. I don't know what my father would say today if he saw the way the Unions have taken over the country. He was 22 stone, and never had a strike in his life."

This record was one that appealed to many, and the family fortunes improved when in 1929, at the deepest point of the Slump, he was transferred to head office on the Tyne and appointed General Secretary of the Association. His son, then 21, came down from Glasgow to help him move house: "I only went to Newcastle for a week's holiday, but one way and another I have never actually left." The same year, father and son were admitted to that temple of self-made men, the Gosforth Masonic lodge.

In due course Westwood became a force to be reckoned with on Tyneside. Football had been an interest for some years, and indeed he had formerly been on the Board of Dundee for a spell. So it was inevitable that he should be invited to join the Board of Newcastle United in 1944, the same year that he was awarded the Barony by Winston Churchill, a close friend from the days when Churchill was Liberal MP for Dundee. He remained on the Board until his death in 1953, when his seat was offered to his son.

But the new Lord Westwood did not take the vacant seat. All through his life, he says, he has accepted seats on Boards only with extreme reluctance. He had a lot to do, dealing with his father's estate, picking up the threads of business interests that were by now very diverse; he wasn't ready for Newcastle, he wanted to wait.

While he was waiting he built up Dundee Ltd, of whom he is still Chairman, into a company with 16 subsidiaries and an annual turnover of £20 million. It's not a well-known name, but they primarily make toys; if your Hornby trainset ever broke, or you ever wrenched the head off a Cindy doll, think of Lord Westwood. In addition, he owned and ran a chain of cinemas and places of entertainment; to this day he still draws on the experience of those years when dealing with football

Eventually he agreed to join the Board of Newcastle United in 1960. He found it bitterly split into two camps, one around Stan Seymour, a local hero and former player who had scored in the 1924 Cup Final, the other around Bill McKeag a cantankerous solicitor, thrice mayor of Newcastle. George Eastham catalysed the rift with his fight to break the retain and transfer system, and Newcastle fought him and the PFA all the way to the High Court, where they were defeated in a celebrated ruling by Lord Wilberforce. The scars were just healing when the Chairman died in 1965. His logical successor, vice Chairman Rutherford, refused to stand and the Board had to find another man who could bring the factions together in some semblance of harmony. Lord Westwood was the obvious choice, and from that time on the reluctant chairman has ruled with a rare mixture of firmness and tact.

But even that did not quench the thirst of ambition. Once established as Chairman of Newcastle, the invisible forces of tradition started to pull our hero towards the League Management Cttee. Rutherford's uncle had been on the Committee, and had been succeeded, almost by right, by another Newcastle director, Wilf Taylor. The latter eventually felt he was too old to remain, and approached Westwood, mentioning that "one or two of the Committee would like you to stand." Westwood 'allowed his name to be put forward by the club', and was duly elected in 1970

Marc

No. 28 April 1975

Four short years later, "I was asked to run for President by several other Chairmen. I think they were impressed by the fact that I had spoken in several debates in the House of Lords . . . they had never had a voice in Parliament before and they thought it might do them some good. I was conned into the job—they told me that it wouldn't involve many meetings, so I agreed to stand." In spite of the implacable opposition of Bob Lord, the title worked its invisible alchemy, and the election was won without undue exertion.

With a track record like that, it would be too much to expect Westwood to push the cause of reform. Nevertheless he oozes complacency and it is easy to see why he gets on so well with Mr Secretary Hardaker.

On the crisis:

"The first thing we must get straight is that there is no crisis. Football is not on the brink of disaster. A struggle, yes, but not a crisis. It's quite false to look at the number of clubs that make money—about 10 last season—and say that football is on the verge of bankruptcy. Most club directors believe, as I do, that the proper way to run a football club is to end the season with a £1 profit. If we think we're going to make money we buy a player. At St James' we don't have many blue receipts from the Inland Revenue, but we do have a lot of good players out on the park.

On money:

"Nearly all the trouble comes from the Government, who take millions of pounds out of soccer every year without putting any of it back. We put up a new stand with more seats, better facilities, everything. It cost us £504,000. And the next day the local authority were round saying that the rateable value of the ground had just gone up.

"We get about £75,000 a year from the development fund, and that will probably rise when the new Lotteries Bill comes into force, which will allow clubs to charge 30% in legitimate expenses, rather than the 10% at the moment. But it would be fatal to allow the Supporters Club on the Board because of that; the first thing they would want is a say in the running of the club. Our shareholders don't interfere with the running of the club, and nor do the Board. We leave that to the manager, that's his job. To allow anyone else to have a say would be like the tail wagging the dog.

On players:

"I have the greatest respect for Cliff Lloyd and the PFA and all they are trying to do. But the players aren't militant; they don't really want power— they just want to niggle. This freedom of contract thing is nonsense. The players do have freedom of contract anyway; any player can walk out and play for a non-League club. He'd probably make more money there. The clubs don't want freedom of contract, none of them would bother to run very

expensive youth schemes if the players were free to walk out at the end and sign for whoever he wanted. The big clubs would just buy cheap out of the third and fourth divisions, and turn those clubs into nurseries. 75% of the players don't want it either. We'll all hear a lot less about freedom of contract at the end of the season when there are 250 professionals on the dole.

On reform:

"If there's one thing I would like to be remembered for in the end, it would be harmony. If we can attain harmony we're a long way towards solving the problems. I see football as a three-legged stool, with the clubs, the media, and the spectators; each of them depends on the other two, and each must give and take and work together towards dealing with the problems. Reform? We don't need reform. And anyway the big clubs would not have it. They just wouldn't accept giving the third and fourth division clubs a vote at the League AGM; it would mean that Workington could cancel out the Arsenal, Stockport nullify Liverpool. Now is that fair? It would make a mock of democracy. It's the same over incorporating the League so that profit and loss are assessed on an overall basis. The big clubs would put in the money and they could never get it out again. They'd never vote for it. It's like that in business. It's the same in life. The big boys run it. It's only fair."

Alan Stewart

No News is Sports News *Hemel Hempstead Evening Echo 3/1/75*

Luton not poised to sign Everton's Royle

By ERIC HARRIS

LUTON TOWN manager Harry Haslam today denied he was poised to sign Everton's ex-England centre-forward Joe Royle.

Farmer not for Leicester

LEICESTER City, in urgent need of a goalkeeper with league experience to replace the injured Mark Wallington, are expected to make an early move.

But today, manager Jimmy Bloomfield dismissed as "paper talk" a suggestion he would be signing Stoke's John Farmer on loan.

NO TOWN BID FOR TOSHACK

JOHN TOSHACK is not poised to sign for Luton Town. Neither is his Liverpool colleague Brian Hall.

By ERIC HARRIS

Boundary Bates and the Virgin Islands

WANTED—an industrial working population; access to main roads and space nearby for facilities and parking; a well capitalised site; and an ailing club. So ran the ad in the mind of Ken Bates, cruising round the north of England in his maroon Silver Cloud in the summer of 1965. Ten years up from London, with a construction company and global interests in investment and property development, he wanted to chance his arm at football. He liked the game and needed another Everest to climb. He saw Burnley, Stockport and Oldham answering his requirements. A cloven butcher and Vic Bernard had taken two of the places; what about the 'Latics?

The patient was ripe for experimental drugs. Oldham Athletic had creditors and shareholders snapping at the window; no money from the supporters; a secretary, named Buckley, shortly to go to prison for fiddling players' expenses (he had also turned down Malcolm Allison as manager for £30 a week); and the police threatening to close the ground for safety reasons. It was an Accrington replay, with United, City, Leeds and Burnley blackening the horizon.

The board was delighted. There were no moguls among them, and no-one who could raise desperate capital. In the autumn of '65 Bates bought 19,500 shares and sank £85,000 of loan stock into the club. Frank Large, Ian Towers, Dennis Stevens and Bloor were signed 'before they could find out I was a millionaire'. He wrote a five year master plan: it was accepted unanimously (had they seen one before?). In January Jimmy McIlroy

came for a five year contract at £4,000 a year. Bates liked his reputation in the area and in Ireland (e.g. Allan Hunter, Ronnie Blair), and his handling of youngsters. The old bicycle and wooden bench that had passed for physiotherapy gave way to a lavish medical room; board room, dressing rooms and social facilities too were re-done. The Boundary Bulletin flooded the town.

The club stayed up: up to 5th place by the next December. The team boasted David Best and George Kinnell: Knighton, Hunter and Blair for a half-back line: Large, Towers and white hope Bill Johnson from Glenavon on the right wing. They sniffed promotion. Bates called for backing from the board, but they were too poor or unadventurous. The chance was gone. The next season the players slipped: Johnson had a tragic injury at Middlesborough: there was no confidence in McIlroy. Bates began to recoup his misfortune. Best, Kinnell and Knighton were sold.

DIRECTOR'S BOX

On Anegada, meanwhile, in the British Virgin Islands he landed a plum. A 199 year lease on four-fifths of the island—as big as Manhattan and 170 inhabitants—with tax exemptions on profits, income, capital and death duties. The price? A £1 million in development. And there were no exchange controls on an island in the sterling area but with dollars as currency. The Anegada Development Corporation was born.

Back out of the sun, the marriage turned sour. His worst mistake, he declared in December '67, was 'not throwing out all the voluntary organisations and quite a bit of the staff' when he joined. But he was loyal to McIlroy: and he kept the board when he could have gone for richer men (he was respectful of local interests, real or imagined?). He started to pull out. 81 acres of Great Budworth, Cheshire, was swapped for a villa in Tortola (the island next to Anegada). And he sold his 10 shilling shares in the club for 6d each to an associate.

In August '68 McIlroy resigned: 'All I can say is that it has been an experience. I have nothing else to say.' Bates followed him in September: 'I feel it impossible to run the club as chairman while living out in the Caribbean'. Harry Massey, a local builder, returned to power. Jack Rowley came back also, to the manager's seat. Together they took Oldham to Division Four.

Bates maintains it was Anegada that forced him to move. I would have carried on, he argues: you need patience, as I always said. He left the club with permanent improvements and himself about £25,000 poorer. He was unlucky or foolish in his choice of manager and the caution of his board. For, fifteen months after, the recipe worked. John Jowe, a textile man from Bury, bought his shares: sacked Rowley and the directors that appointed him: and plucked Oldham from the bottom of Division Four to the Second last year (with five of Bates' team).

But he probably didn't mind. On Christmas Eve 1970 the Virgin Islands offered £4.8 million for the Anegada Development Corporation.

John Willie Lees

No Way The Lads

SUNDERLAND Football Club has the reputation and tradition which has, always, put it in the big league. The last of the founder members of the Football League to be relegated, Sunderland had won the League five times before the first World War. But although it boasts a mighty club, Sunderland is not a big town. With a population of 200,000, almost entirely dependent on the shipbuilding industry, Sunderland is definitely in the second division of English industrial cities.

And it is this clash between the bigtime traditions and the small town community that explains the extraordinary history of the club and its present position. No compromise is ever possible; Sunderland football swings wildly between boom and retrenchment, the open chequebook and the dole queue.

From the very earliest, and particularly in times of Depression, the people of Sunderland were used to style and success; thousands of leisureless working men contributed their ha'pences to see an escapist fantasy. The tradition grew that Sunderland FC was a place for big names – not just the bow-legged youngsters who juggled with a piece of coke, but stars from Alf Common and Charlie Buchan onwards. Sunderland had the gates and the status to attract them.

After the second war, the manager, Bill Murray, spent so much money that his team became known as the Bank of England side. Through the doors of Roker Park passed Len Shackleton, Ray Daniels, Don Revie, Billy Bingham. It was just like Newcastle today, a mess of talents with little guidance, heady entertainment but no medals. Murray was an office manager; he kept to his side of the beige door and the team strode up and down the first division under its own steam. Free enterprise, with no Government interference. But the clock stopped in 1957. Two directors were suspended indefinitely for illegal payments to players (before the maximum wage was abolished most clubs did it, but Sunderland were careless enough to get caught) and Murray was fired. Who was to succeed him?

The directors had two considerations – one was to get a successful man, obviously; the other, to repair the image of the club. This matters more in Sunderland than it would in Manchester or London. For, Sunderland has the mentality of a provincial town, very gossipy and well-informed about itself. People knew the sacking smelt and the directors knew that they knew. In the media rinse of a big city the dirt would have been washed off, but values are different in Sunderland.

Alan Brown was chosen as manager. He came with an outstanding record as youth coach with Burnley; he was a local man and was the first of a new breed of tracksuit managers. The key factor though was his severe and public morality (remorse over his own past had led him into Moral Re-Armament). He was hard on himself and hard on the players; he never asked them to do what he could not. Not only was he upright, he was seen to be upright. That clinched it with the Board.

Brown's effect was immediate. The Bank of England team broke up with astonishing speed. Brown could not handle stars; instead he rebuilt the side with men of his own choosing. Within two years only Stan Anderson was left from Bill Murray's side, and he was a local lad who had joined Sunderland straight from school anyway: "It was quite a shock after being left to ourselves, and only seeing the manager once a week, to have the manager with us every day. It was extremely difficult to adjust." The change was too swift and within a year Brown achieved the unthinkable; Sunderland were relegated. The local paper's Saturday edition went from pink to blue.

The Board stuck with Brown, though. He was a man you either loved or pitied; and it was clear that he needed time before the performance graphs and early morning bathing could take effect. The ageing stars had been wheeled off the stage, and the young turks were running through brick walls and doing overhead cycle racing in the gymnasium. Chairman Sydney Collings, prosperous owner of Central Laundries (and father of the present Chairman) was firmly behind him. And with Brown at least, the club had a clean reputation; no muck, no mud at Roker.

It took Brown six years to gain promotion, and leave Newcastle behind in the second. That summer he resigned. It was a well-judged move; he recognised the limits of his own competence. George Hardwick, a local loyalist, was appointed caretaker while the Board looked for a successor. Willie Waddell and Don Revie were approached, both of them similar to Brown in temperament, but able to handle big names too. In the meantime the Board signed Jim Baxter, and only then appointed Ian McColl, the man who would have to make him play; they had chosen a laissez faire Scot with a big reputation but little experience. McColl, they reckoned, was just the man, being an ex-Ranger and ex-manager of Scotland to handle Baxter, the new Shackleton. He bought Slim Jim's cousin George Kinnell from Oldham, and another Scottish star Neil Martin from Hibs. It was the good old days again. After austerity, reflation and consumer spending; sign up the stars and leave the football to Saturday afternoon. It lasted 2½ years.

For getting along with Baxter, McColl certainly fitted the bill. Ian was with him at the bar as well as on the training field, but so were the rest of the players. Discipline crumbled, morale was low. The good name of the club was being tarnished in pubs all over the town, and in the tight and well-informed circles of Sunderland this mattered. This dirty linen did not wash well with the Board; they could forgive eccentricity in the name of success, but without it? The clean-living lobby on the Board won the day. Ian McColl was sacked and Alan Brown re-appointed. Back to austerity again; a short boom, now a wage and price freeze.

The cycle began again. Sunderland under Brown crashed back into division two. After a brief flurry – Dave Watson, Joe Baker and Dick Malone came for £170,000 – Sunderland did not buy a player for two years. The coffers were dry, and as the club sank to its lowest-ever position, Brown and the directors parted 'by mutual consent' in October 1972.

The directors tried the big managerial names. Contracts were waved at Revie (again) and Brian Clough. But they would both have been very expensive, and after failing to attract either, the Board turned to Bob Stokoe, thereby unwittingly breaking the cycle. Within six months he had won them the Cup, and although promotion did not follow last season, the club are poised to go up now.

But the question persists. Sunderland's fortunes are directly related to the kind of town they have grown out of, and the fabulous tradition behind them. Stokoe is holding his own at the moment, embracing neither the austere discipline of Brown nor the wild transfer excesses of Murray and McColl. But the pressures on him to go one way or the other are intense. In the town they say that promotion will trigger them off, and the cycle will start again. If Sunderland go up this season, Stokoe may well find that his problems have only just begun.

Mark O'Neill

Spot the difference

How the DAILY

TELEGRAPH saw it

No. 26   February 1975

Goalkeeper Boulton is caught on the hop as a white-shirted Velez attacker heads the ball across the Derby goalmouth.

How the SUN

saw it

Derby's Davies uses his head
ROGER DAVIES . . . sent on as substitute, quickly used his head to make a goal in Derby's EUFA Cup match last night. Report: Page 26.

Solution to FOUL HOUSE please.

WEMBLEY POLE-AXE

THE people in the newspaper industry welcome with all their hearts games such as the forthcoming World Cup qualifying match between England and Poland.

It has everything: a chance to hand you part of your daily dose of anti-socialist propoganda — Poland come from "behind the Iron Curtain" and can "sling any dissenting manager into a labour camp" (*Sunday People*, Sept 2); good controversy, for we are led to believe that England's chances of winning are about 50-50; the chance to whip up a drop of nationalist fervour; and, of course, it **is** a vitally important game.

All great stuff, from the *Times* to the *Sun* providing copy desperately needed in a pre-season and early season period almost devoid of genuine news.

All discussion of this match is meaningless, however, if you do not mention one essential fact: **There is not a referee in the world who will send off an Englishman at Wembley in a vital World Cup game.** Leo Horn, the Dutchman, might have done, but he retired, disillusioned and reviled, years ago. This fact is particularly important because of the respective natures of the two teams.

It is said abroad that English teams do not let you beat them — they start fighting. This is confirmed if you look at the fortunes of English teams in foreign competition last season.

In Poland, Ball was sent off for fighting, with England losing 2-0. At Derby, Davies was sent off for butting near the end of Derby's European Cup semi-final second leg with Juventus, when it had become clear that Derby were not going to pull back the 3-1 deficit. And Hunter was sent off for fighting seconds before the end of Leeds' Cup-Winners' Cup Final with AC Milan, which Leeds were losing 1-0. The only team with a clean record was Liverpool — and they won their competition.

Lack of belief in your ability, lack of character and lack of tactical knowledge show in your reaction to adversity and defeat. In spite of the great emphasis on "character" in English football, I do not think that the England national team has much of these three qualities.

The Polish players big problem is that they come from a socialist country, where the law of the jungle does not prevail; so that when an animal comes charging in at them, snapping and snarling, they do not know how to deal with it. This is why they were beaten by Wales, a team far inferior to them in talent. In other words, they chickened out. As they will against England. Anton Malatinsky, manager of Derby's Czech European Cup opponents Spartak Trnava said afterwards, "Derby played like Roman gladiators". England will be more like Philistine butchers.

Although it is said that nothing in football is ever certain, there are two certainties about the night of October 17 — the first is that it will be a thoroughly unpleasant evening, and the second is that England will win.

Terry Bushell

No. 11   October 1973

FAREWELL WITHOUT TEARS

SO on England's Big Night, everything came unstuck. In the recriminations that followed (particularly on television) the aim was clear: blame anything you like, but don't let it get around that England just didn't play well enough; that four points and three goals from four matches is middle-of-the-table stuff, like our international record over the past months.

Sir Alf, having recognised that "We just didn't have the finishing power" (Hector was presumably sent on to put that right in two minutes flat), still appears to believe that we gave two excellent displays against Poland, and luck didn't go our way. This is the type of thinking which, though it may be sincere (and most certainly, who can doubt that, when it is enunciated so correctly) he has been getting away with for too long.

The post-mortem opinions were as useful as the ones the night before, when ITV "marked our card". "Don't knock the players" (Revie), the League programme should have been posponed the Saturday before; Sir Alf had "a hard job" (Clough/Revie). The lads had played their heart out (Dougan/Charlton Bros.). Well, yes, but . . . But, somewhere between all the extenuating circumstances, the Poles got through.

To his credit, Malcolm Allison was the one person disinterested enough to suggest that England's inferior play might be behind the result, but the point was lost in the shouting match which turns every criticism into wishful thinking. And the views were put across with all the swagger which had written off Poland beforehand in a tactical analysis which could hardly have been further off-beam.

The goalkeeper's weakness, Musial's clowning, Gorgon's alleged mental deficiencies were all used as justification for our favourite weapon, the big, high cross which despite some terrible marking, especially early on, the Poles happily swallowed up — just like so many European opponents of British teams before them.

Clough said "I guarantee we'll win" before the match, "Relax, it's going to be all right" at half-time and "It's now time Sir Alf went, and there's a vacant job at Derby" afterwards. The TV boys rub their hands at all this "great television"; it was in fact back-seat driving and bear-baiting rolled into one (a difficult exercise); Clough's law of diminishing credibility.

The match wasn't the bloodbath that many people predicted, especially after the antics of Ball and Hockey in Katowice. Most of the credit for this must go to referee Loraux, who stamped on trouble decisively with the instantaneous booking of Bulzacki for his scything of Channon in the 17th minute. However, it is not the fouls of revenge, which are easily spotted, and condemned by everyone but the use of the foul as a 'legit' tactical device, which should really cause concern.

The best example was McFarland's attempt to pull Lato's shirt off, when he was clean through in the 82nd minute, for which he was rightly booked, and should have been sent off. This was not an isolated incident. All through the match, England's defence was founded on the assumption that should the speedy Polish forwards get through our naturally strained rearguard, they were to get hauled back with anything that came to hand. Thus, dirty defensive play was actually programmed into the English tactical plan, before the match began.

Hunter thumped Lato in the sixth minute, and obstructed him again in the 12th, as he hared after a through ball. Madeley handled the ball as he was caught out of position by a pass that went across him. Hunter gave another warning that he would not tolerate balls played behind him, as he hit Kasperczyk from behind, and McFarland hacked down Domarski in the 33rd minute, and again in the 79th.

The other tactic that so many managers, taking their lead from Sir Alf, have adopted, is letting the keeper know you are around, right from the start. Allan Clarke was delegated this task, presumably because he does it for his club, and hit Tomaszewski so hard after just 40 secs, that the Polish goalie had to have treatment. Just in case the interval had dulled the keeper's recollection, Clarke refreshed his memory 9 minutes into the second half.

So when we say that Alf must go, it's not purely because we want to see England's football lifted out of the sterile, unimaginative rut that Ramsay has ground out through clenched teeth at so many tactics talks; it's not because English supporters would like to see wing-halves and flank forwards given a chance to establish themselves, before they become extinct (there are few enough already in the League, so well have many of our managers learned the Ramsey credo). It is because the whole idea of using illegal tactics as a defensive ploy to cover for inadequacies at the back, and to incapacitate the opposition from keeping our forwards out, is sickening and a travesty of the way football should be played.

If this criterion is to be used to select the new manager, then it becomes only too obvious that Ramsay has nurtured and encouraged a whole host of imitators among the younger managers. McFarland did not learn to play like that at the sporadic England get-togethers. Jimmy Adamsom, another highly-touted favourite, employs Waldron and Thomson at the heart of his defence. At Coventry, Gordon Milne has clearly not discouraged Craven's excesses. And Dave Sexton has picked first Harris and then McCreadie to captain the club. Which leaves . . . . Jago? Bloomfield? Greenwood? none of whom are going to win the League Championship, like Sir Alf did.

Clearly Ramsey has been sowing the seeds that will make his replacement extremely hard to find. The snowball that he gave a hefty shove to on its way down the slope, has attracted so many adherents that Ramsey can be assured that his philosophy will not necessarily be abandoned once he has been dropped overboard.

'OddS SuppORters CLuB

from YOU to US

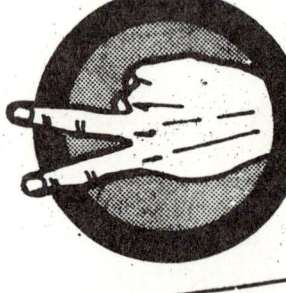

Arsenal. West Brom. Coventry. Liverpool. Chelsea. Leeds United. Bristol Birmingham City. Oxford United. Manchester City. Bury. All these teams have one thing in common.

Don Revie has chosen members of his England squad from all these sides. And what team has had never a mention in this roll of international honour? Aston Villains. Prior to the date of writing, England has displayed poor footballing form into the bargain. So let me suggest to Mr Revie a remedy by quoting again.

Kevin Keegan. Martin Peters. Joe Jordan. Frank Worthington. Mike Channon. Colin Bell. Again, one name is conspicuous by its absence from such a list of England forwards.

I refer of course to our own Hero of the Villains, Arthur Scagfoot. The sooner Don puts Arthur in, the better it will be for football and spectators alike. So here is my selection for an England side which are potential World Cup-winners: Clemence, Lindsay, Yorath, Moore, Hughes, Bell, McKenzie, Channon, ARTHUR SCAGFOOT, Chivers.

Do any readers agree with me?

CLAP YER HANDS
(Ron Plumridge)

★ No.

IT MAY not have escaped your notice that there has been little Supporters Club notes of late. The blame for this must in part be "laid at my door" but I have just been too busy of late to single-handedly tackle the mammoth task of liaising between the Club and its myriad supporters. Cars have to be washed and there's an end to it. I am sorry to report that our fund-raising ventures have not been as successful as was at first hoped, and I must now ask for your generosity, in helping to pay for the coach that took several of us to the London Palladium last month. Quite frankly I had expected a better turn-out and to clear the debts incurred a few of us are organising a Grand Dance in the near future, music once again to be provided by the inimitable Bill Barnum Trio (sadly now of course the Bill Barnum Duo). Many team players have promised to attend with their wives, other social engagements permitting, and it should· be a good time guaranteed by all. Details to cheer you later. Turning to cheerier matters, the Golden Goal jackpot now stands at £450,327, Villains having failed to score in their last ten games. It's an ill wind!

The Manager's Desk...

ASTON VILLAINS FOOTBALL CLUB

A.V.F.C.

Honours:

Lowest League Attendance On Record, 1972 (356)

Last 32 of Quizball 1970-71

Oldest Board of Directors

FA Cup Stealers 1911

League Cup 3rd Round Winners 1965, 1967, 1970

Texaco Cup Qualifiers 1884

Top of the Pops November 1973 with 'You'll Never Walk Again'

HOW TO GET THERE, for those making next Saturday's trip up to Sutherland Argyle.

Ring the AA. Number in phone book.

Take it from me. We aren't going to be in the relegation zone much longer. There's a long way to go yet of this season's campaign, and both remaining matches should prove to be the turning point. You don't need to be a professor to work out that if we can take a maximum eighteen points from these two games, we are home and dry. It's no more than now but that I would like to go on record how these supporters deserve, and I would like to go "ship", how in stressing my appreciation, as "captain" of this "ship", how the supporters deserve, and I would like to go on record now we would never have done it without you behind us, as surely there is no shadow of a doubt we will in the end.

Even the most biased neutral would be hard pushed to it to agree that we have not had the most atrocious ill-fortune this season. Take last week's sizzling encounter with Chessington, a tussle that reached for superlatives — the spoils in our matches this season. We held the Zulus to a share at least some of the sportswriters reaching for the Zulus to a pogrom was just one of them. We held the Zulus to that I know but this is not to shirk the issues 'pogrom' was just one of more than an hour. Yet what modest five-goal margin for more than an hour. I am in no way blaming the players for happened? We lost. I am in no way getting any younger. Our backs this. They did the best they could once again, but Lady Luck played us a cruel blow and three of our most respected and experienced generals were ordered off the field of play.

But let us look on the bright side. The Central League team are playing well, and I must say are a credit to the club. With their never-say-die spirit they are game to the end – the "idle sods" in the first team might care to think about! But this is not to shirk the issues involved. We are a young side, pretty "green", and still have a lot to learn. But we are none of us getting any younger. I wouldn't be a manager if I thought any different. Our backs are to the wall now, so let me just remind you of what I said this time last year:

"Make no mistake. Better days are just around the corner, and things aren't over yet by a long chalk. You have to go some up again."

ASTON VILLAINS FC

GETTING TO KNOW . . .

ARTHUR SCAGFOOT

Name: Arthur Scagfoot
Height: 4'3"
Position Played: Big Centre Forward
Nickname: Prickdust
Favourite Colour: Red
Car Driven: Johnny Mathis
Wife's Name: Scampi
Favourite TV Programme: Any commercials
Favourite Food: with steak in
House Name: Datsun
Favourite Saying: Chicken-in-the-Basket
Anything except "I'm sick"
Hobbies: Pets, gardening (which I combine by burying cats in the back yard)
Likes: Shagging, politics, mixing drinks
Dislikes: Prejudice, queers, reading all that shit about Total Football by Brian Glanville
Advice to Youngsters: Cheat as often as possible
Business Interests: None of your business
Biggest Thrill in Football: Having it away in the tunnel at half-time

Today's Match Ball

Today's Match Ball has again been kindly donated by local haulier Mr Frank Xerox, who reminds patrons that he still has several thousand footballs in his shed which he is willing to sell in part or as one lot.
Thanks Frank.

KEEP OFF THE PITCH

No. 27   March 1975

WELCOME VISITORS

TODAY we bid a warm welcome indeed to our keen rivals Scottish Widows. This fixture in the past has often provided some epic struggles, and today promises to be no exception! Currently in a position of strength in the League, holding the rest up, the Widows bring an important addition to their side in today's visit to Boot Hill.

'Bronco' Scarborough needs no introduction. A great favourite with our own Scrag End during his 4,693 consecutive years playing in the Villains' colours, Bronco made a successful transition to the Widows' colours at the end of last season. Though his free transfer was regarded as daylight robbery on our part by many people at the time, Bronco has for the Widows since made the knockers eat their words tenfold.

Respected for his midfield skills as much as for his professional integrity and his unquestioning of referees' decisions, thus providing a shining example to youngsters both on and off the field, this is the first time the dirty get has been back. In our endeavours today we will surely show him that his influence has not been forgotten.

This afternoon's clash is by way of being a return fixture and if the score stood in our favour at the end of ninety minutes revenge would taste sweet indeed. Our own sortie to The Boneyard earlier this season produced a hatful of goals and some superb entertainment and we were somewhat unlucky to be the unfortunate recipients of a couple of flukey hat-tricks. Hopefully this afternoon the lads will have got their differences ironed over, and we are in for a real cracker!

Rita Scagfoot, attractive wife of star Villains striker Arthur (see facing page) with a cake presented by the Supporters Club to her husband on the occasion of his 100th penalty miss! Rita is currently being bonked by the entire Aston Villains defence!

FOOTBALL LEAGUE DIVISION I

ought to look like this

		HOME					AWAY					Goals	
	P	W	D	L	F	A	W	D	L	F	A	F — A	Pts
VILLAINS	26	0	1	13	5	4	0	0	12	0	78	0	40
Liverpool	27												35
Ipswich	28												34
Stoke	28												33
Burnley	28												33
Liverpool	26												31
W Ham	28												31
Middlsbro	28												31
Derby	27												31
Man City	28												30
Leeds	28												30
QPR	28												28
Sheff Utd	28												28
Newcstle	27												28
Coventry	26												26
Arsenal	28												25
Wolves	27												24
Birmghm	28												23
Tottenhm	28												23
Chelsea	28												19
Carlisle	27												18
Leicester	27												17
Luton	27												

Reviews

ONLY A GAME? — The Diary of a Professional Footballer, by Eamon Dunphy. Edited by Peter Ball (Kestrel Books, £2.50)

EAMON DUNPHY kept a diary during the four months of the 1973/4 season that he was with Millwall. Peter Ball has edited it, added a little material of his own, including a preface by Brian Glanville, and this book is the result.

It is absolutely compelling reading. Dunphy writes about the working life of a professional footballer in an extraordinarily honest, perceptive and sympathetic manner. The quality of the writing is such that parts of it do for football what Hemingway did for boxing and bullfighting.

A multitude of fascinating episodes are covered — the conflict between the manager and the club captain, the efforts of the new coach to establish his position, the relentless ribbing of a confident young player, Dunphy's own reaction to being dropped, the euphoria of playing well against the odds to win, the depression that follows a bad performance, and so on.

The whole diary is given a sharp flavour by the difficulties that Millwall and Eamon Dunphy experienced at this time — the club got off to a poor start to the season, and Dunphy was dropped and sold before Christmas. The tensions provoked by these problems are sensitively chronicled and contribute enormously to the interest of the book. Brian Glanville, in the preface, expresses the view that the book would have been better had Dunphy been writing about a more successful period of his career. One might as well argue that Hamlet would be improved had it ended with the Prince and Ophelia riding off into a Danish sunset.

Eamon Dunphy himself emerges as a complicated person, seemingly full of contradictions. For example, he much admires character, honest effort, loyalty and professionalism, and yet he confesses that he walked out, and later in the book he impetuously demands a transfer. He mocks Trevor Hockey for being a ruggedly effective spoiler, but he is contemptuous of West Ham and their fragile artistry. In one revealing incident he urges the disciplining of a player as a matter of principle, but later he advocates leniency, largely on the grounds of expediency.

Almost every page of the diary contains something of interest, and this is a credit to the careful editing of Peter Ball, who also adds a useful postscript on the subsequent fortunes of the main personalities and a section giving the Millwall results and team listings. However, the chapter in which he gives a journalist's account of one of the matches covered in the diary was marred by a style grotesquely predisposed towards short sentences, and, in six pages, 24 sentences starting with 'But', and 29 with 'And'. And that's irritating. But really.

As for the rest of the book, it is, in the opinion of this reviewer, quite the finest piece of football writing in the language.

Mike Hodd

The People's Game/James Walvin
Allen Lane £4.50

Football became a suitable case for treatment by sociologists and social historians only in the last decade, the result of England beating the dreaded Hun to win the World Cup and hooligans arriving in their hordes on the terraces. The best treatment so far is by James Walvin who studies the case history sympathetically and in great detail from pre-industrial football up to commercial football.

I enjoyed most the pre-industrial section, for Walvin, after an enormous amount of research, links the incidents tightly and grafts them on to the social fabric. The point emerges very clearly that football, in common with every other artisans' and peasants' pastime, is never mentioned by scribes except to be attacked.

As the participants themselves neither codified their games nor set down their feelings and experiences on paper, the only information we have comes from these hostile sources. Previous football historians, confronted with this mass of upper-class hostility, made the mistake of thinking that every time a match was played someone got killed or something destroyed. Walvin not only avoids this error, he goes out of his way to say that this could not have been the case, and each contemporary denunciation is accompanied by his perceptive interpretation.

Carried away by enthusiasm for the first third of the book, I felt my attention wandering and my admiration diminishing as I approached the end.

There is a lot of original stuff in the former; in the latter, much will be familiar to anyone over the age of 25 who followed the game in childhood to the extent of collecting fag cards (and their later equivalents) of players.

Continued

Badlands

SOME 30,000 people turned up at St Andrew's on April 17 for a ritual which is becoming as characteristic of Birmingham as pulling down huge areas of terraced houses and building motorways over the remains. It was Blues' last home match of the season and true to form (this has been going on for three years now) City woke up to beat Spurs 3-0 to help avoid relegation yet again. You could have been forgiven for assuming the lads had just walked off with the European Cup for the third year running, to listen to the supporters. It seemed to sum up another depressing year for West Midlands' football with the clubs, West Brom alone excepted, staggering through the season gripped by an apparent death-wish.

It is a sad indictment of the state of the game here that Coventry can claim to be the region's most successful club. Ending halfway up the First Division, they still had to sell their best player, Dennis Mortimer, to Villa. The dead hand of Ron Wylie, former Villa assistant manager, was evident as soon as his new club visited Villa Park early in the season. Five men were strung across the back with Wylie obviously believing that if you get 42 0-0 draws, you get into Europe (they lost 1-0).

Continued

Although Walvin continues to call a spade a spade, such as Arsenal and Leeds being negative and dirty teams, I disagreed with most of his conclusions, where he abandons his facts and leaps into speculation and analysis.

Admittedly, this speculation and analysis is based on the facts, but the leap from the base into conceptualising is always hazardous; if the scholar has not qualities other than scholarship, he is liable to fall and break his neck, and lose the credit he may have otherwise enjoyed.

Walvin has not broken his neck — it is still an excellent book — but the effect, for me, far from being enhanced by the conclusion, was vitiated.

In disagreeing with Ian Taylor, the foremost football sociologist who links very firmly hooliganism and declining interest with the recent rampant commercialisation, and in asserting that football set in a totally different economic system has exactly the same sort of problems of aggression and violence as ours, Walvin denies all that he has just spent 178 pages in affirming — that football, like every other institution, bears the marks of the society from which it has emerged.

Terry Bushell

No. 27   March 1975

Coventry are not the rich trend-setters they were in the early 1970s. They are still paying back the loan from former chairman (now president) Derrick Robins, who nipped off to South Africa with his secretary and needs the money to finance his one-man service: providing the cricket-hungry Springbokkers with match practice against their own kith and kin (one token black excepted).

The age of the big-spending chairmen is over in the West Midlands — Robins in South Africa, Clifford Coombs in Heaven and Doug Ellis in disgrace — which is one of several reasons why the area is now not just a backwater but a dried-up creek. Probably the main reason clubs are up the creek is sheer bad management.

Ron Saunders at Villa had bad luck with injuries and bought good players in Mortimer and Andy Gray. But he also spent £90,000 on the world's most fanatical goalkeeper, John Burridge, who, however, was not fanatical enough not to get married during the season; his hands have not stopped trembling since. Saunders found that reserve keeper Jake Findley was no teetotaller but at least he kept his mind on the job. There were mutterings about Saunders' ability by the end of the season. People remembered when Norwich's John Bond had said: "Saunders is good for 18 months. He gets teams fit but as a long-term manager he won't bring success." He has now been at Villa Park for two seasons.

At City, the season will best be remembered as the one when the Blues' board finally got round to sacking **Freddie Goodwin** (the team had started better than usual by taking two points from the first seven matches). Goodwin, it is not easy to forget, spent £1,115,000 in five years, accumulating the most expensive and overpaid reserve team in history. Badloss finally went, only to be replaced by somebody called Willie Bell, whose chief virtue in the board's eyes was that he cost £4,000 a year less than his free-spending predecessor.

Birmingham's board may not contain the finest football brains in the country but they can at least remember the time Badloss badgered them for six months for £90,000 to buy Gary Sprake. After Badloss complained that not to be given the money would amount to a vote of no confidence in him, Clifford Coombs wrote out the cheque. It is now costing Blues absolutely nothing, except hospital bills, to get rid of the Welsh fumbler.

To his credit, Bell has quietly pruned the playing staff of 17 deadbeats, including Roger Hynd. Roger, it will be remembered, has a famous uncle, one Bill Shankly, and on Willie's behalf, Roger asked him to ring Blues' chairman and put in a good word when Badloss got the chop. He did and Roger thought he'd get a free transfer to Walsall, picking up a couple of grand for himself in the process. "Oh, no Roger," said Willie, once confirmed as manager. "We want a fee for you."

Wolves went down, despite beating Birmingham three times during the season. Nine days after the Liverpool game, the Board assembled at the scene of the crime. That week had seethed with furious plotting, as vice chairman and chief shareholder Harry Marshall lobbied the three other directors for changes 'near the top' by which he meant chairman John Ireland, as well as manager **Bill McGarry**.

"We must give this club a new image, and take it into the 1970s," said Harry, but the end, when it came, reeked of the 1950s. Press, radio and TV crews had been huddling around a lamp post for six hours, when the door opened and club secretary Phil Shaw walked out, said: "Are you ready, lads?" and read a two-sentence statement. Then he went back in again.

McGarry had been sacked, his career just a pawn in the old-fashioned game of boardroom power politics. Ireland at least voted for his friend, but Marshall had done his work well, and the other four were solid. Ireland hung on to the chairmanship, but McGarry's body was the price he had to pay.

How much of the plot was Dougan's work? There have been strenuous denials from both him and Marshall that he had anything to do with all this talk about 1970s images, but the day after Wolves went down, Derek's Wolverhampton house, that he had been trying to sell all season, after buying another in Kettering, was taken off the market.

Which brings us to West Brom, and all the proof you need that managing is about players, and not about administration and finance. Johnny Giles (now known as the Little Wonder at the Hawthorns) was kept free of administrative duties and concentrated on trying to put back what master mechanic Don Howe had spent four years taking out. And after a bad start, Albion played football as it should be played, mixing hard running with skill and inspiration. You don't get rid of the Leeds habit that easily, though, and Albion did their fair share of clogging (the Little Wonder himself was sent off at Luton for a truly classic chop on Ron Futcher).

So Albion went up, and no-one in West Bromwich is carping about the £80,000 that Johnny Moneybags made in just one week. He looted half of it from the Irish in his Dublin testimonial match against Don Revie's XI. The match was a goalless draw as Leeds United get-togethers normally are, but it netted Johnny nearly £50,000, not the £20,000 that *FOUL* 32 predicted. The rest, unbelievably, was his promotion bonus.

Will Milne and Saunders last another year? How long before Sir Alf (he already controls transfers) takes over at St Andrews? Where is Giles's next £50,000 coming from? All these questions to be answered in the next episode...

Anthony Hollis

No. 33   May/June 1976

Mark O'Neill visits the city where fighting in the streets has emptied the grounds, and discovers that English crowds have not yet learned the extent of their power.

LIKE everything else in the Province, football in Northern Ireland has been savagely affected by barbarism and religion. The blow has been mortal in two cases — Belfast Celtic and Derry City — and almost in two others — Distillery and Cliftonville. For the moment the sport is kept alive at League level by sympathetic distillers, a Sockmaker, and by the eagerness Irishmen to collect in social clubs and disperse their wages. But the margin of survival is slender.

The sectarian ball was kicked off in 1886 with the foundation of Linfield. It quickly became, like Rangers in Glasgow, the Protestant club. Same colours, same Union Jack snapping in the brisk Belfast air, same following, in bias and numbers (60 supporters' clubs all over Ulster) and, since 1950, the same policy of excluding Catholics (with the exception of their trainer, an irresistible jester named Gerry Morgan). In 1891 the Catholics dutifully followed suit. Belfast Celtic was started and in the words of one of the founders: "We want to call the club after Glasgow Celtic and our aim is to imitate them in their style of play, win the Irish Cup and follow their example in the cause of charity." Their strip was the same and their ground named — yes, you've guessed it — Celtic Park. They chose players of both religions but drew their support from Catholics only.

The first major flare-up came in 1912 when 70 were taken to hospital after the match at Celtic Park. Then in 1920, in a match against Glentoran, a club from a very Protestant part of the city, a man started shooting into the crowd and the game was abandoned. In 1938 their main stand was burned down. But the last hurrah came on Boxing Day 1948, and their match against Linfield at Windsor Park.

A crowd of 40,000 watched a ferocious game. One Linfield player went off with a broken ankle, another with bad chest injuries, and a man from each side was sent off. At the final whistle the score was 3—3, with Jimmy Jones the Celtic centre forward at the opposite end from the dressing rooms. The players sprinted like scalded cats for the tunnel, but Jones — 653 goals in his career — was caught by the Linfield fans before he could escape. He was mauled and thrown over a wall; one or both legs (reports differ) were broken. He later received £4,364 in compensation and Windsor Park was closed for a month. According to Celtic's account, this was the last straw. "If this is what sport had come to, we couldn't continue," Cyril McAlinden, one of the directors, told me. In the new year they announced that the club was to close, and it has not played a game since. The ground still stands, though, and though the stands have suffered fires and extensive vandalism, the pitch is still in excellent condition, like a cemetery garden.

What about the Belfast Celtic supporters? Most of them drifted out of football, to follow the Gaelic sports, that prosper in that part of town. The rest transferred their allegiance to Distillery, another team in Belfast, or to Derry City, the only other recognisably Catholic team — though 80 miles away. In Celtic's place play Crusaders, a north Belfast team, to make up the 12 of the Irish League (the small number means that they have to have seven trophies, to make the season last).

The Troubles have resurrected the bogey, and two teams in particular have suffered. Derry City's ground is situated in Brandywell, a Provisional area of Belfast, and within easy bullet range of where the 13 were murdered on Bloody Sunday. Derry were ordered to play their home games at Coleraine, 40 miles away, because the other teams were too frightened to go to Brandywell. Soon they found this uneconomical as well as demoralising. As the Troubles receded, they returned to Brandywell when the Army said it would be safe to play there. But the other 11 still would not come and the

League refused to compel them. So Derry City had no alternative but to fold up. Their place in the League was taken by Larne, a solidly Protestant town.

Cliftonville, in Belfast, have a social club, but because of the position of Solitude, their aptly-named ground, in the middle of a trouble spot, they have very few supporters. Their match against rivals Linfield used to keep them going, but the police will no longer permit the fixture to be played. Still, their chances are better than Distillery's. A motorway was planned to go through their ground, but then

GO-SLOW

a bomber did the Council's demolition work for them. They are playing at Crusaders' stadium, but may not be able to for much longer because of the effect on the pitch, which is very low-lying, and a few hundred yards from the sea. Even with £100,000 compensation (the motorway has not been built yet), their situation is desperate.

It is the social clubs that have kept the football going. Attendances are a quarter or less than the pre-1968 level, but nearly every team boasts a prospering social club. These clubs have thrived during the Troubles. Most of the pubs have been bombed or boycotted because people fear the lack of protection. Safe, restricted premises do a roaring trade, whether they are run by Sinn Fein or Linfield. Football supporters are very grateful to have somewhere to go. Linfield stopped being self-sufficient out of soccer alone in 1965, and reckon on about £15,000 a year from their supporters.

Another essential wet-nurse is sponsorship, which provides over £20,000 a year. With less and less entertainment available, interest in football may be on the increase, even if it is not reflected in the attendances. The four companies — Guinness, Hennessey, Texaco and the sock-makers Blaxnit — spread their money around the League, and consider it well spent.

Where the clubs ought to make a fortune is from flogging talented pixies to England, but here the Irish League loses out. English scouts swamp the market, herding players across the Channel like novices into a convent. They are helped by the extensive coverage the newspapers give the English clubs (at one game I went to, the FA Cup quarter final results were given before the Irish League scores). Irish boys are a soft touch. What job in Ulster can compare with the hope of life in the First Division? All the same, Irish League teams cannot do better than the record of £30,000 Linfield got from Ipswich for Brian Hamilton. The main fears in the English mind seem to be: why hasn't he played in England before, and will he make it as a full-timer? Irish League part-timers are on a maximum wage of £6 a week (plus bonuses: basic is up to £9 next season). So the English clubs may get nothing out of him for three months and even then cannot be sure he will adjust. This is not really a valid argument, but it works. Sheffield Wednesday have offered Linfield £16,000 for Paul Malone, their best player; I doubt if Linfield will be able to resist the temptation after April.

The religious ghost haunts the Irish League even more as a result of the Troubles: Glentoran tried to sign a Catholic but were told by the para-militaries that it would cost them more than the transfer fee if they did. Linfield say that they dare not do so at the present time (which may be a useful way of getting off the hook). The taboo goes further than that. One sports editor told me that it was more than his job was worth even to mention religion in his columns. He was proud to say that he had kept off the pages a story about a city councillor complaining that the Irish rugby captain, McBride (a Protestant from Ulster) had stood to attention for the Republic's anthem. Stories as innocuous as that are dangerous, he said. He forecast that Pat Jennings and other Catholics would refuse to play in the April international against Yugoslavia at Windsor Park, if it takes place at all.

These undercurrents were present at the game I attended between Linfield and last year's champions, Coleraine. Even though there were hardly a hundred of them, the end affected a style halfway between the North Bank and urban guerillas, scaling fences and raking round the ground in heavy shoes. The atmosphere was modestly tense. Recently there has not been any riot at a football match, but the possibility is always there, especially in Belfast. There were imitations of England in the chants as in the barracking. The crowd — which could not have numbered more than 3,000 — kept up a vivid commentary; this was more Irish than English I thought, but then I have spent too many silent afternoons at Craven Cottage. But momentum was always dampened by the low standard of play and the vast size of the stadium with barbed wire overhanging a moat and heavy policemen in dark green uniforms. Too much has happened to let them take a chance.

The loss of partisanship between Protestant and Catholic has been a severe blow, though it is retained in the Texaco and Blaxnit trophies when teams from North and South compete. In England and Scotland particularly crowds and profits depend a great deal on the edge that rivalry provides. Religion and sectarianism add a vital ingredient; Glasgow Celtic fans would happily see their team finish third bottom if Rangers were relegated. This nastiness swells the English terraces. In Northern Ireland the risk is too great. After all that has happened on the other side of the turnstiles, it is only too probable that tactics learned on the barricades would be practised in the football ground. If you can drive out the paratroopers, what chance of defence have two club commissioners and a handful of police? The English clubs can thank God that aggression is confined and tribal. After Belfast you realise that English crowds have not learned the extent of their power. In Northern Ireland the clubs count their 25p and keep their fingers crossed. In this half-light between bankruptcy and violence the Irish League stumbles on.

Windsor Park

Simple Pye-Men

REMEMBER Ken Bates? He was the man with the maroon Silver Cloud (see *FOUL* 22) who bought his way into Oldham Athletic in 1965, made himself chairman and sank over £100,000 into the club, made a series of spectacular signings and sacked everyone in sight, but sold out in 1968 to go to live in the Virgin Islands, leaving the club in a worse mess than ever.

Well he came back, and in 1971, with the profits of his Virgin Island property speculation founded an investment bank in Dublin — the Irish Trust Bank. Also on the Board was Freddie Pye — wealthy scrap-metal dealer and currently joint chairman of Stockport County. Ken Bates was drummed out of his directorship of the bank in 1972 by the Irish banking authorities who said in a High Court action that they thought he was an 'unsuitable' person to be on the board of a bank, and pointed out that Bates had been chairman of a holding company in Burnley which had run from a profitable position to a million-pound loss in double quick time. (They didn't mention the damage he had done to Oldham Athletic.)

It came as no surprise, then, to anyone who knew the track record of the men involved, when the Irish Trust Bank closed its doors in February of this year, leaving its shareholders and depositors with a fistful of worthless paper. It cost Freddie Pye over £500,000 and also the forfeiture of his scrap-metal business, which he had used to guarantee the ill-fated ITB.

None of the activities of greedy businessmen in the North-West would matter all that much, if it wasn't for the fact that these men always seem to get involved in football clubs. Worse, they tend to involve footballers in their affairs. Albert Quixall, who played for Oldham in Bates' time, and is 'my best pal' (Freddie Pye), lost nearly £2,000 that he had in [ITB shares. Among bank depositors, who can also be assumed to have lost their money, are Bobby Charlton, who is employed by one of Pye's travel firms, Malcolm Allison, whom

Pye almost tempted to Stockport last autumn (see *FOUL* 31), and George Best, who was backed by the ITB when he took over the former Waldorf Hotel in Manchester.

The collapse of the bank also throws Pye's rescue of Stockport County into jeopardy. He swears that the receiver can't touch any of the money he has pumped into the club (along with four others, he put £50,000 into Stockport's ailing coffers last summer), but it does mean that there won't be much more where that came from. He says: "I am now trying to buy back a business that I have spent a lifetime building up — and I don't have any money left."

A sad tale, then, and one which underlines yet again the risks involved in any club letting itself get into hock to the men with the wide smiles and fat cheque-books. Still, there's one faint consolation for us. Freddie Pye says: "I think that these days Ken Bates has completely lost interest in football."

Sanders of the River

Remember the million-pound sports centre that Fulham announced they were going to build with the Hammersmith Borough Council on the site of Craven Cottage? That was some 16 months ago, and since then not one labourer has been seen at the cottage, (apart from on the pitch). What has happened to it?

"That's a very good question", was the response of Mr Jimmy Hill, who, apart from spending his Saturday evenings at Television Centre, is also Fulham's 'Commercial Consultant': "Everyone was very keen on the idea, but it just does not seem to be happening. What will materialise is anyone's guess."

The scheme has to be put in the context of the complete redevelopment of Thameside round the Fulham bend. All the warehouses have now moved nearer the mouth of the Thames to cope with the container traffic, leaving behind them huge spaces that can be transformed by developers into very lucrative blocks of riverside flats. Two sites in particular, were keenly sought after, the Stevenage and Eternit wharfs, and the developers who won the race to purchase and apply to develop them were J Sanders & Company. But Hammersmith, the planning authority, refused planning permission for blocks of flats unless J Sanders also agreed to embark with the Borough, on a scheme to provide some desperately needed sports facilities. And thus the scheme

was hatched to make Craven Cottage into the Hammersmith Sports Centre, open seven days a week, and with facilities for practically any sport to be played there, a real community centre.

This agreement was finalised between the three parties in October 1973 and a plasticine model (now lost) was shown to the Press. The plan was massively supported by the Sports Council, who have been trying for years to get League clubs to co-operate in opening up their grounds to the people who live nearby. They had approached 22 clubs with the idea, and three of them were interested, Sunderland, Sheffield Wednesday, and Bournemouth. But of all these, Fulham, with an enthusiastic council and a committed developer, were by far the best bet.

However, even though a deal had been done, J Sanders were in no hurry to start work, since there was, and is, very little in it for them, and Hammersmith felt they had done their bit in getting the agreement signed. The onus was on Fulham to push ahead, but just when they should have been united, there was a split on the Board. A very rich business consortium had approached director **Eric Miller** with an idea to turn Fulham into the London Leisure Centre, with an indoor stadium on the lines of the Houston Astrodome, artificial grass, and a capacity of 40,000 all seated. Miller thought this a splendid plan, and tried to persuade the Board that a Leisure Centre of this size and opulence was just what the community wanted its local football club to turn into.

The Board were rather taken with this, until it was pointed out to them that Hammersmith would never allow

planning permission for the London Leisure Centre while there was still a chance of their scheme, and that it was such a vast project that it would doubtless turn out like the Brighton Marina (second public inquiry now under way). So although it was finally turned down, the Leisure Centre had diverted the attention of the Fulham Board away from what was practical, and into the realms of pipedream, while months were wasted.

Ironically, during those wasted months, J. Sanders discovered that they could not sell the 114-flat Stevenage Wharf, even though they are a subsidiary of the second largest property company in the country— MEPC—and only want £6 million for it. So on February 1, three executives from J. Sanders fly to the Middle East to offer a portion of Fulham to the Arabs. They are prepared to throw in a hydrofoil service to the West End and the City, which should be a great help to any Fulham fans who want to go to the Bank after the match.

Craven Cottage won't change much, either, for at the moment the economic situation makes the financing of the Centre almost impossible, and with the gigantic failure of the Sobell Centre in Islington to cater for the needs of the people who live in the area, the idea is looking less and less feasible. Nevertheless, J Sanders say that they have set aside the money to develop the Fulham scheme, and so have Fulham. Fulham deny this, and say they have no money to set aside, but that "discussions are going on and the matter is under constant consideration."

And for some years to come, no doubt.

THE VILLAGE HERO

AS it was with Kennedy's assassination, so nearly everyone in Stoke can remember exactly how they heard the news of Gordon Banks' car crash last year. The final sequel to that Sunday, Bloody Sunday, too place at the Victoria Ground on December 12 when Gordon, halo glistening in the driving rain to supplement the half-power floodlights, took his last mythology of the "all-time-greats" of the game.

The crowd atmosphere was nervous and uncertain. Was it a funeral with a live body, or a Royal Variety Performance? (Sir Alf was there). We all wanted to savour a few final touches but knew that he couldn't be the same. We feared embarrassment. But Stoke City had thoughtfully provided a pre-match relief to the tension — Stoke ladies v. Midlands ladies. Here was No. 7, the real live Norma Huntress, before our very eyes. In fact, apart from a certain re-positioning of the protective hands in the defensive wall, it could have been the real Stoke City. One or two late arrivals, with wet specs, actually thought it was.

And so to the main match. The choice of opposition, Man. Utd., had attracted local adverse comment but its logic was quickly apparent in the first half. This was Banks' night and it wouldn't be fair to play a visiting team who would actually try to score against him. But it was worth 50p just to see Eusebio, "Oozeybow" as the Potteries tannoy-announcer had it. He was like Sister Theresa amongst the Calcutta poor as he distributed the ball and scored a nice goal before being replaced in the most incongruous substitution of the year by Alan "Tank" Bloor.

Bobby Charlton, now mature enough for Stoke, looked the answer to their midfield problems and we feared a sensational comeback with Waddo signing the lad. Banks comprehensively beat United's leading scorer in a half-time penalty competition (sign him as a forward, Doc.) and George Best set up two goals in as manu minutes for United after the break. This definitely signalled the end of Gordon's activity for the evening as Docherty instinctively sat upon his illusory two points just when the rugby phrase of "playing on the blind side" had assumed a new and sombre significance. (Knowing Idi Waddington's capacity for crackpot ideas, it's amazing he had't asked the League for the goals to be placed at the corner flags so that Gordon's career could continue)'

And after it all Gordon is given £15,000 which he doesn't need. In the days of the maximum wage there may have been some justification for generous testimonials to big stars, but surely not now. Gordon had done as well out of football as football has done out of him. For example, the picture in the sycophantic programme showed him turning on the Blackpool lights but omitted to say how much it cost the Blackpool ratepayers. More than his train-fare, I'll bet. Think what the Lord Mayor of Stoke, who is a member of Banks testimonial committee, could do with that £15,000 in his Xmas fund for the needy and the elderly of the City. And incidentally what about the other injured party in Banks' crash? The last we heard, shortly after the accident, was that her sight was failing too as a result. You could hardly find anyone in Stoke now who

Jennings' new goal

FOUL Ad-Feature

Next month he stars for British Leyland in a Unipart commercial (by Saatchi and Saatchi), in which he lunges around the goalposts dressed as an oil filter.

Not very dignified, we thought. However, Jennings says he enjoyed it (not to mention the fee) and can't think of any type he wouldn't do — "unless it's something ridiculous, you know."

Adweek 27/3/75

knows what happened to her. After all, Banks was convicted for the offence.

But for all that, it is not hard to understand why he has been canonised in the Potteries, which Dave Hadfield (Foul 13) accurately described as the biggest village in the world. Banks was the village hero, the only thing in Stoke about which superlatives could accurately be written and who would keep Stoke in the programmes of the world as long as he was playing football. And without him there could well have already been a return to Second Division

football at the Victoria Ground because, no messing, he was the Greatest. He made mistakes, it is forgotten, for example, that the famour League Cup Semi-Final last minute penalty which he miraculously saved from Hurst was given away by his own rugby-tackle) but he made less than anyone else. It was worthwhile to go to the Victoria Ground week-in week-out just to watch him — consistently superb. Thanks for that memory, Banksie●

Malcolm Clarke

EDDIE KELLY'S transfer request has been agreed by Arsenal, writes VICTOR RAILTON.

Kelly told: You stay

ARSENAL today told Eddie Kelly: "You must stay at Highbury."

Evening News (same day)

By VICTOR RAILTON

Manager Ron Greenwood missed his side's 4—0 defeat at Manchester City on Saturday to watch Hull play at Southampton.

I believe his targets were forwards Roy Greenwood and Malcolm Lord.

Daily Mirror 19/8/74

Manager Ron Greenwood, who is expected to name an unchanged side tonight, missed Saturday's 4-0 defeat because he was at Goodison Park watching Kevin Hector and Joe Royle.

Sun 19/8/74

BRING BACK WARD!

Sun 16/8/74 (Northern Edition)

BRING BACK SNOW!

Sun 16/8/74 (Southern Edition)

HAPPY F.A.MILIES

IN THE aftermath of England's failure to produce the expected victory against Portugal Don Revie was found by Brian Glanville to be pondering the fact that the road ahead of him could well be long and that his task would not be made easier by the obvious need to broaden the footballing horizons of the Wembley crowd and of the English footballing public in general.

So it is ironic that Revie's attempts to 'reach' the crowd in an effort to hoist the red white and blue and banish nationalist apathy have so far served to undermine his rebuilding of the England team. It is odd that he is also sensitive to the reactions of a group of people whose knowledge of football he has scant regard for—"Our crowds have been brought up to admire one thing from this game, goalmouth incident" (*Sunday Times* Nov 24)—but it is a fact that he is more preoccupied than most managers with the opinion of the fans. This need not be a bad thing, but in the context of international football and coupled with the stress which Revie places on Nationalism and 'family togetherness' it prompts a sense of foreboding.

In League competitions the occasional poor display by an individual is expected and can be covered by his team-mates. Matches at international level, however, are 'flag wavers' and occur far less frequently for erratic form to be tolerated. The off-form player cannot rely on his colleagues, most of whom are preoccupied with staking their own claims to a place in the side. Against this background the England manager chooses his squad from a range far wider than that available to League managers so it is understandable that Revie is striving to build a stable 'family' unit, a nucleus around which a side can be constructed and to which new faces can be added.

Revie's predecessor was a great 'family' man. He spent a decade trying to build England sides around a fairly constant nucleus of players who had been with him since the early, heady days of success. But families are hierarchically structured and usually subject to paternal authority. Families can be very inward looking, outsiders are looked upon with suspicion. Obedience to the father figure and family values is highly important and loyalty is prized above all.

That Ramsey's 'family' survived for so long is not wholly unconnected with nationalism—that very expression of crowd response which Revie is at present trying to encourage in an effort to shift the dust from the Wembley crowd. Ramsey and his men might have

disappointed in terms of entertainment but they never *disgraced* England.

So it is not surprising that we have under Revie's promptings arrived at a point where Glanville complains that "the ill mannered chauvinistic Wembley crowd (is) now scarcely distinguishable from the fearful mob in Rome", (itself a chauvinistic remark).

It is the first time in my memory that the opponents' national anthem has been jeered as forcefully as was the case before the match against Portugal; just as the hesitant mouthing of their own anthem by some of the England players was surely unprecedented if not unprompted. To be played into the arena in red white and blue strip to the strains of Land of Hope and Glory might well engender a mood in which the encouragement of the crowd will serve (in the words of David Lacey, *Guardian* Nov 20) to make "Don Revie's side mightier yet", but the euphoric potential of such an occasion depends ultimately on England 'producing the goods'. Nationalist fervour will certainly swell the volume of encouragement which greets an impressive England display but, it will also hasten the rumblings of discontent if the team fails to play its part.

So the uncritical acclaim which greeted the start of England's performance against Portugal eventually died and was replaced by cries of "what a load of rubbish". Revie said he was disappointed with the crowd but he could hardly complain when he himself had stoked up the fires of nationalism and generated expectations greater than the scoreline of a football match.

Nationalism is of course inevitable when the talents of different nations compete on this basis, but the danger is that it will overshadow the event which people have come to watch. When this happens in football the result becomes more important than the quality of the performance—witness the enthusiasm which greeted England's late win against Czechoslovakia and the three goals which came at the end of a badly sagging performance.

The borderline between national pride and chauvinism is thin and by appealing initially to nationalist fervour Revie is restricting his own scope for movement and the time available to him to 'come good'. His appointment as successor to Ramsey produced groans from many anti-Ramseyites because he, like Ramsey, is more vulnerable than most to criticism. His Leeds United were characterised by their readiness to run the whole gamut of so called 'professionalism' at the slightest sign of things not going their

way. Leeds were not the only rough-house outfit around but no other team clogged quite so readily, so comprehensively, so effectively or quite so much as the Don's boys (good 'family' lads all). A few more displays like the Portugal one will, if the crowd react with similar fickleness, bring about a similar approach at international level.

This is how Revie's teams will become indistinguishable from those of Ramsey. The sight of Revie and his England 'trustees' retreating into a defensive familial shell will be a familiar reminder of Ramseyism. Back will come those players known for work rate and punctuality (although that would not necessarily apply to the timing of tackles or to the converting of goal chances). Players noted for their independence will be elbowed to one side. The 'family', far from being a flexible unit ready to absorb new talent, will close in on itself to the exclusion of the more precocious talents and we will settle down once again to a period of crushing boredom which will be justified by the avoidance of defeat at the hands (feet?) of the 'continentals'.

Revie has in the past been something of a pioneer in introducing 'foreign' ideas to our domestic game and the memory of some excellent performances by Leeds United bears testimony to this. It would be ironic if his willingness to absorb lessons from overseas was hampered by the chauvinistic impatience of the England crowd—a response which he has himself encouraged. Revie has the ability to restore the footballing fortunes of England but he must play down rather than appeal to the nationalist spirit which will dominate crowd reaction with very little provocation. By doing so he will buy himself time, crowds will display less impatience if their hopes are not prematurely raised on the strains of Elgar, and Revie's chances of building a harmonious and flexible family unit will be greater. ●

Barry Purchese

No. 26 February 1975

I WOULD SAY THAT IT SURPRISES ME...

WHEN PEOPLE COMPARE ME TO ALF RAMSEY...

AFTER ALL, HE'D CREATED A BORING UNSUCCESSFUL TEAM...

HE WAS DEVIOUS & SECRETIVE...

HE WAS PARANOIC ABOUT CRITICISM...

AND HE WAS AN UNPOPULAR FIGURE WITH THE PUBLIC...

SO I JUST SMILE AT THE SUGGESTION...

BECAUSE I KNOW I'VE MADE A LOT OF PEOPLE VERY HAPPY!

FAIR-PLAY LEAGUE

AS EXPECTED, Liverpool and Chelsea clinched their respective ends of the Trident Fair-Play League. Chelsea coasted home by nearly 100 points to give them a marvellous double — relegation and the title of "dirtiest team (nearly) in the first division".

Liverpool finished their season in style, by conceding just 10 points at home to QPR. Before the game, they were presented with the Fair-Play Trophy by League Secretary Alan Hardaker. *Foul* readers may remember Hardaker's ill-tempered letter in issue 24, in which he revealed considerable unconcern for what Trident were trying to do. He wrote:

"*...I have to inform you that the Trident Television Fair-Play League was instituted without any prior consultation with the Football League, nor do I have any knowledge of the prizes great or small which they are offering.*"

One presumes that his presence at Anfield on April 26th indicated an increased familiarity with Trident's efforts, possibly even official recognition? Trident hope to continue the League next season, even without our publicity which has been, sad to say,

the only consistent support it has received. The League has been a worthy experiment that, despite official and media apathy, has managed to provoke a genuine interest among fans. *Foul* readers have shown this, and if you

wanted further proof, you could always try telling the Kop that their team didn't win anything this season! A national newspaper would do well to adopt the Fair-Play League. See to it, Fleet Street.

		Play-ed	Free-kicks (1pt)	Penal-ties (5pts)	Book-ings (10pts)	Sendings Off (25pts)	Total points
1.	Liverpool	42	430	6	9	0	550
2.	Carlisle United	42	496	1	9	0	591
3.	Newcastle United	42	545	4	18	0	745
4.	Coventry City	42	561	4	19	1	796
5.	Leicester City	42	633	5	14	0	798
6.	Sheffield United	42	502	5	25	1	802
7.	Tottenham Hotspur	42	543	5	21	1	803
8.	Ipswich Town	42	650	1	16	0	815
9.	Derby County	42	535	5	27	0	830
10.	Stoke City	42	581	5	20	1	831
11.	Everton	42	626	4	19	0	836
12.	Leeds United	42	560	2	27	1	865
13.	Middlesborough	42	632	4	19	1	867
14.	Wolverhampton W.	42	590	3	24	1	870
15.	Queens Park Rangers	42	596	6	25	0	876
16.	Luton Town	42	627	4	21	2	907
17.	West Ham United	42	629	6	27	0	929
18.	Arsenal	42	616	6	27	2	966
19.	Birmingham City	42	648	4	28	1	973
20.	Burnley	42	679	4	32	1	1044
21.	Manchester City	42	699	1	30	2	1054
22.	Chelsea	42	667	4	41	2	1147

FOULNEWS Taking Umbro

Question: What do Wales, Southampton and West Ham have in common?

Answer: Admiral, the football club's friend.

Each of the three sides had a crucial (and televised) game this spring, and true to form, Admiral stepped in with a never-to-be-repeated offer to join the gravy train and rip off the kids. The deal was in each case much the same as the one that Manchester United signed a year ago, and that Godfather Revie negotiated first for Leeds, then for England (see FOUL 27). It goes like this. Admiral pays the club a flat fee, plus a percentage of the price of each shirt sold in the shops. And in return they are allowed to redesign

the strip in their own lurid style, and possess the sole rights to sell the things to any kid who wants shorts, shirt or tracksuit in his team's colours.

There's a catch of course. Admiral prices are always a spectacular mark-up on the price the kit sold for before the deal. But the clubs don't care. Why should they? After all, the kids who are buying at these inflated prices are only those kids who are so devoted to the club that they are willing to step out into the street or playground dressed in the club colours, and any kid like that is ripe for exploiting. Just so long as the cheque from Admiral has floated into the club's bank account.

One team, however, doesn't have the same mercenary attitude to its supporters, and it's refreshing to say that of all people, it's the Scottish Football Association. They signed a deal, not with Admiral, but with UMBRO. Admiral, of course, made an offer, but the SFA turned it down. Why? In the words of SFA secretary Willie Allan: "There were three reasons. First, they played around too much with the basic design. Also the reproduction quality at retail level is much better with the Umbro design than with the Admiral one. Third, just compare the retail prices of our kit to the England stuff put out by Admiral."

We did. They're cheaper.

Like England, Scotland have signed a complex deal, which involves sliding scale bonuses for progress in the next World Cup. There's one difference, though. None of the England players, who are in effect walking billboards, get a penny of the money — but the Scots deal includes Player Pool bonuses from Umbro.

And another thing. The SFA are only on a royalty, not a fee plus royalties. That means there's another difference. Willie Ormond had nothing personal to gain by choosing one firm rather than another. Perhaps that's why the kids and players were thought of, rather than the bank balance.

No. 33   May/June 1976

THE international season will soon be under way again, and with it will rise sales of the products of Cook and Hurst (Leicester) Ltd, sportswear manufacturers. For it is they who have hired the England football team to sport the word 'Admiral' over their tracksuits.

Cook and Hurst are not letting on how much they paid the Football Association to enter into the Admiral deal. Nor, unsurprisingly, are the F.A. The reason for this is that the England team are on a very complex bonus system, which means that if the Admiral tracksuits are seen in the streets of Buenos Aires in 1978, the FA will receive a lot more than if Revie's boys have as little success in qualifying as Ramsey's did. They are even on a sliding scale for qualifying for the European Nations Cup finals in 1976. Two things, though are certain. England are tied to Admiral for the next five years. And it is the FA, not the players, the walking billboards, who will receive the loot.

The man behind the deal is, inevitably, Godfather Revie. He has had tie-ups with Admiral since May 1973 when he signed Leeds up to them soon after the ill-fated experiment with 'artist' Paul Trevillion, Thus it was only to be expected that he would continue his relationship with them when he changed his job. And sure enough he had not been England manager for many days before he approached the International Committee with the idea that they might put the contracts for the the commercialisation of the national team out to tender. Cook and Hurst, predictably, were the firm selected; Revie the mediator had worked another deal. Or, in the words of the FA: "You had better speak to Mr Revie about that, since a lot of the negotiations were dealt with by Revie himself."

The only catch was that Admiral wanted to design the kit themselves, following their triumph of vulgarity with Luton Town's bright orange 'Da-Glo' gear. This the Don persuaded the International Committee to agree to, and that is how the nu-style England colours came about. No doubt the advantages of the deal were such that the Don could afford to ignore more than one England player who said he could not find his team-mates under floodlights.

'No, as a matter of fact I quite enjoy speaking at lunches, but it would be rather difficult to fit in . . . I'm very busy at this time of year you know. No, not watching players, but all the contracts fall in at the beginning of the season, so I have a few deals to fix. And of course I can't do that sort of thing for nothing . . . How much did you say? Well, I'm not *that* busy. Look on it as expenses and cut down on the guests. Okay? See you there then.'

WILSON

SCHMILSON

The scene is the Grandstand studio, 12.15 on a Saturday afternoon. Outside there is snow on the ground, so much so that thirty-two League matches have already been postponed. Frank Bough is introducing the day's line-up.

BOUGH: . . . So why don't you just keep warm indoors and enjoy the tasty little menu we'll be serving up for you this afternoon. Later on we'll be going along to RAF Cotsford for the programme of indoor horse-racing, but first we'll be hearing from Bob Wilson, and that's straight after the news headlines, read for you now by Kenneth Kendall.

Pause. Nothing happens.

BOUGH: Oh! No Kenneth Kendall. Well in that case let's go straight over to our Football Preview, and Bob Wilson. Bob! . . . Bob?

There is a quick flash of Bob Wilson putting his jacket on and trying to pick up his notes at the same time.

BOUGH: Well, while we're waiting for Bob let's just reflect shall we how few matches there are actually being played this afternoon, because, quite obviously, of the terrible weather conditions. Bob?

WILSON: Yes indeed, Frank.

He waits for his autocue to start. Nothing happens. A long pause. He starts sorting through his notes.

WILSON: Yes indeed, Frank. Well! As you rightly said, Frank, the weather has indeed taken a hand. . . for the worse. And you can see from our caption –

Pause. No caption.

WILSON: – the list of fixtures postponed makes a considerable inroad on the, er, list of fixtures scheduled for this afternoon's Football League programme of matches.

He sorts through his notes.

WILSON: Including the top Second Division clash between top-of-the-table Torquay and promotion-chasing Tranmere, who will no doubt remember their last encounter two seasons ago, when back in 1972 they met at, er, at. . .

CAMERAMAN'S VOICE: A cafe on the M6!

WILSON: . . . At, thank you, a cafe on the M6. Tranmere are in the white shirts and darker shirts.

He looks to his right. There is a clip of film of the 1922 ('White Horse') Cup

Final. Wilson's phone rings. He picks it up, listens, puts it down, and consults his notes.

WILSON: I've just heard in fact that ten more fixtures have been postponed out of this afternoon's remaining matches, and they're the ones at Stranraer, Molyneux, The Dell, Charlton, Wolves, the Baseball Ground and, er, Southampton. Southampton have been maintaining a good run of late, as John Motson found when he went down this week to talk to Pompey's manager, Lawrie McMenemy. . .

There is a clip of film with numbers in front of it. John Motson is having his hair combed, while McMenemy straightens his tie.

MOTSON'S VOICE: . . . I won't ask you any embarrassing questions about promotion, just the usual crap.

McMENEMY'S VOICE: Ha'way! I could do without all this pratting around, but.

WILSON: Well! Lawrie McMenemy in frank mood there, pulling no punches as we know he can so well! Like Southampton, Stoke's name also begins with 'S'. Stoke haven't been enjoying such good form of late, as they did so convincingly last season. Here we see them taking full use of their home advantage when they entertained Burnley recently up at Turf Moor. . .

There is a clip of film of Torquay versus Tranmere.

MOTSON'S VOICE: You seem to be going great guns this season, Lawrie. . .

WILSON: Well, it just isn't our day is it? It seems the gremlins have defeated us. One piece of good news I can confirm is that there'll be at least one match on today, and that is the fixture at Brechin City, so all those of you who've already set out for that match. . . er, well, Frank?

CAMERAMAN'S VOICE: He's gone to the toilet, you've got another four minutes.

WILSON: Well! With so few matches being played this afternoon it's certainly going to be hard on goalkeepers, er, and with snow-affected pitches so much in the news, er, viewers may be reminded of the goal scored by Steve Heighway in the 1971 Cup Final, when the goalkeeper left his near post unguarded. . .

There is a clip of film of Bob Wilson leaving his near post unguarded in the 1971 Cup Final.

WILSON: It was a goal that was to prove decisive, as up till then both teams had been evenly matched in all departments. Let's just take a look at it again with the benefit of the action replay cameras, and con-sider what the goalkeeper should have done. . .

There is a list of fifty-four postponed matches.

MOTSON'S VOICE: Oh and another great shot by Mahoney!

WILSON: Frank? FRANK! Er, starting with the left-hand column first, the list reads, Arsenal versus Birmingham, Coventry versus Derby, Everton versus. . .

CAMERAMAN'S VOICE: Oy! Has anyone ever told you you've got a face like a lemon-squeezer?

Rangers: Ungrateful Dead

ON THE MORNING of December 11th, some 200 men wearing dark suits and plain shirts and ties with *RFC* embossed on them will file into McClellan's gallery in Glasgow. The event that pulls them there is the annual shareholders' meeting of the Rangers Football Club.

Rangers are unlike any other Scottish — or indeed, English — club in that they are a public limited company. Shares in the Rangers can be bought on the open (well almost) market. This autumn trading has been very heavy, with shares passing hands at £8 or more. Most of the buying has been done by two garage owners, **Jack Gillespie** of Lenzie, and **Tom Dawson** of Helensburgh. They want to get on the Rangers Board. And they have been buying because they know they will never have a better chance.

The last five years have been tumultuous ones for the Rangers. January 1971 saw the horrific disaster on the Cairnlea staircase at Ibrox, when 66 men were killed and hundreds injured while the Rangers players celebrated a Colin Stein goal on the pitch below. Then, in 1972, years of tribal warfare on the part of their supporters erupted in the face of the police batons in Barcelona in a riot so fierce that Rangers were banned from Europe, even though the occasion of the riot was their victory in the European Cup Winners Cup Final.

Then last autumn, in a Glasgow court (see *FOUL* 24), Sheriff James Irvine Smith found in favour of a Mrs Margaret Dougan, who was suing the club for the death of her husband in the disaster, stating that: *'the said accident was due to the fault and negligence of the defenders'*. He added: *'Rarely can an organisation of the size and significance of Rangers FC have succeeded in conducting their business with records so sparse, so carelessly kept, so inaccurately written up, and so indifferently stored'*.

This was sensational stuff. The Board of the Rangers is a pillar of the tightly-knit Protestant mafia that controls Glasgow, professional men running the city in a professional way. Rangers don't employ Catholics, and indeed are so extreme that they have only had one director in their entire history who was not a Freemason, a cult that ensures its ascendancy by the strict operation of secrecy and tradition, a tradition that is embodied in the club, which embodies all the old-fashioned virtues of self-discipline from below and authority from above.

Incompetence, though, is something else. The Rangers Board have been made to look inept in the eyes of their friends in the professional classes. And it is this feeling that Gillespie and Dawson hope to capitalise upon. They would have struck last year, but the Rangers lodged an appeal against the Sheriff's judgement, an appeal that they later abandoned on advice from all sides that they could never hope to win. But it served its purpose: the Board kept the shareholders quiet by

W.O. - Mysteries of the Organism

The Scottish football team returned to Glasgow without the World Cup. Many tears were shed at the airport, not least those of Willie Ormond. They were shed because Scotland, the only country in the tournament that is not a nation had lost its only chance of establishing its nationhood in the eyes of the world. The great Tartan Dream was over.

The sense of expectancy all over Scotland when the team left for Dortmund is hard to explain in rational terms. There is an intangible feeling that a new era of Scottish history has opened. The economy will be transformed by the wealth of the North Sea, and oil will join whisky and footballers as Scotland's major exports; political independence seems that much closer with seven SNP members in the English Parliament. Football means more to the Scots than to any other people, because the only times that Scotland can express itself as a national entity, separate from the rest of Britain, is when the national side is playing football. It was not that the Scots expected their team to win; more that they were relying on the dark genius of their footballers somehow to take the world by storm, to fight Bannockburn in Dortmund. Too much emotional capital was invested in the football team this

Scottish Daily Record

summer for defeat not to hurt badly.

So the myth that is being created is one that has turned failure into success. After all, it was not a beaten team that was returning — it was the first side in history to return home unbeaten from a World Cup finals without the Cup. In the toughest qualifying group of them all, they held the Reigning World Champions to a draw ('a moral victory' said the Scottish press), drew against another of the most fancied teams, and were eliminated through an African team giving its all against Scotland, and then throwing in the towel against its other two opponents. "If we had got through that group we would have won the Cup," said captain Bremner. "The best team in the group went home," pleading *sub judice*.

But there's no hope of that happening this year. And in the past 12 months the cards have been shuffled. Chairman **Matt Taylor** has died, and director **Davie Hope**, who got landed with the buck in court, has 'retired'. Tom Dawson, at whose garages Taylor's lorry fleets were serviced, has wheedled the proxy votes on Taylor's shares out of his widow; that's 40,000 to add to his own 20,000. Jack Gillespie has 26,000; so, in uneasy coalition, they claim to control 86,000 of the 346,000 votes. The Board can only muster 70,000 between them.

The fight, then, centres around who can control the missing 190,000 votes, most of them in small holdings, although the Rangers lawyer, Browning, controls 17,000, and he will certainly vote with the Board. The Board are prepared to fight dirty. They moved the date of the AGM forward in the hope of finding Gillespie unprepared. But as soon as the Rangers sent out letters to the absent shareholders asking them to give their vote to the

Board, Gillespie's letters were in the next post, chronicling the incompetence and wasted opportunities of the old men at the top.

Gillespie is utterly unacceptable to the Board, although even he is a Mason. Loud, brash, indiscreet with journalists, wearing flamboyant Hawaiian shirts rather than three-piece suits, he embodies all the qualities that the patrician elite feel menaced by. Any man that can spend over £200,000 on a football club's shares has a) done rather well out of selling cars, and b) has ideas as to how to get his money back – and it is Gillespie's rampant commercial sense that scares the canny, cautious men in the Ibrox boardroom. They are very happy to squeeze money out of their support – the Rangers Pool pulls over £450,000 a year from the pockets of 670,000 Rangers fans – but they are not prepared to see their dignity imperilled. Nor are they prepared to give their army of supporters and shareholders any say in what kind of club they want. The fact that Gillespie is the largest private

shareholder will not entitle him to any kind of power. Gillespie is a loser.

The reason is Tom Dawson. As Matt Taylor's heir apparent, he is in an extremely powerful position. There is not much that the Board can do to keep him out, and indeed there is no great reason why they should wish to. But the price of admission is steep. No seat on the Board unless Tom double-crosses his mate Jack. Tom knows full well which side his bread is buttered. He will vote the way he is told. The wind of change that Gillespie symbolises will blow vainly for many years yet.

Chairman **Rae Simpson** is in his mid-fifties. He will be succeeded by **Willie Waddell**, the former manager, when his time is up. Dawson is only 44. As Davie Hope says: "If Dawson gets on, that will seal up the Board for a generation." The trauma of the Disaster will gently fade in the memory. Grass will grow on 66 graves. But the Board's theme tune will still be "We Shall Not Be Moved".

Alan Stewart

---

said Jim Holton. Dissenting voices were muted.

A less emotional analysis might cast a few shadows upon this defiant tartan front. Football, more than any other game, is an expression of the characteristics of a nation, and this is particularly true of the Scots. Scottish football reflects the 'terrible balance of arrogance and insecurity, the conviction that you're one of the chosen by very virtue of being Scottish, and also a desperate fear that maybe you're not, and there's nothing whatsoever that you can do about it.' * Nothing has ever illustrated this more clearly than the progress of the team in Germany

In their first game they insisted on squandering their genius, impressing their superiority upon a team from Zaire that was only too aware of it, showing off, not so much to the opposition as to each other, and neglecting to score the goals. Against Brazil, and again in the Yugoslavia game, the players showed the other side of their Scottishness. The insecurity that riddled their play against the Africans drained away, and they set out to show the world that not only were they a prouder nation than their much-vaunted opponents, but that they were better footballers too. Bremner and Hay crossed the

Alan Sharp on 'This Week', 13.6.74

invisible line between showing off to the others, and inspiring with their example; remorselessly and relentlessly, they crushed their opponents with the arrogant assertion that, on the night, they were the chosen ones. But because of what happened against Zaire, the flame that burned so brightly in the other two games turned to ashes.

It would have been better if the team had actually lost to Zaire. Then at least the reason for the failure would have been out in the open and, as it turned out, winning by only two goals had exactly the same effect as losing. But the fatal flaw, the urge to self-destruction, has bitten too deeply into the psyche of Scottish footballers to be forgotten, even admidst the pain and tension of the World Cup. The abiding images of the game are of Hutchison, fresh on late in the day, showing he too could be one of the lads as he beat man after man on a long, mazy dribble back to his own keeper, and Bremner, instead of driving on the team to score the goals that would have kept them in the competition, casually playing keepy-uppy in his own half.

What then has been learned from the miserable experience of Germany? First, that no amount of organisation, pressure or financial motivation can persuade a Scotland team to try in a match they con-

sider not to be worth the effort; but that if the opposition is famous enough, they can swamp the best teams in the world. Second, that even if there could be no place for Johnstone or Hutchison in the final lineup, enough wayward talent was harnessed to show that if the occasion is right, a Scotland team can actually play for each other. The defence made only one fatal mistake in three games, in front of a goalkeeper who can finally lay the ghost of Frank Haffey, and behind the first real centre-forward Scotland have unearthed in a decade. And the Scots have rediscovered that, even now, for sheer inspiration, exuberance and pride through football, no nation on earth can match them.

So the great World Cup adventure was not entirely wasted, even if the Cup itself did not come home. All the major fears proved groundless. The team did not indulge in Anglo/Tartan squabbles, or degenerate into religious feuding, in spite of IRA threats to knock off the Protestants in the side; the manager did not suffer intolerable interference from the SFA officials (one of his predecessors actually resigned during a World Cup); nobody was sent off, or arrived drunk for a match. Only one fear was justified – they could not rouse themselves properly to beat the worst side in the tournament.

Alan Stewart

O's
Unlucky Man

"Now that supporters are getting fewer, the clubs' cavalier attitude to those who remain is no longer good enough." (FOUL 9)

A perfect example of this 'cavalier attitude', bordering on contempt, has been provided this month by Orient chairman Arthur Page, who decided to disband the official Supporters Club — replacing it with a "Sportsman's Club" at four times the price — and to ban from the ground for life a 54 year-old supporter who has been following the club since 1925.

The whole sorry episode also illustrates how increased emphasis on commercial management is divesting Supporters Clubs of what little influence they have ever been allowed to exert.

George Taylor, 54, is the archetypal small-club supporter. First taken to watch Orient when he was five years old, he became steadily more involved with them to a degree not possible at bigger clubs. As travel secretary of the Supporters Club for 11 years, he put in hours of unpaid work at the ground, and was publicly commended for it by chairman Page.

A typically menial job was to be at the ground at 6.30 the morning after each away game to unpack the skip brought back by a Supporters' coach. Others included weeding the terraces, cleaning and painting.

This is the man of whom Page now says: "We can do without his type"

Trouble started when Page, keen as most chairmen to keep supporters at a distance, gave a firm of outside caterers an exclusive contract to run all the bars on the ground. This included the Supporters Club bar, traditionally run by club volunteers as one of the more agreable ways of helping out.

George Taylor and three other club officials resigned: the dynamic new caterers walked out after a month. Taylor resisted appeals to go back, but, prompted by friends and sympathisers, began organising his own coach to all away games.

Though all profit from these trips was contributed to Supporters Club funds, Page began to turn the screws. Mrs. Taylor was sacked from her job of laundering the playing kit; so were two unpaid match-day stewards, whose crime was to travel on Taylor's coach.

Players were told that under no circumstances were Taylor or his band of supporters to be given complimentary tickets — a common practice when there are tickets to spare for games involving a long and expensive trip.

Taylor himself says he was under surveillance at all home games: a claim borne out when Page sent a letter banning him, because "loyal supporters" allegedly saw him touting coach tickets inside the ground — something he doesn't need to do, since there is always a full complement who travel with him.

This is supposed to have happened at the pre-season friendly with QPR, when, Taylor says, "I was standing with club officials for the whole game."

Since the ban was first publicised by a local paper, despite Page's desire to hush it up, Taylor has received countless letters and phone calls offering support. There is talk of a petition being raised, and even of suing the chairman.

"A wonderful spirit in the club has been typified by supporters George Taylor and Les Banner and their band of helpers who have quite voluntarily been at the ground night after night working on redecorations and improvements".
— Orient chairman Page, 30/6/69

"This man Taylor is a troublemaker and we can do without his type at the ground. He has constantly tried to stop the Supporters Club from functioning properly, and we have finally lost patience with him".
— Orient chairman Page, 3/9/73

But the supporters, as usual, are quite powerless. Clubs have a legal right of admission, and can, as this case shows, ban anyone on a whim.

What is most absurd is that the situation should occur at Orient, the worst supported club in division two.

The management are trying to pacify increasing numbers of dissenters with a "Sportsman's Club", offering little for £1 membership except a 'chance to meet the players' — which used to happen quite naturally when the team were allowed to frequent the tiny Supporters Club bar.

But the moral of the story would seem to be that as long as supporters accept sops like this, and let commercial enterpreneurs take over more and more of their activities, they will remain hopelessly ineffective and impotent.

No. 11   October 1973

Best of the B.G.s

Creamed

How well I remember, in 1943, being given by a kindly tennis coach, living near my boarding school, a copy of the *Topical Times* sporting handbook for 1935.

Westwood was chosen as one of the five outstanding sportsmen of the year. *Eheu, fugaces!*

World Soccer, May 1976

My own view is that Anderlecht's heads had drooped, their hearts had sunk and the game was in West Ham's pockets when poor Frank Lampard made that awful, uncharacteristic error, and presented Anderlecht with their equaliser at the most delicate of moments; three minutes from half-time.

On the aeroplane home, I tried to console him by reminding him of Disraeli's aphorism: the defects of great men are the consolation of dunces.

Sunday Times 9/5/76

WELL, what do YOU think Frank Lampard's reply to Brian Glanville was? Entries (not more than four words, please) to FOUL House. Winner receives autographed copy of Milan telephone directory.

No. 33   May/June 1976

A HERO TURNED BORE

Eamonn Dunphy
on Brian Clough

TO those of us in football resigned to the one-dimensional nature of the Game's leadings pros, the arrival of Brian Clough on the scene was something of a relief. Here at last was a man casting aside the "cloth cap and muffler" mentality, with revolutionary ideas and an uncompromising way of expressing them.

Professed socialist, relentless Ramsey-basher, a leading cadre in soccer's revolution — and the brilliance of his young Derby side served only to confirm the notion that the Messiah had arrived.

Now, a million words and a good many boardroom battles later, his caravan has come to rest in elegant Brighton. There, like a bemused Heathcliff lost in a Noel Coward set, he continues to launch his seemingly endless verbal assaults on the football world.

I went to meet him there wearing my journalistic hat. I must admit I was curious, for the enchantment of the early days had worn a little thin in recent months. It seemed as if the value of what he was saying had diminished proportionally to the amount of space taken to say it. His thoughts had become a commodity whose main value was in boosting the circulation figures of Fleet Street's less reputable organs.

Arranging to interview him through a mutual acquaintance, I had confirmed the date personally, before turning out for Charlton against Brighton on the Saturday previous to our meeting. So I was a little surprised when Clough asked "What's your first name, lad?" Was he trying to put me down, or had he really been that remote from Saturday's proceedings at the Valley? I'd interviewed many other people in the game — Revie and Allison among them — and they had all known my name, or at least pretended to. For there is an affinity among football people, regardless of station, a sense of shared experience that can break through the normal journalist-pro relationship. Clough seemed unable to acknowledge any such rapport: indeed, he made it clear that he disapproved of players talking to the press, let alone messing around with tape recorders. It seemed that his passion for free speech extended only to himself, except when, as he put it, "I feel players are able to handle journalists."

Nevertheless, although receiving the Village Idiot treatment, I suppose I could claim to have extracted my journalistic pound of flesh. Clough was, as ever, free with his opinions. On the morality of the transfer system "Anyone that I've bought has done alright" On West Ham "they haven't learnt to defend." Every sentence contained its own built-in headline.

Yet when it was over, I felt curiously empty. An unimportant personal reaction, perhaps; it certainly has no validity in the wider context of assessing Cloughism. He remains a superb manager, a leading apostle of skilful football and, in strict football terms, a man of substance.

I just fear he is no revolutionary. In fact he now represents proof of the observation that "Every hero becomes a bore at last."

No. 16   March 1974

FOUL's Golden Classics

DESIDERATA

YOU ARE an apprentice of the Football League, no less than the Teams and the Stars; you have a right to be there.

Go placidly amid the noise and haste of the penalty area and remember what peace there may be on the wings. As far as possible without surrender be on good terms with the Ref. Speak your truth quietly and clearly; and listen to others, even the dull and ignorant; the Eddie Bailys too have their story.

Avoid loud and aggressive persons, Brian Clough is a vexation to the spirit. If you compare yourself with others, you may become vain and bitter; for there will always be someone to remind you of Dave Mackay. Enjoy your medals and caps as well as your plans for an FA Coaching Certificate.

Keep interested in your own career, however humble; it is your only possession, as you left school at fifteen without a trade. Exercise caution in your business affiars; for the world is full of the trickery of players' agents. But let this not blind you to what virtue there is; many persons strive for high ideals; remember Ron Greenwood.

Be yourself. Especially, do not feign injury. Neither be cynical about training; for in the face of all aridity and disenchantment it is better than the White City dog track.

Take kindly to the counsel of the years, gracefully agreeing to sign for Stoke City. Nurture strength of spirit to shield you when you are offered in a player-exchange to Rochdale. But do not distress yourself with transfer requests. Many fears are born of fatigue and a spell in the reserves. Beyond a wholesome discipline, be gentle with yourself, especially the night before a big match.

You are an Apprentice of the Football League, no less than the teams and the stars; you have a right to be there. And whether or not it is clear to you, no doubt the League programme is unfolding as it should.

Therefore be at peace with your Manager, whoever your directors decide he shall be, and whatever your labours and aspirations, in the noisy confusion of the six-yard box keep your shinguards on.

With all its sham, drudgery and broken dreams, it is still the Toughest League in the World. Be careful. Strive to stay onside.

No. 23   November 1974

TWO NORTHERN CHAIRMEN

1: Peter Swales

It has not been a good season for Chairmen. Before October we saw Leeds' Manny Cussins paying his manager £98,000 to go away, and since then Tottenham's Sidney Wale has presided over a club which has collapsed into Division 2 in the hands of his own appointee. These two men are complete opposites – Cussins a self-made man who wanted a slice of the glory and was prepared to pay for it, and Wale a conservative, small-minded local businessman who inherited the club from his father. But they share one characteristic: neither demonstrated any ability to run a football club before he got the job.

One man who has served an apprenticeship and earned his place on the back pages, is Manchester City's Peter Swales. A local man who shrewdly anticipated the boom in consumer durables, built up a chain of electrical and television shops (White and Swales) sold out at the peak, and then built up a second chain of retail outlets to rival the ones he had just sold, he has proved his talent for running a business. For eight years he was Chairman of non-League Altrincham, founded the Northern Premier League and was its Chairman for three years, before an invitation came from City to join their Board in April 1971. Two and a half years later he was Chairman.

Unlike the suave Lord Westwood, Swales is forceful, blunt and a bit shabby. He admires Sam Longson and Bob Lord – he would probably like to be as blunt and patronising as them, but feels it inappropriate for a young man at a big city club. He insisted on my Petering him, but everyone at the club called him Chairman. He claims to have been a City fan all his life, but essentially likes running things. Reluctantly he admitted that he would have joined the United Board had they asked. The Chairman of Liverpool once drunkenly asked him to join the Anfield Board, but the offer was never followed up. The Altrincham experience has left him with the conviction that the League should be thrown open to non-League clubs for promotion and relegation, and a profound contempt for badly-run

Third and Fourth division outfits, who take the £30,000 League hand-outs earned by clubs like his, and "piss it up the wall". Even though football clubs are different from business, he believes his business ability is transferable:

"There are three major differences. First you are not in football to make a profit; the whole point is to plough all the money back into the club. Secondly, in business you are trying to eliminate competition, to have a monopoly; football clubs depend upon the existence of other clubs to play against. The third difference lies in your relationship with your staff.

"In business you are in continual touch with your management, criticising them, telling them what to do, and if they don't do it, doing it yourself. This is just not possible with football. Here I have appointed a manager, and I have to let him get on with it . . . If he comes to me and says I want to buy such and such a player for a couple of hundred grand, my decision as to whether or not we do it is not based on what I think of the player, but on whether or not we can afford him. It's the hardest thing in the world not to interfere, the temptation is to let your heart rule your head and ring the manager up every day. Expressing an opinion of what the manager should do is the right of every

fan who walks through the turnstile. But it's not mine."

If you think that is frustrating, just imagine what a Chairman feels who, like Portsmouth's John Deacon, has sunk half a million of his own money into the club. Swales denies that he has put any of his own money into the club, and says that none of the other directors have either, apart from the money they used to buy their shares. If that is true, then his sums don't add up. City, he says, will have spent a million on ground improvements by next summer, and he has spent a million on players. In return they have received some £600,000 in outgoing transfers, some £70,000 a year from the Development Assn., and £30,000 a year from the Social Club. They owe money on the HP for some of the players, but do not have an overdraft at the bank. How is it done? Swales dismisses questions with a smile.

What, then, can a Chairman do? "It's up to me to appoint the right man to manage the club, and then create a mood, an atmosphere in the place in which he can do the job. Of course you make mistakes. FOUL seems to think that Chairmen should be supermen who never make errors, but you've got the easy job. We're all human, and we often get things wrong. I made a mistake with Ron Saunders. Johnny Hart had been appointed from within, and he broke under the strain of managership. I thought it would be too big a risk to appoint Tony Book, the same thing might happen again, even though the players came to me and said that was what they wanted. I weighed up all these factors and I came to the wrong decision. Ron Saunders was a good manager – he has proved that before and since – but he was not a good manager for us. I admitted that. I'm learning all the time; I didn't realise then how important the players are. I do now." One feels that Swales approves of Cussins' actions in sacking Clough, but not Wale's determination to stick by Neill.

In 1971 Manchester City had been bitterly divided for seven months between two irreconcilable factions on the Board. The established faction,

'I don't even have the right to express an opinion...'

led by Chairman Albert Alexander and his son Eric, was challenged by a rebellion led by double-glazer Joe Smith, who spent £110,000 on getting on the Board. Mercer was identified with the former and Allison sided with the latter. It was paralysis. Swales was drafted in to solve the split, rather like Lord Westwood at Newcastle. He worked fast and mysteriously. Within months Smith retired from the fray, saying: "I didn't realise what running a football club would involve. I do now," and sold all his shares back to the Board at a loss. Soon after, Albert Alexander died and his son became Chairman, but resigned in October 1973 pleading pressure of work. With both factions routed, Swales was the obvious choice. How did he do it?

"Graft. Bloody hard work. Every director is in charge of one aspect of the club's administration." He obviously hit on the age-old solution to curb radicalism, give everyone so much work to do that they don't have time to conspire. "And running the club on businesslike lines. We do know how to balance the books, even if we can't pick footballers. And between you and me we've got one or two homers in the side."

That home is the only ground in the country that does not have an 'end'. The City heavies stand peacefully on the Kippax which runs the length of the pitch, and there is seating everywhere else. Even if you forget that United are in the same town, the docility and lack of atmosphere is baffling, and in the face of it Swales' formula of graft is impotent. But it might change. The ground is an oasis in a desert of demolished housing. Soon Moss Side will be one of the most densely populated areas in Europe. If anyone can involve the new hordes in the Club, Swales can.

Meanwhile, what does the future hold for him? Like many Chairmen, he moved into football because he was bored with running successful businesses, and wanted to try something with more risk. City are not a success, yet. Despite all the blood-letting on the Board and three managers, they are still the same mixture of explosive talent, irritating introspection, and unpredictable bursts of violence. They are many years away from establishing another consistently successful side.

But Swales is already looking forward to the day they do. The North West is represented on the Football League by Matt Busby and Bob Lord. No future there. So Swales has moved in on the FA; already he sits on the International Committee. The octogenarians at Lancaster Gate must be bracing themselves, because none of them are in his class as an operator. Manchester City itself may just be the apprenticeship for something else.□

Alan Stewart

'Running a business is too easy... Stockport County was a challenge'

2: Dragan Lukic

Everyone in Stockport knows the Belgrade Hotel. Inside it there was an impressive bustle of people, salesmen from Edinburgh, councillors from Newcastle, Frankfurt businessmen on their way to Manchester Airport. Surveying the scene was the proprietor, owner of two other hotels, anti-Nazi Partisan in Yugoslavia, later a prisoner in German, Communist and British camps, but since 1969 chairman of Stockport County, Dragan Lukic. A sturdy, impressive figure of a man, well preserved and at the peak of his powers.

The contrast between his business and his football could not be more striking. The profits from his hotels this year will be £300,000, and in addition he has won a 99 year lease to develop a 160 acre site on the plush Cheshire side of Warrington, in a triangle formed by the three motorways. It will contain a golf course and a leisure centre, 'a family place, no single people or men who have just come for a game of golf and a pint.'

At Edgeley Park the prospect is gloomier. Single people are welcome, with or without a pint, for attendances are 40% of break-even point and the current deficit is about £150,000. There are only two operative directors, Lukic and vice-chairman Alan Kirk, and they have paid the players' wages many weeks of this season. Of the other two directors, one lives in Guernsey and was last seen at Edgeley Park in October '72, the other is in his 70s, has acute deafness and recently had a bad accident. Since relegation in 1970 they have applied for re-election twice, and are currently in 21st place. Only Doncaster have had more managers since the War, and the present incumbent, Jimmy Meadows is in his second stint. Until seven weeks ago, the club had no scout for three years; they have a playing staff of sixteen, and some of them may go part time next season.

Lukic avoided talking specifically about the problems of Stockport by generalising about the state of football and the moral decline of the nation. He insisted that the club's plight be seen as part of football's crisis as a whole: 'if you judge chairmen on whether they make a profit, then there are 81 chairmen who are failures. But they still keep pumping their money into clubs because they know that for every club that packs up, then a little piece of football dies. But income and expenditure have never been related. If I ran the League, the first thing I would do is say no more transfers on the HP. Every player's fee must be there in cash before his registration may be accepted. That would bring down the fees. And I think that clubs like Stockport should pay nothing in transfer fees anyway. If players didn't join us they would go out of the League altogether.'

He feels particularly strong about players who, he feels, are just taking the money out of the game that men like himself put in: 'There were £8 million of transfers last year, and of that 10% went to the Benevolent Fund, and to the players themselves. That's £800,000 lost to the game. Forever. If I appear on tv, I put that fee into the club. I am only there because I am chairman of Stockport, so that money belongs to the club. If Keegan, say, makes money selling cars, he should pay it to Liverpool. Without them, he is nothing; once he no longer plays, then no-one will be interested in him.' None of his own players face this problem: 'If any of them had outside interests then I would fire him. Footballers are inept businessmen, and it affects their game.'

His blame of the players has much to do with his contempt for them: 'It's not like running a business; there is so much more man management to do. They gamble, they have debts, they have family problems. It all affects their game on a Saturday. And I can't do their playing for them. And it's also not like business in that I can sack my manager here at the hotel, nobody takes any notice. I sack the manager at the club or one of the players, and it's

Continued

115

SCOUSE BENNY

"Give the ref a chance, lads! Back ten yards. . . !"

ARGENTINE BEEF

THOSE OF YOU who may think that England is the only nation afflicted by strikes, might be relieved to hear that we are not alone. Argentina was recently hit by a stoppage that overshadowed our trifling industrial disputes — this one concerned football.

It seems that referee Jorge Alvarez so enraged fans in Rosario with a last-minute penalty decision, that one of them took him to court for alleged 'sports fraud'. Now, the Referees Association weren't too chuffed about this trespass on their authority, and so called a strike of all members. More than 100 scheduled matches were cancelled, while the boys in black campaigned to have the sports fraud law repealed and Alvarez released.

Poor old Jorge was allowed out, but only for treatment on his right eye, injured by a cob of concrete hurled by a less legally-inspired Rosario fan. The case continues. In the meantime, I hope Tommy Reynolds doesn't get any fancy ideas. . .

CUP FINALITY POINTS

ONE OF THE more unacceptable faces of lunacy that always seem to afflict Cup Finals, was the hokum surrounding the ball for this year's Final between er, between er, I've forgotten, but it doesn't matter. Anyway, the company who provided the match ball hit on an elaborate publicity stunt which involved flying it down under escort from Leeds only hours before the kick-off. The ball, we were assured, received 'V.I.P. treatment' — what? A four-course meal and drinks on the plane? A shag with a stewardess? I demand an explanation. Incidentally, the same company has signed a long-term contract for providing balls for the F.A. (sic), so watch out next year when it's parachuted down to the stadium inside Bernard Manning.

While on the subject of the Cup Final, I might just report that I watched the game on ITV, and found that my 'enjoyment' was considerably impaired by an occasional high-pitched whine on my television set. On ringing up to complain, I was told that it was Alan Ball. . .

BYE-BYE BENNY

BEING AN EMOTIONAL sort, I find it difficult to remain unmoved while the good ship *Foul* slips below the waters of oblivion. But I remember, and draw strength from the words of my ancestor, Admiral Horatio Benny, R.N., as his flagship sank slowly under him at Trafalgar. Surveying the disaster around him, he screamed his defiance at the heavens:

"Fuck this for a lark, I'm going home." I'll see yiz. ●

Continued

all over the newspapers and I have people ringing me up demanding to know why I did it.

Jimmy Meadows knows all about the Stockport sacking game. He was first fired in 1969 for playing Bill Atkins against Orient; the then chairman, Vic Bernard, had given him express instructions to leave Atkins out of the side as he knew Portsmouth would withdraw their £22,000 bid if they saw him play. Meadows wanted to keep Atkins at the club, so he played. Bernard was right; Portsmouth did retract their bid, Atkins stayed, Meadows got his cards.

Why does Lukic do it, if he despises the players so much? 'I'm a masochist I like being whipped. But seriously, I look upon Stockport as my home town, and now I'm an institution in my home town. Football has given me back my self-respect, and I have been able to give something to Stockport. Also I was bored. Running a business is too easy, you know what is going to happen, you know you are going to make money. I can tell you exactly how much money each of my hotels will make next year. There's no challenge in that. But in football there is a challenge. In football, nobody knows what is going to happen, and you can't control it. You just have to do what you can.'

But Slavonic sentiment isn't the whole story. Lukic plans to save Stockport County by joining with the local authority in developing a site in the Bredbury area in the North of town into a sports centre and leisure complex, of which the football club will be part. Talks have begun with the Corporation, two possible sites have been mentioned. Lukic's big card with the burghers from City Hall is that if County went out of the League or out of existence, professional football would not return to Stockport; he points to Barrow, Gateshead, Accrington. The point is not lost on the city chieftains. League football is a non-recoverable asset.

Now if this scheme goes through, Lukic would be sitting very pretty indeed. Edgeley Park, an excellent site in the middle of town would be sold, and since the ground is steeply mortgaged to him, he would get all his money back. The Council would then provide architects, surveyors, drainage men and park officials free of charge, the club would be swallowed up by the sports complex, and he would end up as part-owner of a very prosperous leisure centre — in addition of course to the Warrington one.

With Stockport County, as with his hotel business, Lukic is utterly autocratic. Because he virtually owns the club he can do things that big city chairmen who have rivals on the Board, and are watched much more closely by the press, cannot do. But even in so businesslike a mind it is hard to believe that the profits from the sports centre were his intention right from the start. He went into Stockport County originally for reasons of sentiment and because it was a challenge. He stuck with it from pride, and from local patriotism. But now the idea of the Council-aided sports centre has turned all the drawbacks to advantages. The wily partisan may well escape from his prison yet again.□

Mark O'Neill

PARIS 1975

MY journey to Paris on May 28th, 1975, started from a soggy Second Division match at Elland Road fifteen years earlier. It progressed via Hull, Sunderland, Carlisle, Liverpool, Sutton, Colchester, Manchester, Wolverhampton and Tottenham, with many stops in between, and frequent diversions to Villa Park and Wembley. It was usually made in the company of the same travellers. Sometimes we all agreed it would be the last such journey. But in our more ecstatic moments we pledged to meet up on the day Leeds United reached the European Cup Final.

Of course, promises made in the slightly-addled state of post-match euphoria are apt to take no account of practical probelms. Firstly, tickets; 10,000 was a ridiculous allocation to the club—no chance of getting one there. But days of effort produced the magical slip of paper—anybody wanting to know the hang-out of the widest boy in London, please send s.a.e. to me. The other big obstacle was finding a means of transport which would return me to work by 9 a.m. on May 29th, but more of this later.

The Gare du Nord looked and sounded like the Gelderd End after a Lorimer special, and was attracting a largish growd of baffled French commuters. One of them told me that he'd studied English for several years, but had not come across this word 'Weregonnawin', although he did understand 'European Cup this year'. At this stage, the general mood was boisterous but not malicious and the good spirits predominated until we reached the Parc des Princes.

Looking back, there *were* indications of what was to follow — a scrum of Yorkshiremen helping themselves to the contents of a wine supermarket, and a French waiter peering from group to group of white-bedecked Leeds fans, anxiously trying to identify the particular party who had spent the afternoon drinking at his street cafe, only to leave before the bill came.

The nearest Metro station to the ground is situated in a large, elegant square. One of my few happy memories of the whole day is of emerging from underground to a barrage of sound with white, blue and gold everywhere. It was the meeting of two cultures — Paris on a warm, sunny evening with all that is chic, and the more earthy elements of English football supporters, noisy, colourful and revelling.

We got to the ground much too early. I'd been fingering my ticket nervously all day; in flashes of sweaty apprehension, I'd imagined it slipping irretrievably down some French grid, so it was a relief to get inside. The bar underneath the stand was open, and doing great business. Before long, the barman had become familiar with 'three halves of lager, mate', and was even taking English money. An hour before the kick-off, a roar from upstairs told us that the team had come out for a look at the pitch. A stampede for the staircase — the way blocked by a one-legged French official in a beret (honest), trying to collect ticket stubs. He didn't appreciate the urgency of the situation and was pushed aside.

* * *

I enjoyed waiting for the kick-off; lots of songs, a few lagers and, best of all, knowing that, short of an earthquake or a sudden attack of blindness, I was going to see my team play in a European Cup Final. The game itself is no longer news. In any case, I could not even attempt an objective account of penalty refusals or Lorimer's disallowed goal. All I can tell you is that for about ten seconds after Lorimer's shot hit the net, we were all convinced that Leeds had won the European Cup, and that it was a pretty good feeling.

The effect of the referee's decision to disallow the goal is well-known. The youth who had been analysing the game quite sensibly for me at half-time stamped on his seat. It broke, and he threw the two halves down the terracing to join numerous other bits of orange plastic. A sheet of glass landed squarely on the head of someone in front of me; he didn't flinch, but just picked up the biggest piece and threw it further down the steps. And so it went on — Bayern scored, and just to rub it in, did it again. For genuine Leeds supporters, the tragedy was that Liverpool, or Celtic, or Manchester United fans in the same situation would have got behind their team and yelled them back into the game (although they might have still destroyed the stadium afterwards).

When the line of riot police, armed with crash helmets, truncheons and shields, formed up at the bottom of the stand, my feeling of disgust at being associated with events going on around me was compounded by fear, and I left the game a few minutes early. Outside, the trouble continued: to the family whose front room window was smashed by a brick, sorry; I saw him pick it up and was too cowardly to stop him.

I left the area of the ground and once far enough away to feel safe, reviewed my position — overwhelming disappointment, a feeling of total flatness, a night to kill in Paris, nowhere to stay (I'd thought we'd be out celebrating), and an acute sense of shame. We drank in Montmartre — the 'SuperLeeds' banners at least ensured prompt service and free passage down the pavements — and tried to work out why the riot had occurred.

The usual arguments about social problems obviously applied to some extent, but this particular burst of aggro was directed at something specific, compared to the usual premeditated frolics of a Saturday afternoon. Being abroad, a sense of immunity from prosecution, drink, the effort and expense of getting to Paris (these were ordinary blokes with ordinary jobs, for whom this game was an alternative to a summer holiday), all contributed. But above all, it was an irrational response to something every Leeds supporter had seen before — failure at the last hurdle, often connected with a bad refereeing decision.

To understand this you'd have to be a Leeds supporter and be familiar with the list of occasions on which it has seemed easier to blame the referee than the team. It began when Ken Burns disallowed Lorimer's free-kick in a Villa Park semi-final against Chelsea; we all hoped it had ended after the Cup Winners' Cup Final in Salonika. Yet it had happened again, the killer blow to a side probably past its best, with no chance of that particular line-up reaching a European Cup Final again. Worst of all, perhaps, was the knowledge that our much-abused Leeds team had lost the chance to silence a decade of criticism.

My own immediate future looked pretty bleak too. I did get a bed for the night; I did oversleep and miss my plane; the ferries were on strike; so were those planes that weren't fully booked; and yes, I should have been at work an hour ago. When I finally did get a flight back, I arrived home to find the most ghastly sight of all staring up at me from the door-mat — a copy of every daily newspaper for May 29th, which I'd ordered before leaving. ●

Philip Augar

IN THE PRESENCE OF THE LORD

WITH the exception of West Ham's Reg Pratt (due to retire later this year), nobody has been chairman of a League club for longer than *Bob Lord*. This is his nineteenth year in the Burnley chair; longer than half the club's supporters have been alive. As a study of how one man can gain control of a football club, and then personally guide its destiny, the case of Bob Lord is unique.

Football could have died in Burnley, just as it is surely dying in Bury, Barrow, Halifax and Rochdale. The reason that it has not, and the reason that any one outside NE Lancs has heard of the town, is because of his vision. When all is said and done, this fact at least, cannot be taken away from him. He says that he realised the heart of the matter very early in life: "I knew, when I was your age, that Burnley, with a population of 74,000, could never support a successful League club on gates alone." But instead of trusting to luck, as have other clubs, to throw up a player every two or three years, whose sale will command a fee large enough to clear the overdraft, Burnley

have evolved the System. This has taken twenty years to put together, and the fact that Burnley were relegated 3 years ago was only due, in his view, to temporary defects. To a less committed observer however, the composition of the present team makes it less than a 'typical' Burnley side.

Two preconditions were necessary. The first was laid when Burnley acquired the 79-acre Gawthorpe Hall, with its seven training pitches, all weather surface, and staggering appreciation in terms of wealth. When granite-hearted Alan Brown heard the news (it was he who spotted Gawthorpe first, taking tea there with the caretaker), he reputedly embraced the two messengers and pronounced "now we'll get somewhere with our youth policy". Who was actually responsible for the purchase of this Lancashire gold mine has been lost to the chronicler, but we know who takes the credit.

The second was, and is, the inexorable continuity of the Plan, which ensures turnover at first team as much as at youth level. Not Ray Bloye's instant jam today and bouncing cheques

tomorrow (where will the bills be sent?). "I have never sold a player either too early or too late," says Lord, and will produce chapter and verse to support his case, whether it be the sale of Jimmy MacIlroy or Dave Thomas. Examine the records of Harris, Irvine, Coates and Elder, all fat fees who contributed little to the clubs they joined after leaving Turf Moor.

These conditions of employment are most attractive to the schoolboy star, and, more important, his father. Burnley have established a reputation for being the good shepherd to the lost youths who come to them, talented striplings for whom the

reward is the offer of a first team shirt. Lord stresses the benefits of the warmth and homeliness of a small town compared to the anonymity and fleshpots of the metropolis.

How has Lord guaranteed this continuity? Only by a gradual process of elimination of the Lordless elements in the mixture. He joined the Board in 1951 with the minimum 35 shares, and admits "they let me on by accident, while the team was in Turkey". Within four years he was chairman: "When I became chairman, it was the custom that each chairman should do the job for three years and then retire to let another member of the Board take over. Now that's not the way to run a business. . . When I became chairman there were nine directors." Now there are just four others.

He sees his operation as successful only if every turret is manned by a private picked for that very post and none other. Lord remarked on the voluntary unanimity of the directors, adding that he does not vote himself. The training staff and managers — men like Dougal and Bannion — are and have been men with claret blood in their veins. This did not save Alan

Brown, whose youth policy produced the League Championship side of 1960. He left for Sunderland in 1957, "but I had not spoken to him for twelve months before then. He was getting too bigheaded for his own good." Bob Lord also abhors what he euphemistically calls 'wastage'. Harry Potts, manager of the triumphant team of the early sixties, agreed to be moved upstairs to the post of 'general manager' soon after his fiftieth birthday (Jimmy Adamson is twelve years younger). But he did not succeed in creating sufficient work for himself, and had to go in July '72. Lord claims to have awarded him "the biggest golden handshake that had ever been seen in football. I like creating records."

Driven by this singleminded devotion, it is difficult to see why Lord has had so little effect on the League Management Committee. He tried to get on it for ten years before reluctant acceptance, but the reason, by his own admission, "was one of status". What reason could he have anyway, for proposing new statutes which, if resulting on the reorganising of other clubs along his own lines, would only be at the expense of Burnley? "The task of the League is purely to organise and administrate the four divisions, and not to meddle in the domestic affairs of the clubs."

In particular, this autonomy must be maintained against a move by the supporters to have any say in the running of the club. "It took me until 1962 or '63 to make sure we could control who got onto the Board. Even now it is theoretically possible for the shareholders, collecting all the dead votes, to vote someone on, since "I do not own a majority of the shares, and nor does the Board as a whole". But given his opinion that "it is fatal to allow shareholders to elect any Tom Dick or Harry," it is clear that such a proposition is to all intents and purposes impossible.

His devotion to the Plan means that it must also be defended against interference from supporters. "We don't recognise *any* supporters associations. I don't mind them existing – just won't have anything to do with them. I never go to Supporters' Dinners; it only costs them a fiver or so, but then they think they own you. In particular we never accept money from supporters associations; they hand you a couple of cheques for a few thousand, and the next thing you know they are demanding a seat on the Board in return. There is all the difference in the world between a supporter's viewpoint, and a director's viewpoint.

Where, then, is the Plan leading? Certainly not towards the democratisation of the League, or of Burnley FC. In fact, it is leading in the opposite direction. In the words of the pilot: "My ambition, what we are aiming for, is for the Club to function completely without any money coming through the turnstiles at all. That is the road to Utopia."●

No. 16   March 1974

Alan Stewart & Mark O'Neill

FIGHTING HK FINALLY GO DOWN TO WELSH

No. 32   April 1976

IN a pulsating clash at the Football Club last night the powerful Welsh side eventually overcame a fighting Hongkong team by 57 points to 3.

Hong Kong Standard 11/9/75

No. 23   November 1974

I understood then, for the first time, why some fellers who had the choice of a ball at their feet or a girl in their arms usually chose the girl. "Not me. When they passed me love letters under the desk at school—I flicked them back. I never squeezed the spots on my face because I wanted to be repulsive and keep the girls away."

Alan Ball in The People 29.9.74.

Yeovil say Oxford slope is too much

YEOVIL TOWN, the club with the notorious sloping pitch, refused yesterday to play their FA Cup second replay

Daily Mail 27/11/75

No. 32   April 1976

BRIAN CLOUGH had an almost impossible task in occupying the chair vacated by Don Revie.

Leeds have been a shadow of their normal selves and this is supported by players who have played against them in the past month.

RODNEY MARSH, Manchester City, who beat Leeds 2-1: "I was impressed with them at Maine Road. I had so much respect for them and I was proud to be a fellow professional. They behaved responsibly and players such as Johnny Giles and Norman Hunter got on with the job without any moans.

"I think dignified is the way I would describe them."

News of the World 15/9/74

COOKE: Any one of several teams could win the league. Do you feel this indicates the high quality of the English game or its mediocrity?

CHARLTON: I think the clubs with the best players don't always have the best method of play. Stoke probably have the best players in the First Division but they don't have the best way of playing.

COOKE: Are sufficient good minds coming into the game to ensure its future good health?

CHARLTON: Yes, but I think we've got to be allowed to work at our ideas and not be knocked down by the dirty word "method."

Evening News 12/4/75

No. 29   May 1975

119

UNITED WE FALL

ALL those drear Saturday afternoons, standing in the Stretford end or resting easier in the cantilever — occupied territory they call it now — I've watched them, the growing sorrow of the late sixties turning to that bitter hysteria which now greets a goal. Amidst the curses and those vague doubts about the will of God and the wisdom of referees, always the thought, "That muther in the box, they pay the bastard enough, why can't he DO something." I could never figure why the guy in the overcoat couldn't diagnose it, until I realised that no amount of foresight in '74 can ever cater for the lack of perception in the late sixties.

Manchester United were to so many people, and unhappily even to themselves, little more than a brilliant forward line. It was enough, enough to conquer Europe and a million hearts. Law, Charlton, Best, *they* were the Reds. It was a myth, it was a lie, but at that point it didn't matter, it was only later, later when the cracks appeared and rebuilding was needed that a sound knowledge of the foundations was both crucial, and painfully absent. Looking back, the man at the centre of the grace and style which made that team was not one of the above but rather one Patrick Crerand. They didn't sell his picture down the souvenir shop, didn't call him King, the girls didn't shout and swoon when he came to the touchline to take a throw-in, but all the time, it was Crerand, tackling, passing stroking the ball around, creating in a way that few players can, who set that team in motion.

As Law and Charlton aged we saw George pick up the crown, the afficionados did not fear time, the young saviour was at hand, why worry; no-one noticed the fading of Crerand and the hole left by his departure. That was the error, the tragic flaw, and having watched those poor bastards suffer like Sisyphus against Liverpool this Christmas I'm willing to invoke Sophoclean proportions.

It seems a maxim that if you don't score blame the forwards. But that's just not good enough. That ball must be in a position for them to score goals with it, and it is put there by the schemers, the midfield players, the Crerands. Don't give me this bullshit about Denis Law being inspired by the fresh Maine Road air. How do you explain it Mr Docherty, just that the boy scores goals when someone gives him the ball within about thirty yards of white wood, and City have the men to give him that ball.

The strange case of "The king is dead; long live the king" should, it won't, but it should, prove once and for all where United needs lie. Don't sack Macari, he's small, not very strong, but give him that ball where he can do something with it, and the chances are he too will prove his worth. Right now the poor sod has little better to do but run for a series of ridiculously optimistic long balls. Like one or two other players in that team he is forced by lack of the essential link men to play an unnatural game; is it any wonder he has lost his rhythm? It's diabolical to watch the way the last two years of this sort of stuff have hacked away at the style of Martin Buchan, but that's another story.

The heart of this cry from the terraces is the almost carnal desire I feel to see a great midfield creator once

again grace the Trafford turf. Greenhoff is showing great promise, but more in defence and gaining possession than in terms of setting up attacks. There was a time last year when I thought the call would be answered. They were moving for Hartford or Currie, but whichever paranoid Deity controls soccer looked unkindly, and the Lancashire brass was spurned. Now the fools seem to have given up. I'm of the opinion we should arm the Stretford end, send them on a scheduled flight to Madrid airport, then threaten to terrorise the fascists till they hand over Netzer. There would be a solution worthy of the red and the white.

Other oversights have cost Busby his happy old age (if he doesn't feel guilty, he bloody well should). We needn't bother with defence — any team that could win the league with Pat Dunne, Shay Brennan, and Tony Dunne — clearly didn't need a defence. Except for centre-half. After Busby allowed himself to be outmanouvered by Spurs for the signature of Mike England in 1966, it was clear that the centre could not hold, and that anarchy was the best any one could hope for. We got Ure, and then we got Sadler, and Edwards and James, and others I may have forgotten, all players of some mild quality, but not IT. A centre half has to be as solid as a rock and all the aforementioned had a little too much of plastic about them. I left out one name, the latest, and despite all Brian Glanville's accusations of bestial origin and psychopathic leanings, I still believe that James Holton esquire is the best thing Docherty has done for Manchester and the best thing to happen at Old Trafford since they used to play a radio recording of the Benfica game at half-time. When he takes those enforced legal absences he's missed, like a junkie misses his needle

The most mindless aspect about the criticism heaped on Holton has been the "a disgrace to the tradition of Manchester United" approach. Remember the long regretted Maurice Setters, the human scythe, so much a part of the early sixties team. And of course, young Jim's precursor, Norbert Stiles. Now that boy was rough but he was vital to any success that was achieved. Just as we never gave Stiles the credit he deserved so we never gave enough attention to that midfield position. Even Crerand had a way of going into a tackle with right leg splayed forward to take the ball but the left one dragging behind to win it if the sucker went the other way. Then for the lean years, the centre park became little more than surrendered territory. The hard man, the ball winner, the third link that no-one appreciated till too late, and Willie Morgan has to play midfield.

The thought of Morgan brings us full circle, for there is a player of large talents, who must squander them in midfield because of that central error. They never replaced Crerand. Busby, McGuinness, O'Farrell, Docherty are all in their way to blame. But George Graham, I mean alongside the memory of Crerand, the man, for all his hard work, is the real insult to a tradition. There's still a gaping hole that no shit-kicking 15-goal-a-season forward is going to fill. Gunther Netzer, won't you please come home? ●

Tony Wilson

No. 15   February 1974

LETTER

Dear FOUL,

There will be precious little "alternative" about your paper if you print many more articles written in the cretinous manner of Tony Wilson's "United We Fall" (FOUL 15), whose style — if I may adopt Mr Wilson's idiom — makes Julie Welch read like Ruskin. Surely FOUL represents a reaction against the inanity, affectation and hyperbole of current football journalism, yet here was an article which brought these vices onto its own pages.

Mr Wilson feels an "almost carnal desire" to see a great midfield creator rather than any "shit-kicking 15-goal-a-season forward". Carnal desire? — it can't be true, not in FOUL, any more than the absurd affectation of "Norbert" Stiles or "James Holton esquire" (what does that achieve?).

But amid all the shit-kicking, the poor sods and the bullshit comes, incongruously, this gem: "That was the error, the tragic flaw, and having watched those poor bastards suffer like Sisyphus against Liverpool this Christmas I'm willing to invoke Sophoclean proportions." The point of the Sisyphus legend, of course, is that the suffering is caused by repeatedly reaching the very verge of success, being denied that success and having to start again — is this really what happened to United against Liverpool? Even allowing for the hyperbole, just how pale an imitation of Geoffrey Green this is may be illustrated by quoting that writer's use of the same legend in his report of the Cup Final Replay in 1970, after another frustrating season for Leeds: "Leeds, like Sisyphus, have pushed three boulders almost to the top of three mountains and are now left to see them all back in the dark of the valley" (*The Times*, 30th April 1970).

Clearly it would be wrong to condemn your paper on the grounds of one puerile article, but its inclusion was nonetheless disturbing as it suggests a possible compromise of your standards. The argument was sensible enough but it was almost completely obscured by the manner of writing — not only no alternative to what we read elsewhere, but a gabbled hotch-potch of all that is bad in those other writers. Leave Sisyphus and shit-kicking to Printing House Square and Fleet Street, and concentrate on the reasoned and witty writing at which FOUL excels.

Yours
Sean Magee
London N6

No. 16 March 1974

PARROTS

"SPURS are a world-wide institution and there's no way I'm going to give up the fight to try and save them. The chairman is probably eating his heart out but keeping a stiff upper lip. That makes it tough for me, but I don't lose any sleep over it."

Reading Terry Neill's terrible bromides in the *Daily Mirror* last March (*you* try eating your heart out without moving your lips) made me pull down from the shelves George Orwell's essay *Politics and the English Language*. Whose gist was that slovenly diction and hackneyed prose is a sign of the greater idleness and reactionary way of thinking permeating social, business, literary and political life.

I'm not suggesting that Spurs' bad play is a cause of Terry Neill's not being able to string his words together very well, but I do think that to trot out the same old cabbage in interviews is merely diverting attention from the actual problems being 'faced'. Whenever Neill was called on to account for himself last season — plenty of times, in the London area — out came the familiar backs to the wall and driving seats and socks needed up-pulling. Not because he had to say these things, but because it was expected of him: assuming sombre mien and delivering guff on *The Big Match* earned Neill the compliments 'frank', 'brave', 'no-nonsense' etc.

This has been the year of the continuing 'No Way' syndrome, of being over the moon one match and sick as a parrot the next. Everything footballers are saying now — or rather, are reported as saying, a different matter — is as much fashion and imitation as the suits they wear; it all gets turned into variations on the same reactions, pleasure and moans, so it begins to be indistinguishable from ghost-writing. Dropped stars might as well nail a bulletin to their Tudor front doors: 'Say I am sick'.

The press is entirely to blame for this. The weekly stream of hacked-out copy can be expected in match reports, just the names and details changed, but it now seems to be spreading to news and features also. To note that Alan Taylor is over the moon at scoring or that John Mitchell feels 'fabulous' at being selected becomes as prosaic and finally dispensable as writing down the facts of Taylor's bargain transfer or Mitchell's raise from the reserves. It's something to do with the hand-in-hand nature of stories and incidents, and the emotions that go with them — just as the whole aim of a football report will be geared towards justifying the final score.

This isn't the same as defining why a team won or lost: the exigencies of match reporting mean that seven-eighths of what actually happened on the field will be ignored if it doesn't tally with the result (unless, of course, it can be turned easily into the 'Robbery!' headline-category). The match report's idiot brother, the television commentary, makes this sort of practice easier to grasp, as well as throwing up one or two abuses of its own.

We all know what Coleman is like — verdicts on saves or near-miss free kicks delivered as if burned into stone tablets; Davies's mind and mouth will be a minute behind what he's watching: "He got to it, but only just... though the only just was the determining factor";

Hill will pick out some piece of individual skill not because it's particularly enlightening, or can be deduced by the viewer, but because it's *obvious*: pick yourself a Man of the Match and you can justify or point to *anything* he's done. Going to ludicrous extremes, Moore will add a spurious commentary to some pirated European clip — the 'incredibles' come out just as easily as if he'd actually been there.

What I'm trying to say is that all these reactions are programmed, after the fact: Spurs lose a few matches, so Neill is wheeled out to proclaim that he's keeping his chin up though his heart is in his boots — what else can he say? They win a couple on the trot so then it's a case of we think we've turned the corner at last though it's early days yet... don't you just long for Revie to come on television after another enigmatic England performance and announce: "Fucked if I know what to do for the best!"?

So let's not laugh too easily at the thousand post-mortem interviews where "there it was in the back of the net" — it's the same as you'll see in a thousand match reports. If *Foul* has proved anything it's that between players and spectators there's an enormous common scorn and loathing for such offences against the game as Bob Wilson's lunchtime preview. We obviously all feel the same resignation towards the press, the snake pit separating the sport from its public. Trample the Monte Frescos! This spirit must not disappear. If it does, then I'm afraid our pig is dead.

Andrew Nickolds

No. 30 June 1975

"The level of discourse . . .
was here on the level of the
public bar.**"**

BRIAN GLANVILLE

4 We'll get you in the end

Although *FOUL* staggered on for another four issues after no.30, they were somehow something of a parody of what had gone before, and never quite recaptured the original spirit. Anyway, the valedictory articles in no.30, (reprinted in this chapter) still contained the essentials of why *FOUL*'s departure was significant, and what it had achieved in its lifetime, even if they turned out to be slightly premature. Fortunately, they also found time to stick the knife in Don Revie one more time . . .

FOULMO!*!*!!UTH

IS THIS THE END?

STORY SO FAR: October 1972. In a small town in East Anglia — just a 4th division football team — is born FOUL, spawned by a dedicated band of enthusiasts who see the land of Football being over-run by Cloggers and Con-men. Its dreams and its potential are being choked and drowned by petrol and cigarette smoke: but its dictator, the dreaded Sir 'Alf Wit, and his henchmen at The Leeg and The Sweet F.A. tell the people that all is well.

The friends of FOUL spread across the nation, are recognised by the men of Tee Vee and the Press Gangs, only to be spurned and rejected. 'You say nothing original,' scorns Jeff Fowell. 'You have had no effect,' says the venerable Des Hack. You *know* nothing, you *are* nothing.

Football men are divided. The Cloggers and those who pay Them are outraged — some even threaten violence. 'I'll throw them in the bath!' screams Big Mal, fearsome South London boss-man.

A year old and moved to London,

FOUL needs money to spread the gospel. Rich friends are sympathetic; the willing workers, unbeknown to many fans, continue to help for no financial gain. And the new ideas began to gain acceptance. Sir 'Alf fails the people again and again; the Press Gangs turn against him and ask What's Wrong With Football?

The Sweet F.A. take action to pacify everyone. Changes are made in the secretariat, and the eldest of the elders brought together to Make Recommendations. Sir 'Alf is deposed, the Press Gangs feign sympathy, then welcome his successor — The Godfather!

Meanwhile, confusion reigns. The players elect a wicked Northern Hunter as their ideal warrior — then change their minds within nine months; denied firm leadership, they launch an unconvincing campaign for freedom from their masters. The Leeg are appalled as the players rebel and the people desert them; but refuse to implement real change.

FOUL demands a shift of power, with the players and people given a

voice, but its message is not always heard. Its supporters are loyal and responsive, but not numerous enough. 'Where can I find this FOUL?' ask others, in vain. An increased price has to be asked, yet still bills are not paid. 'Advertise your wares with us, that we may stay alive', beg the friends of FOUL. The call is unanswered, and the Rich Ones worry more and more. FOUL is much loved, but under-nourished. . . too weak to do its job as it should, with helpers constantly at its side. For they, too, must earn their daily bread.

And then. . .

'Enough!' cry the Rich Ones. 'No longer can we support you. Much as we love you, you must make your own way in the world or die.'

So. . . are there no Friends able to save SuperFOUL? Must the forces of The Leeg and the Sweet F.A. rule un-opposed? The voices of the Batt Man and the Coal Man go unanswered? Can our hero be struck down at 30?

IS THIS THE END???

A legend from mythology, a legend about power and strength, life and death; a legend so terrifying it can have only one fatal end . . .

The Godfather, Part II

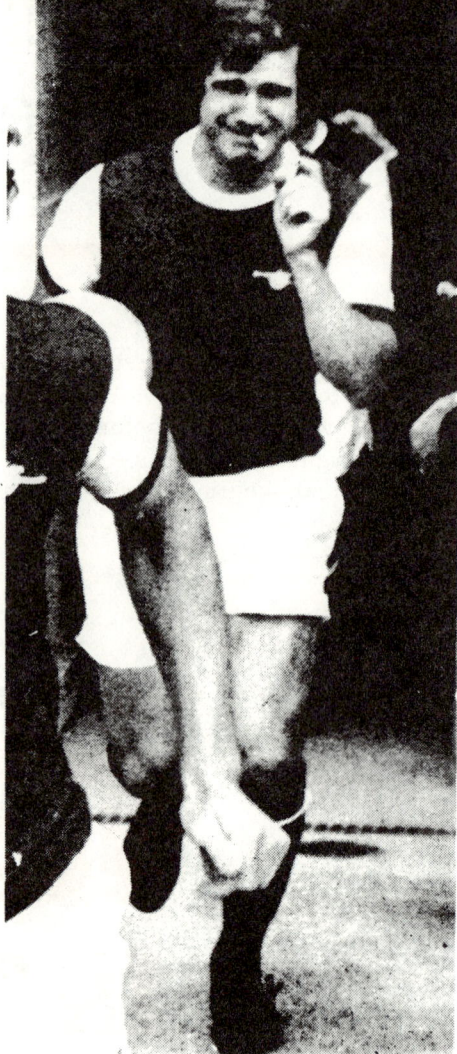

(ON THE basis that football is an accurate mirror of society, for this last issue of *Foul* I thought I would tell you a story, with a little quiz at the end to test your apprehension of the tale.)

Once upon a time, the rulers of a certain country found themselves faced with a crisis. Although there was an obvious solution to the crisis, it would have meant them losing their wealth and power; therefore they searched around for another solution.

They hit upon the idea that what was needed was a strong national leader, one who had proved his abilities as leader of a small group in hostilities with other small groups. The man they chose had a bad reputation, one of ruthlessness. This was unfortunate (the reputation, not the ruthlessness: they were not averse to the latter, only concerned about the former). So the first thing to be done was to change the man's image. This was easy, for the newspapers, being owned by friends of the rulers, helped by depicting the man's group as a cosy family affair, the members of which loved each other as brothers, loved the leader as a benevolent godfather, and dutifully worshipped their children and their country's gods.

The first thing the man did on his new appointment was authorize a new uniform. Uniforms meant a lot to him. He had done the same when taking over his group many years before.

And so, with a new uniform, with much appealing to his countrymen's patriotism, and amid much public calling on his god for help, the chosen man shed his former image and took his place as head of the whole show.

Consider how far he had come: from boss of a small gang which disposed of opponents in a most primitive way, especially when defending its home territory, to someone who rubbed shoulders with the highest officials in the land; from a street-corner thug to a member of the establishment. Once on top, he disavowed some of his earliest methods (although he did go on record as saying that the answer to hooliganism was flogging).

What sort of man was he? We can best answer by pointing out what type of society it was. . . A very primitive society, which, though it could produce things in abundance, could find no way of distributing them properly, or of averting periodic crises.

In this primitive society, prowess manifested itself mainly in two ways — force and fraud. From the lowest to the highest, from delinquents to rulers, a sort of low cunning was a highly prized characteristic. They called it "astuteness". This man, like the men who had chosen him, possessed this characteristic to a remarkable degree. The biggest change he underwent was from an early reliance on bare-faced ferocity to a later subtlety in execution.

WHO WAS HE?   (a) **Al Capone**
                                 (b) **Adolf Hitler**
                                 (c) **Don Revie**

<u>WARNING</u>: PLAYING FOOTBALL MAY DAMAGE YOUR HEALTH

THE GODFATHER's previously blissful relationship with the national press is becoming a little cooler. There's no danger yet of a return to Ramsey days (like the Berlin international, when the press first heard his horrendous team changes over the stadium loudspeaker), but the Don fears that he and his lads are not getting an entirely fair deal.

The McGhee/Clough/Powell triumvirate, anxious to maintain the coffee-and-biscuits intimacy of Revie press conferences, has managed to persuade him that it's all the fault of sensationalist sub-editors composing misleading headlines.

Don has therefore summoned Sports Editors of all the pop papers (*Times*, *Telegraph*, *Guardian* need not apply), to attend England's summer get-together in darkest Cockfosters, where he'll put them straight.

Meantime, those Fleet Street reporters whose allegiance is in any doubt have been taking every opportunity — the Keegan affair was a perfect one — to establish whose side they are on.

A Long Goodbye

Brushing a tear from his eye and a moth from his wallet, GEOFF McDONALD bids a last farewell to his faithful readership.

AS RINGO STARR once remarked, this famous business can get out of hand. The champagne and knighthood bit is okay, you can get used to that, but it's not being able to get round the pub for eighteen pints of wallop with your mates, it's having to walk around with your head in a brown paper bag for fear of the fans with nail scissors. And worst of all, it's having to write for Fleet Street under silly names like Chris Lightbown, and appear on television with a hairpiece stuck on your chin. Where's the sense, where's the style, where's the glamour in that? As Teilhard de Chardin has written: 'It's a mug's game. I'd as soon muck out the Bishop of Bruges.'

The sad truth, *Foul* fans, is that the game is up for us selfless servants of all that is of good report in our national sport; we can no longer bear the strain that is the price of international stardom; we are off to join the circus. Stanley Baldwin, politician, statesman and father of the quicksilver Chelsea striker was once heard to comment (to Wally Barnes, I believe) that it's time to pull out when they start naming international centre-forwards after you, and if ever a wiser sentiment was expressed I was out of earshot. With Mike England's retirement to the BBC, the Peter Mellor Final and Malcolm Macdonald's hatful at Wembley still fresh in our memories, we feel that we have chosen an appropriate moment to step out of the spotlight. We are confident that we leave the game in good hands; as Brian Moore is fond of saying, 'Apres moi, The Persuaders'.

But we cannot leave without saying what a very great pleasure it has been to have you take us into your homes, to laugh at our jokes, to nod sagely with our editorials, and to pass us around among your mates at work, or on the terraces when you have felt the need of something to take your minds off the game. It has been the thought of you, the little people who agree with every word we write, that has given us the will to keep going when the pressures of our enormous wealth have constrained us to chuck it all up and vote Tory. It hasn't always been easy, with Don Revie on the line begging us to tell him how Colin Viljoen measures up against Alan Ball, to remember that our views cannot be leaked, not even to the England Supremo, but that our first loyalty must always be to you, the readers. For, as D.H. Lawrence asked, 'A writer/Without readers/What is he/

But a clown?' Yet we do not regret our three years on the razor's edge. We may be bald, haggard and hooked on cowgum, but we are able to reflect with pride on all that has been achieved; to change the face of journalism; to become legends in our own time; but above all to be a source of pleasure and amusement to you, the humble men on the terraces who would be at a loss as to what to think about were it not for our gentle guidance.

Perhaps the most moving moments of my time with *Foul* have been the mornings when Alan or Steve would phone me at home and say, "Geoff, there are a couple of hundred letters for you here", and I would dutifully drive round to the office and spend perhaps as much as two or three hours just sifting through them. How very gratifying it is to learn that one's labours have not been in vain, and while it would be an exaggeration to say that all the jokes in *Vince of the Villa* got the recognition they deserved, it is nonetheless encouraging to receive the praises of men like Eric Idle and J.K. Galbraith, of women like Simone de Beauvoir and Isobel Barnet and, of course, of you wonderful little people from places as far apart as Halifax and Ho Chi Minh City. Even the pathetic begging letters from Sam Leitch and Billy Wright sometimes find a way to one's heart. It is at times such as these that one is most apt to recall the words of journalist Tom Wolfe: 'Hot shit!!! Who'd be a bus-driver??!!**???**!!?'

Regrets? There have been a few. . . but then again, what else can one expect? One's commitment to *Foul* and the *Foul* ethos has from time to time obliged one to turn down what would, under other circumstances, have been most attractive offers. It would, for example, have been fun to prepare a biography of George Best, but one would hardly have been able to give such a project the benefit of one's whole attention, with the likely result that the finished article would have fallen short of that standard of excellence to which *Foul* readers have become accustomed. Yet how keen was one's regret when it was noised abroad that George — ever a capricious lad — had turned around and handed over the commission to the first hack to heave into view! And when one sampled the fruits of that unfortunate collaboration tears filled the eyes. One felt that a grave injustice had been done to the book-buying public.

One would also dearly have loved to accompany Il Glanville on his fact-finding, stone-turning, muck-raking, graft-probing tour of Italy and Eastern Europe — a tour that, in the fullness of time, is all but certain to come up with a story of some description. Perhaps if I had been at his side the great man would not have lost heart so easily and turned towards his unsubstantiated allegations of goals and excitement at Brisbane Road. If you are reading this Brian, and I know you always like to keep up with the really important writings, my message is this: Don't give up. Perhaps if your grasp of Serbo-Croat had matched your mastery of the Italian language it would have been a different story.

Then there are the innumerable stories, interviews and exposes that the pressures of space and deadlines have prevented us using. Brian Clough's account of his weekend with the Revies, for example, fairly bristled with human interest and carried a big punch, but its style was weak and we have always insisted on handing our public a clearly-written as well as a pungent and witty twelve pennorth. Similar arguments persuaded us to give a reluctant thumbs-down to the word-for-word transcription of that lively dialogue between Ron Saunders and the directors of Norwich City on the occasion of Aston Villa's triumph in the League Cup Final. This, we felt, was a document of real interest to the soccer-minded public, yet the language was of such a vulgar nature that no guardian of decency and clean-living could think of publishing it. Our motto in these matters has always been a phrase made popular by the Caesar Marcus Aurelius: "When in doubt, don't."

Yet, what are these regrets when weighed against the achievements of the *Foul* era? When we first hit the news-stands, football was thriving as a national hypocrisy; Denis Law, Bill Shankly, George Best, Ian Moore and Gordon Hill were still active, but so, too, was Norman Burtenshaw. Chelsea were in the First Division, Middlesborough and Huddersfield in the Second. Now, so widespread is disenchantment among intelligent men that clubs are having to talk of half-price admission for those with an IQ of over 80. Hugh Johns has to go about with an armed escort. The Stretford End are putting up a candidate to oppose Winston Churchill come the next election. Married women are sending back their locks of Charlie George's hair. *Foul*'s fearless stand has given Football the Manipulator a big push towards the exit, and we urge you, the little folk, to carry on our good work, in Soren Kierkegaard's colourful phrase, "by voting with your feet".

Goodbye. We love you.

Last Ball

GO ON, they said, write about the last three years. You can have 700 words. Trends, developments, that sort of thing.

But it is too close, really. Things have changed a bit. Arsenal haven't won anything over that period, which can't be bad. And in spite of Norman Hunter winning the PFA Player of the Year award the season before last, the continuing presence of Storey and Chopper Harris, indeed the continuing supply of candidates for the Foul Award, the game has become a bit more civilised. Only a bit perhaps. Too many coaches and managers still ask 'how long will he run for me?' rather than 'how skilful is he?' when selecting a player. Cynicism is still rampant. Referees still wave the book at the first sign of dissent, while watching blithely while leg-breaking tackles fly around. A commentator can still say happily, as David Coleman did in the England v Wales game, 'Francis *had* to foul him', when Leighton James had bamboozled his opponent and was then pulled back by the shirt. And maybe the mediocrity of the first division last season says there is a long way to go.

But it still seems that there is a trend towards better days. In the last four years, Leeds and Derby twice have won the first division. Leeds were still a 'professional' side with all its bad connotations. But they also won the title by playing positive football of the highest order. In Europe, the evidence has been wholly positive. Ajax and Bayern Munich have been European champions. You couldn't ask for better representatives for positive creative football. In the World Cup, if the final was a disappointment, the presence of Holland and West Germany gave the same message, as did the early failure of Italy, and the absence of that terrible stereotyped English team.

Perhaps the most encouraging sign of all, though, was what happened in the lower divisions of the Football League. In the second, Manchester United, Norwich City, Sunderland and Aston Villa came out top. Hardly surprising, except that they all succeeded by positive football. It was especially good coming from Villa. When Ron Saunders manages a side which has small ball players, and attacks away from home, the wind of change begins to show signs of becoming a gale. If the sadness at Sunderland's ultimate failure could be assuaged, then the surprising pleasure one could get from Villa does it.

Lower down too, success went to the teams who played positively, rather than just being organised big runners. Plymouth, Blackburn and Charlton all gave a surprising amount of pleasure last season. Even by encouraging wingers. All good stuff, and something which gives me a lot of hope that the trend for positive football will continue.

Off the field, though, the same old faces still rule in the same unimaginative reactionary way. Alan Hardaker shows no signs of realising that what was good enough for 1888 is not necessarily ideal in 1975. Fans are still treated with absolute contempt by the clubs who need them. Sponsorship is producing abortions all over the place — the Texaco Cup and England's shirts being two manifestations we can do without. And of course the thing which would give positive skilful football its greatest boost, cutting down on the number of games, is further away than ever. While football is run in the way it is, our hopeful trends will have a hard struggle to exist — even as hopeful trends. In the end you can only salute the players, and the managers, for a brave fight against a stultifying structure and abysmal leadership. They, who receive most of the bad publicity going, should only receive our thanks for continuing to produce the creativity they do.

Peter Ball

'A team of eleven Berti Vogtses would be unbeatable'

from Shoot's Kevin Keegan Column

VOTED: LD'S MOST E MAGAZINE

125

A Long Goodbye

Brushing a tear from his eye and a moth from his wallet, GEOFF McDONALD bids a last farewell to his faithful readership.

AS RINGO STARR once remarked, this famous business can get out of hand. The champagne and knighthood bit is okay, you can get used to that, but it's not being able to get round the pub for eighteen pints of wallop with your mates, it's having to walk around with your head in a brown paper bag for fear of the fans with nail scissors. And worst of all, it's having to write for Fleet Street under silly names like Chris Lightbown, and appear on television with a hairpiece stuck on your chin. Where's the sense, where's the style, where's the glamour in that? As Teilhard de Chardin has written: 'It's a mug's game. I'd as soon muck out the Bishop of Bruges.'

The sad truth, *Foul* fans, is that the game is up for us selfless servants of all that is of good report in our national sport; we can no longer bear the strain that is the price of international stardom; we are off to join the circus. Stanley Baldwin, politician, statesman and father of the quicksilver Chelsea striker was once heard to comment (to Wally Barnes, I believe) that it's time to pull out when they start naming international centre-forwards after you, and if ever a wiser sentiment was expressed I was out of earshot. With Mike England's retirement to the BBC, the Peter Mellor Final and Malcolm Macdonald's hatful at Wembley still fresh in our memories, we feel that we have chosen an appropriate moment to step out of the spotlight. We are confident that we leave the game in good hands; as Brian Moore is fond of saying, 'Apres moi, The Persuaders'.

But we cannot leave without saying what a very great pleasure it has been to have you take us into your homes, to laugh at our jokes, to nod sagely with our editorials, and to pass us around among your mates at work, or on the terraces when you have felt the need of something to take your minds off the game. It has been the thought of you, the little people who agree with every word we write, that has given us the will to keep going when the pressures of our enormous wealth have constrained us to chuck it all up and vote Tory. It hasn't always been easy, with Don Revie on the line begging us to tell him how Colin Viljoen measures up against Alan Ball, to remember that our views cannot be leaked, not even to the England Supremo, but that our first loyalty must always be to you, the readers. For, as D.H. Lawrence asked, 'A writer/Without readers/What is he/

But a clown?' Yet we do not regret our three years on the razor's edge. We may be bald, haggard and hooked on cowgum, but we are able to reflect with pride on all that has been achieved; to change the face of journalism; to become legends in our own time; but above all to be a source of pleasure and amusement to you, the humble men on the terraces who would be at a loss as to what to think about were it not for our gentle guidance.

Perhaps the most moving moments of my time with *Foul* have been the mornings when Alan or Steve would phone me at home and say, "Geoff, there are a couple of hundred letters for you here", and I would dutifully drive round to the office and spend perhaps as much as two or three hours just sifting through them. How very gratifying it is to learn that one's labours have not been in vain, and while it would be an exaggeration to say that all the jokes in *Vince of the Villa* got the recognition they deserved, it is nonetheless encouraging to receive the praises of men like Eric Idle and J.K. Galbraith, of women like Simone de Beauvoir and Isobel Barnet and, of course, of you wonderful little people from places as far apart as Halifax and Ho Chi Minh City. Even the pathetic begging letters from Sam Leitch and Billy Wright sometimes find a way to one's heart. It is at times such as these that one is most apt to recall the words of journalist Tom Wolfe: 'Hot shit!!! Who'd be a bus-driver??!!**???**!!?'

Regrets? There have been a few. . . but then again, what else can one expect? One's commitment to *Foul* and the *Foul* ethos has from time to time obliged one to turn down what would, under other circumstances, have been most attractive offers. It would, for example, have been fun to prepare a biography of George Best, but one would hardly have been able to give such a project the benefit of one's whole attention, with the likely result that the finished article would have fallen short of that standard of excellence to which *Foul* readers have become accustomed. Yet how keen was one's regret when it was noised abroad that George — ever a capricious lad — had turned around and handed over the commission to the first hack to heave into view! And when one sampled the fruits of that unfortunate collaboration tears filled the eyes. One felt that a grave injustice had been done to the book-buying public.

One would also dearly have loved to accompany Il Glanville on his fact-finding, stone-turning, muck-raking, graft-probing tour of Italy and Eastern Europe — a tour that, in the fullness of time, is all but certain to come up with a story of some description. Perhaps if I had been at his side the great man would not have lost heart so easily and turned towards his unsubstantiated allegations of goals and excitement at Brisbane Road. If you are reading this Brian, and I know you always like to keep up with the really important writings, my message is this: Don't give up. Perhaps if your grasp of Serbo-Croat had matched your mastery of the Italian language it would have been a different story.

Then there are the innumerable stories, interviews and exposes that the pressures of space and deadlines have prevented us using. Brian Clough's account of his weekend with the Revies, for example, fairly bristled with human interest and carried a big punch, but its style was weak and we have always insisted on handing our public a clearly-written as well as a pungent and witty twelve pennorth. Similar arguments persuaded us to give a reluctant thumbs-down to the word-for-word transcription of that lively dialogue between Ron Saunders and the directors of Norwich City on the occasion of Aston Villa's triumph in the League Cup Final. This, we felt, was a document of real interest to the soccer-minded public, yet the language was of such a vulgar nature that no guardian of decency and clean-living could think of publishing it. Our motto in these matters has always been a phrase made popular by the Caesar Marcus Aurelius: "When in doubt, don't."

Yet, what are these regrets when weighed against the achievements of the *Foul* era? When we first hit the news-stands, football was thriving as a national hypocrisy; Denis Law, Bill Shankly, George Best, Ian Moore and Gordon Hill were still active, but so, too, was Norman Burtenshaw. Chelsea were in the First Division, Middlesborough and Huddersfield in the Second. Now, so widespread is disenchantment among intelligent men that clubs are having to talk of half-price admission for those with an IQ of over 80. Hugh Johns has to go about with an armed escort. The Stretford End are putting up a candidate to oppose Winston Churchill come the next election. Married women are sending back their locks of Charlie George's hair. *Foul*'s fearless stand has given Football the Manipulator a big push towards the exit, and we urge you, the little folk, to carry on our good work, in Soren Kierkegaard's colourful phrase, "by voting with your feet".

Goodbye. We love you.

Last Ball

GO ON, they said, write about the last three years. You can have 700 words. Trends, developments, that sort of thing.

But it is too close, really. Things have changed a bit. Arsenal haven't won anything over that period, which can't be bad. And in spite of Norman Hunter winning the PFA Player of the Year award the season before last, the continuing presence of Storey and Chopper Harris, indeed the continuing supply of candidates for the Foul Award, the game has become a bit more civilised. Only a bit perhaps. Too many coaches and managers still ask 'how long will he run for me?' rather than 'how skilful is he?' when selecting a player. Cynicism is still rampant. Referees still wave the book at the first sign of dissent, while watching blithely while leg-breaking tackles fly around. A commentator can still say happily, as David Coleman did in the England v Wales game, 'Francis *had* to foul him', when Leighton James had bamboozled his opponent and was then pulled back by the shirt. And maybe the mediocrity of the first division last season says there is a long way to go.

But it still seems that there is a trend towards better days. In the last four years, Leeds and Derby twice have won the first division. Leeds were still a 'professional' side with all its bad connotations. But they also won the title by playing positive football of the highest order. In Europe, the evidence has been wholly positive. Ajax and Bayern Munich have been European champions. You couldn't ask for better representatives for positive creative football. In the World Cup, if the final was a disappointment, the presence of Holland and West Germany gave the same message, as did the early failure of Italy, and the absence of that terrible stereotyped English team.

Perhaps the most encouraging sign of all, though, was what happened in the lower divisions of the Football League. In the second, Manchester United, Norwich City, Sunderland and Aston Villa came out top. Hardly surprising, except that they all succeeded by positive football. It was especially good coming from Villa. When Ron Saunders manages a side which has small ball players, and attacks away from home, the wind of change begins to show signs of becoming a gale. If the sadness at Sunderland's ultimate failure could be assuaged, then the surprising pleasure one could get from Villa does it.

Lower down too, success went to the teams who played positively, rather than just being organised big runners. Plymouth, Blackburn and Charlton all gave a surprising amount of pleasure last season. Even by encouraging wingers. All good stuff, and something which gives me a lot of hope that the trend for positive football will continue.

Off the field, though, the same old faces still rule in the same unimaginative reactionary way. Alan Hardaker shows no signs of realising that what was good enough for 1888 is not necessarily ideal in 1975. Fans are still treated with absolute contempt by the clubs who need them. Sponsorship is producing abortions all over the place — the Texaco Cup and England's shirts being two manifestations we can do without. And of course the thing which would give positive skilful football its greatest boost, cutting down on the number of games, is further away than ever. While football is run in the way it is, our hopeful trends will have a hard struggle to exist — even as hopeful trends. In the end you can only salute the players, and the managers, for a brave fight against a stultifying structure and abysmal leadership. They, who receive most of the bad publicity going, should only receive our thanks for continuing to produce the creativity they do.

Peter Ball

'A team of eleven Berti Vogtses would be unbeatable'

from *Shoot's* Kevin Keegan Column

VOTED: WORLD'S MOST HORRIBLE MAGAZINE